Values & Public Policy

Values
&
Public
Policy

Gerald P. Regier, Editor

© Copyright 1988 — Family Research Council of America, Inc.

All rights reserved. No part of this publication may be reproduced in any form without the prior written consent of the publisher.

ISBN 1-55872-000-6
Library of Congress Catalog Card Number 88-81831
Printed in the United States of America

Family Research Council of America, Inc.
Gerald P. Regier, President
515 Second Street, N.E.
Washington, D.C. 20002
(202) 546-5400

Cover Design by: Darby H. Waters

The Family Research Council of America, Inc. is an independent, nonpartisan, non-profit research/resource/educational organization that examines social policy issues. The Council assists policymakers, scholars, government officials and the general public by providing objective analysis of issues affecting the family. The purpose of the Council is to ensure that the interests of the family are considered and respected in the formulation of public policy.

The Family Research Council has drawn together professionals from across the nation, in a variety of academic disciplines and professions. Council members are highly credentialed and respected in their professional communities and desire to provide their expertise and research to policy debate on family issues.

515 Second Street, Northeast ● Capitol Hill
Washington, D.C. ● (202) 546-5400
Gerald P. Regier, President

Table of Contents

INTRODUCTION
    Values and Public Policy
    Gerald P. Regier

Part I - AIDS AND AIDS EDUCATION

Chapter 1   AIDS and the Family 1
               Vernon H. Mark, M.D., F.A.C.S.

Chapter 2   Values and Education 15
               William J. Bennett, Ph.D., J.D.

Part II - ISSUES IN BIOMEDICAL ETHICS

Chapter 3   Surrogate Mothers: The New Bondswomen 25
               Abigail Rian Evans, M. Div., Ph.D.

Chapter 4   Pathways of Change in Biomedical Ethics:
               The Changing Concepts of Parenthood
               & Personhood 45
               Rita L. Marker

Chapter 5   The Human Unborn: Research Subject,
               Organ Donor, or One of Us? 67
               Joseph R. Stanton, A.B., M.D., F.A.C.P.

Chapter 6   Research on the Psychosocial Impact
               of Abortion: A Systematic Review
               of the Literature 1966 to 1985 77
               John S. Lyons, Ph.D., et al.

Part III - AGING AND FAMILY RELATIONSHIPS

Chapter 7   How Old is "Old Age"? 91
               Peter Uhlenberg, Ph.D.

Chapter 8   Aging and Lifelong Learning 103
               Robert Strom, Ph.D.

Table of Contents

Part IV - TEEN SEXUALITY: RESEARCH, PUBLIC POLICY AND PROGRAMS

Chapter 9   Decision Making in Adolescent Pregnancy: A Review of Intrapersonal and Interpersonal Factors 119
Everett L. Worthington, Jr., Ph.D.

Chapter 10   "Don't Tell My Parents" — Parents' Rights Regarding the Provision of Contraceptives to Their Children 181
Lynn D. Wardle, J.D.

Chapter 11   The Benefits of Legislation Requiring Parental Involvement Prior to Adolescent Abortion 221
Everett L. Worthington, Jr., Ph.D., et al.

Chapter 12   Fathers and Teenagers: Social Facts and Biblical Values 245
Stephen M. Clinton, Ph.D.

Chapter 13   Teen S.T.A.R.: Sexuality Teaching in the Context of Adult Responsibility 261
Hanna Klaus, M.D., F.A.C.O.G., et al.

Part V - THE FAMILY AND THE STATE

Chapter 14   The Anti-Family Economy 273
Joseph Sobran

Introduction

VALUES AND PUBLIC POLICY

Gerald P. Regier
President, Family Research Council

"Values and Public Policy" at first glance is regarded as either a misnomer (because of the perception that public policy is always neutral), or it is considered a contradiction in terms (because of the perception that values are not allowed in public policy).

On the contrary, values *are* of critical importance in the formation of public policy. Policy makers in the public arena as well as scholars in the research arena are products of the values they have formed over the years. These values reflect the political, educational, religious and cultural presuppositions which they have accepted as fact.

Philosophical presuppositions are not bad or wrong, they are merely foundational presumptions which a person has accepted as fact and which influence subsequent value decisions. They are foundational beliefs which influence how a person accepts data and how a person builds upon that data. A person then constructs his or her world view based on this foundational information. These presuppositions, which are founded primarily upon scientific and historical information, become the core basis for the formulation and the acceptance of certain values.

Therefore, individuals come to different value positions based on different presumptions. For example, if a person accepts the presupposition (based upon the information to which he has been exposed) that life is merely birth to death, and that there is no afterlife, he will have certain values and presumably live according to those values as a result. Conversely, if a person accepts the presupposition (based again upon the information to which he has been exposed) that God creates life and that man will live eternally, he will also in turn have certain values and presumably live accordingly.

So there are different resulting values based on diverse presuppositions. These values which overlap one another are commonly referred to using the following designations:

- traditional values
- liberal values
- libertarian values
- conservative values
- family values
- biblical values
- Judeo-Christian values

It is important to reiterate that these values are not based on whims, speculation, or even hopes, but on evidence and data.

The life-long challenge for each of us then becomes to take the truth we know and to match it constantly with other data we were heretofore unfamiliar with ... and to test it. If it stands, we add it to our own value system; if it does not stand the test then we regard it as untruth, or as truth based upon an untrue presupposition.

Let me illustrate by referring to modern day attitudes concerning child care. There are different presuppositions concerning care for children, each of which is based upon a body of information. The first is that care by the parent is preferred and critical to the normal development of the child. The second is that although care by the parent is preferred, it is not critical to the normal development of the child. The third is that it is sometimes desirable for care to be provided to the child by someone other than the parent.

Proponents of each of these views rely upon research to support their positions. In fact, different conclusions are sometimes drawn from the same set of data — an indication that one's world view may influence one's interpretation of research information. Ultimately, of course, one must attempt to evaluate the research evidence as objectively as possible so that arguments and positions unsupported by evidence are distinguished from those supported by sound reasoning and data.

VALUES AND PUBLIC POLICY

One's values are critical to policy direction; values have become an integral part of public policy. This is legitimate and right, and, therefore, we must bring to light research data which supports the values which we hold dear. Research cannot be contrived or developed simply to support one's position; but *valid* research *must* be a part of the public debate. Unfortunately, when one comes to accept a presupposition it is extremely difficult to change that view even when presented by research to the contrary. This is the challenge of policy debate.

Public policy then becomes the expression of our ideas based upon research. Ideas do have consequences, because ideas are simply values expressed. Therefore, it is our right and our duty not only to point out the fallacy of another's ideas, but to present our own ideas clearly and accurately ... to present the data in a compelling manner, so as to be a positive proactive force in the formation of public policy.

FOUNDATIONS OF PUBLIC POLICY

After eight years of working in the public policy arena I have come to see and understand that public policy is built upon four pillars. The *first* of these pillars is *values*. Depending upon one's core presuppositions, a variety of values are behind the ideas being presented in the public arena. This is not only unavoidable but desirable. It is what government is all about. It is what the "public square" is all about. It is the free exchange of ideas based on values which have been formed by a combination of evidence, experience, and expectation. As these differing values are presented and discussed, a consensus is developed resulting in a policy.

The *second* pillar is *data*. An idea flowing out of values can only be expressed effectively if it is supported by convincing and compelling evidence, data and facts. Traditional values and Judeo-Christian values have suffered in the past because they have not been presented with proper research and evidence to make them compelling. It is not because there is not sufficient data, it is simply because this data has not been gathered, analyzed and presented in the public arena.

As you can see from the following presentations, this is changing. There *is* data available which gives credence to basic Judeo-Christian values. This data has not been presented to policy makers in the past. The Family Research Council's primary focus is to ensure that such data becomes a vital part of the public policy debate.

The *third* pillar is *credible spokespersons* and presenters of data. Facts cannot be gathered and presented by just anyone. I have attended many congressional hearings. The witnesses range from scholarly experts to blue collar workers. All testimony is heard; however, it is the data presented by the credentialed spokesperson that will live on in the policy debate. In fact, it is essential that data be presented by recognized experts in order to be persuasive, accurate and compelling. It is the experts presenting their data and research who command the attention of policy makers.

The *fourth* and final pillar in building public policy is the *implementation* process. Ideas based on values and data must become effective functioning policy. Ideas begin as rhetoric, move to discussion, are considered, and then become actual policy. It is a process which demands considerable expertise and understanding of the governmental system; and it will not be effective unless this final step of implementation is carefully planned. A clear strategy must be developed and followed which will move these ideas from rhetorical ideas to actually becoming working, functioning policy. There are many good ideas based upon credible research data which never become policy simply because no one shepherded them through the implementation phase. This has been a major breakdown point in the policy making process which we must correct and which we must master.

CONCLUSION

We at the Family Research Council are committed to bringing values into public policy in a responsible manner. That is why we have hosted a conference each year in order to bring together credible professionals and academics with policy makers and practitioners. In this framework research can be presented based on presuppositional values which have a high regard for life itself, a high regard for the family unit as being in an *a priori* position to the State, a view of man as a moral being with responsibility and accountability to a Creator, and a view of marriage and parenthood as sacred covenants and commitments to be honored and protected.

The following presentations were given at the Fourth Annual Family Research Council Network Conference. The theme of the conference, "Values and Public Policy", is explored in these issues. You will see that values *are* important in the public policy process, and you will see that values do make a difference in what ultimately ends up as a policy recommendation. This research is presented so that it can be used in public policy debate for years to come — to be used by policy makers at all levels of government, including the United States Congress, the Executive branch, the Judicial branch, the Statehouses, the medical profession, the local school board, and the community.

We hope that this book is an informative and helpful tool to add to the policy debate at all levels, and that it will contribute to the strengthening of the family unit in America.

The papers contained in this book were presented at the Values and Public Policy Conference, October 1987, in Washington D.C.

The annual conference, sponsored by the Family Research Council of America, Inc., brings together researchers, academics, policy makers and opinion leaders nationwide to examine current research and policy on family issues.

PART I

AIDS AND

AIDS EDUCATION

1

AIDS AND THE FAMILY

Vernon Mark, M.D., F.A.C.S.
Associate Professor, Harvard Medical School

Editor's note: Following is the edited transcript of an oral presentation.

I heard Dr. James Dobson recently talk about a conversation he had had with his father, telling him how difficult it was for him to raise his own children, particularly through the vulnerable period of adolescence. He marvelled at the fact that his father had done this so well and said to him, "Dad, I just wanted to thank you for the wonderful job you did in raising me when I was an adolescent." He noticed that his father, who was a minister, was embarrassed by this accolade and said, "Well, I really have to be honest. I didn't do anything. I didn't even notice that it was happening."

Dr. Dobson made the point that, indeed, something has changed. We don't have the same society that we did when he and I were in high school — when there wasn't any drug culture and when promiscuous sexual behavior was almost unknown. There is something that's changed to break down family values. Dr. Dobson's point and this section on AIDS dovetail in terms of what we can do to stop what is really a voluntary epidemic.

AIDS is an infectious disease which is transmitted for the most part by voluntary activity. It is not casually transmitted. The involuntary victims are those who have received tainted blood in transfusions or infants who have been infected by contaminated blood flowing from an infected mother's circulation. But that represents only a relatively small number of the victims. For the most part, the victims of AIDS are the victims of a voluntary transmission through contaminated needles and sexual intercourse.

When we look at AIDS in terms of public policy, I think we have to be ruled by one emotion; and that emotion is compassion. We have to be compassionate toward the people who are infected and we have to show that compassion by objective things that we accomplish. For example, I think we have to have a medical subsidy for the treatment of AIDS-related diseases that are presently not covered by health insurance. It is cruel and unconscionable to allow people who are infected with any disease to suffer without adequate medical care.

Also, I think that we have to respect confidentiality, we have to pursue counseling, and we have to pursue workman's compensation insurance for those people who are so ill that they can no longer work because of this devastating disease.

There is another aspect to compassion, however. We must be compassionate not only towards the people who have the disease but also towards those people who are potential victims of this disease.

There are two preventive techniques about which Congress has been talking and for which legislation has been proposed: public education and public health measures.

Public health measures are focused on two kinds of activities: 1) identification of who is infected and infectious; and 2) accountability —so that the people who are infected and infectious do not transmit the disease to those who are uninfected. It is important to realize that whatever public policy we pursue, we must have the basic information to determine correct policy, so that the money we spend is not wasted and that it is going to help people who are ill and help others to remain healthy.

How much should be spent and who should it be spent on? That question can only be answered by determining how many people in this country are infected, how far this infection has spread into our population, and how rapidly it is spreading (by which we mean that we've got to do more than one mass testing to determine the rate at which this infection is spreading).

There are different views on AIDS. There are some people who feel that this disease is so menacing that it may end civilization as we know it. And there are others, like Dr. Jaffee from the Center for Disease Control (CDC), who, when asked about the chances of AIDS infecting people outside the high-risk groups (the homosexual community, intravenous drug abusers and their consorts), stated, "The chance of that happening is zero." (New York Times, June 15, 1987). And furthermore, when asked if he could look into the future and see whether this was going to affect the general population, he replied, "I don't see it." Now this is the chief epidemiologist of the Center for Disease Control. Obviously, there's a difference of opinion.

The CDC has had the power to do population sample statistics — anonymous random testing — for the last two years. There are no civil or other rights of privacy that are invaded by doing this kind of testing. Even the American Civil Liberties Union has come out in favor of random testing. But no plans or contingencies were made by the CDC. On June 1, 1987 the President ordered them to carry out such a test, and to have the plans available to him by the middle of July 1987. As of October 1987, not only are there no plans for carrying this out, but there's been a public statement by Dr. James Mason (head of the CDC) that such tests are not going to be carried out, at least not in the near future. So we will have no information as to whether the disease is spreading widely or rapidly.

Dr. Mason gave three reasons for saying that testing was not the proper thing to do. First, he said that if we begin widespread testing in populations that are relatively uninfected, we're going to get a lot of false positives. An answer to that was given by Dr. Robert Redfield, chief virologist at the Walter Reed Army Hospital. He and his colleague, Dr. Burke, have been carrying out widespread testing in low prevalence groups for the Department of Defense. They have a false positive rate now of only one in 135,000. The idea that there will be a lot of false positives in a low-risk group is incorrect. When someone made this statement at a Congressional hearing, Dr. Redfield challenged them. They replied, "Well our laboratories are not as efficient as your laboratories." Of course, the answer to that is to use Dr. Redfield's laboratories and to make all laboratories equally efficient.

Secondly, Dr. Mason said there would be a lot of false negatives. He based this objection on a recent study in Finland which shows that about 5 out of 22 homosexual men did not have sero conversion — they did not produce positive antibodies to the AIDS virus — for a year to 30 months after infection. That's a small study — and therefore should be repeated with a larger sample.

At the present time the CDC is promulgating public policy on the basis of the number of people who get sick. Now AIDS is called a "lenti" virus, which means "slow". Not only is it slow in producing positive antibodies, but symptoms may not occur for months and sometimes for years after infection. During this time, the people who are infected are still infectious.

How can you follow an epidemic by looking only at the end stages of the disease? It would be comparable, for example, to following the prevalence of tuberculosis in our society by looking at only those patients who developed the fatal miliary tuberculosis. It would be like trying to determine how many people were contracting syphilis by looking at only those people with syphilis of the great vessels of the heart, or syphilis of the brain. It doesn't make any sense. It does not give us an accurate picture.

"Ah," they say, "That isn't all. We've been doing some tests in sexually transmitted disease clinics in New York and Denver in which we find that women who attend these clinics have a very low rate of contracting the AIDS virus." It turns out that these people are volunteers. These aren't mandatory random tests, these are voluntary tests.

That brings to mind an old story about statistics. There was once a magazine in the United States called the "Literary Digest". It conducted in 1936 the largest presidential preference poll ever taken up to that time. There were perhaps a million people who were contacted about their preference for Landon or Roosevelt. That poll came out showing that Landon was going to be the next president of the United States. Of course, as you know, he only won two states. The "Literary Digest" went out of publication.

What did they do wrong? They contacted all of these people as efficiently as they could — over the telephone. However, in 1936 there were a lot of people who voted who did not have telephones. So it is very easy to make a statistical error, particularly when you're relying on voluntary compliance instead of using random statistical samples.

The third, and probably the most cogent, reason given by Dr. Mason is that people would refuse to be tested. I don't know what kind of testing he is talking about, but there isn't anyone who has a good reason for refusing to be tested in an anonymous test, where we pool the samples. There is no way of checking back to determine the results; and if he's worried about the fallibility of the government, he can always farm this testing out to a polling organization and use HMO's to draw the blood so that government workers are not actually involved. Dr. Mason's response has been very disappointing because he has left us in ignorance.

In the absence of firm data, we have the prevailing point of view espoused by Dr. June Osborne. Dr. Osborne is a very prestigious physician and head of the School of Public Health at the University of Michigan. She has been responsible for the position taken by the National Academy of Sciences on AIDS, and she's been very important in public policy.

At a meeting at which we both testified, she said that the older methods of tracking the AIDS epidemic — by identifying who is infected and who is infectious, and then having accountability in some way or other, so that the virus is not transmitted — is counterproductive. Not only would this not work, but it would infringe on civil rights. She feels that the newer method of preventing infectious disease embodies education — value-neutral education — so that people can know the facts and act on them. And, of course, in that value-neutral education is embodied the various preventive techniques generally now categorized as "safer sex".

Let's look at this values-neutral education. Among the most compliant group, which are the homosexuals, there were two studies reported at the recent AIDS conference in June 1987. One study had about 5,000 homosexual men at several centers. With repeated counseling about 2,500 of them gave up having anal intercourse. But of the 2,500 who continued to have anal intercourse, about 70% (30% of the total) continued to have unprotected anal intercourse — one of the most high-risk forms of activity for the transmission of the AIDS virus — and 40% of the entire group were under the influence of Amyl Nitrite at the time of sexual intercourse to enhance their pleasure.

In another group of over 500 homosexual men surveyed, over 90% knew that anal intercourse was dangerous and that wearing a condom might reduce the chances of being infected, but of the 500 over 60% — almost two-thirds — continued to have unprotected anal intercourse. In that total group, one third had sexual intercourse while their brain was poisoned with either alcohol or some other drug, so that the chances of compliance with an "adequate technique" (the efficient use of condoms) is probably substantially reduced.

Another study done in San Francisco between 1980 and 1984 in the male homosexual community found that safer sex techniques were able to reduce the incidence of rectal gonorrhea by 73% — a remarkable change for the better which shows that they were trying their best to reduce sexually transmitted diseases. However, during that same time period and in that same group there was an increase in seropositivity to the AIDS virus from 24% to 68%, so that techniques which were useful in reducing rectal gonorrhea were not useful in preventing infection with the AIDS virus.

I asked the person in charge of the San Francisco study how he could explain this paradox. He said that, of course, gonorrhea has a very limited period of infectiousness, whereas the AIDS virus is almost continuously infectious. Even one or two episodes in which precautions were not taken would cause infection with AIDS, whereas the most infectious period of gonorrhea produces clinical signs and symptoms. So much appears in the literature about the fact that safer sex techniques are working because other sexually transmitted diseases are being reduced; however the San Francisco study, which is published in the medical literature, is very much to the point here. You can't tell what's happening to AIDS by looking at what's happening to other sexually-transmitted diseases in the homosexual community.

Dr. Gordon Dickinson was head of a study of heterosexual groups in Miami. In a group of men who were infected drug addicts but who were apparently faithful monogamous partners to their wives (at least their wives were faithful), there was a failure in condom usage of about 18% over a period of a little over a year. Even in an apparently monogamous relationship using condoms, there was in fact a definite failure rate of about one out of six.

In World War II, condoms were issued to 16 million men under arms. Condoms were freely available. The compliance rate was so poor that "prokits" and then oral sulfathiazol were used, and in 1945 we had the biggest rise of syphilis in the history of the United States with over 400 cases per 100,000 of the population. During any period of war, where there's a transposition of populations, there will be an increase in sexually transmitted diseases. But this indicates that the efforts of the Department of Defense were not effective.

It's useful to see how effective Dr. Osborne's techniques were in 1986 in terms of preventing other sexually transmitted diseases. Dr. Jonathan Zemmelman of the Department of Sexually Transmitted Diseases of the CDC found that during 1986 there were 13 million new cases of sexually transmitted disease. That's a conservative estimate. It includes such things as Hepatitis B, 500,000 cases of Herpes Type II (which is the venereal herpes), 2-3 million cases of gonorrhea, 5 million cases of chlamydia, over 90,000 cases of syphilis — and that's not even taking into account AIDS.

Although it's been around for some time, venereal warts is a recently publicized disease, produced by the human papilloma virus. There were a million new cases of that in 1986. We have newly discovered that it is associated with squamous cell cancer of the vulva, cervix, anus, mouth, and precancerous lesions of the penis as well. If it weren't for AIDS, this disease would be the most important sexually transmitted disease of the 80's and 90's. And there doesn't seem to be any diminution of the spread of this disease. It is, in fact, spreading very rapidly.

Dr. Thomas Becker, of the CDC, and his group have also begun new tests for venereal herpes. Venereal herpes, like AIDS, is not curable. It can be treated, but the virus stays in the dorsal root ganglia around the spinal cord and the cranial nerves. Of course, they say it's no worse than the common cold, except for those infants that are born when their mothers are infected and have the blisters. Between 500 and 1,000 children are affected every year. These infants get an infection of their central nervous system, producing either death or a loss of brain function. This is a menengioencephalitis.

The CDC says, "Well, we've somewhat miscalculated here. Actually, we find now that venereal herpes is present in one out of every four adult Americans and that there are now 40 million Americans infected with venereal herpes. We made a slight error in our previous estimates."

Now, I'm not suggesting to you that AIDS is as infectious as herpes, but I am saying that if there is even a slight miscalculation on the optimistic side, it doesn't have to be nearly as infectious in order to produce a national tragedy.

Is there another method of education, an alternative to Dr. June Osborne's suggestion? I don't want to single out Dr. Osborne, because she merely represents a whole group of educators. But in looking at the data, I'm not convinced that the kind of sex education they're proposing is at all effective. And I also want to tell you that the medical profession has a very substantial role in the containment or the noncontainment of sexually transmitted diseases through their educational programs in medical schools.

I got involved in this debate through my wife, who has a Ph.D. in the Humanities. She began looking into some of the sex education courses that our oldest son had when he was a medical student. She found that the course work in medical school — the so-called nonjudgmental courses — actually consisted of pornographic material from Denmark and New York. She found that 91% of medical schools used such material and the educators responsible for this were Dr. John Money of Johns Hopkins University (who has now apparently modified his program to some extent), Dr. Paul Eberhart of the University of Indiana, Dr. Mary Briggs of the University of Minnesota, and many, many others.

The material used by these educators has been used as a standard for other educational institutions, like colleges and high schools. They have set the standard for sex education. It's strange that even at the present moment with all the sexually transmitted diseases and with AIDS, there is still a group of medical educators who are influential in the American

Medical Association, in the Department of Health and Human Services, and in the CDC, who are still following precisely the same course that they did before. They do not want to give up the gains that they have achieved in terms of sexual freedom. As a result, we are getting a very ambiguous message in trying to control a public health problem — to the extent that we're not even allowed to determine how serious this problem is.

What is an alternative AIDS education or sex education program? My wife and I in our book *The Pied Pipers of Sex* suggested that sex education is needed, but that it must emphasize two things: responsibility and accountability.

When we talk about "safer sex", (i.e. using condoms), what is it safer than? What is "safe sex"? "Safer sex" is a comparative; it means it must be safer than safe sex. Safe sex is abstinence outside of a faithful, monogamous marriage, in which both partners are uninfected. Certainly wearing a condom in promiscuous sex is not safer than that. At best, safer sex can only be called "less dangerous sex".

I would like to close by mentioning teenagers and some of the problems that have arisen, and some of the debates that I've been a part of in a few Congressional hearings. I represented one side, and three other doctors, including an associate dean of a medical school represented the other side. They were telling the country that it's not going to be possible to change the sexual habits of teenagers because teenagers feel that they are immortal, that they cannot be destroyed, no matter what they do. They're probably not going to use condoms very much because they're not afraid.

Now this is a strange self-fulfilling prophecy that's being foisted on teenagers. If you'll remember, one or two years ago there was another pronouncement made about teenagers to explain why there were so many teenage suicides and why there was such a large amount of chronic alcoholism and drug addiction among teenagers. The reason given was that teenagers are afraid that they're going to be destroyed in an atomic holocaust. So in two years, teenagers supposedly have gone from being extremely frightened to feeling immortal. It's an unusual change in mental behavior.

From the point of view of neurology and neuropsychology, there are parts of the brain which are definitely related to our ability to plan for the future and to see the consequences of our behavior. That's not simply a psychological attribute. It is a neurological function of the brain. To suggest that all teenagers don't have that part of their brain functioning is absurd.

It is possible to have a national hysteria which will sweep over and change behavior as a matter of conditioning — a self-fulfilling prophecy. In this case it is almost a political statement. This is extremely dangerous. It is unwarranted. It is an abuse and an unjust criticism of teenagers who are perfectly capable of determining their future.

We have a great awareness now about adolescence, and a whole area of medicine devoted to adolescence. Sixty years ago there was no such thing as adolescence, because when people got to be 12, 13, or 14 years of age they were at work. When they were 16 or 18 they had a family. They seemed to have skipped over this period completely and they were able, strangely enough, to think about the future and the consequences of their behavior.

But now we have a whole new problem — a problem which is a result of miseducation — and it can be corrected by proper education. It is not a malfunction of the brain. It is something which is reversible. People who have not lived in another generation, as I have, just can't conceive of the fact that there can be whole generations of teenagers that are not drug addicts, that are not promiscuous, and that are not chronic alcoholics. But I can guarantee you that such is the case. This is a function of our society, of our culture, and of miseducation.

A very high official made a statement at a recent conference. He was in favor of education, of religious education, and of value education. But he said, "I'm sorry, there's nothing we can do about teenagers. They're lost. They are on their way, they're promiscuous. There's nothing we can do to change their behavior. But the thing that we want to do is get the preteenagers who have not yet had sexual intercourse and give them religious values." Think about that. They're going to take one segment of the population, 11 to 14 years of age, and give them value-oriented education — only them and no one else.

How often is that education going to be given to them? An hour a week? An hour a day? Two hours a day? What about the education they're receiving during the rest of the day? (This criticism, incidentally, was brought up by a very liberal Congresswoman. And then she stopped to think: of course we can't touch that — that's freedom of speech. We can't touch the pornographic television programs, the video cassettes, the movies, the magazines, and the culture of their peers.)

What I am suggesting to you is that in order to save the 11- to 14-year-olds we cannot focus on children 11 to 14 years old and let everyone else go by the board. What we have to do is to change our education, not only for teenagers and children, but for adults — for parents as well as their children. We have to make a total commitment if we're going to have an education which is going to be effective. We can't do it piecemeal — it won't be effective. And in order to do this, we have to know how serious the problem is.

AIDS is a serious disease for those people who are infected. If it's not a national threat, it has to take its place among other serious diseases — cancer, heart disease, stroke — and it has to compete for the available health care dollars. It can't be given preference if it's not a national emergency. If it is a national emergency, then public health regulations, which are some of the most powerful laws we have in this country, are going to have to supersede other legal considerations.

Editor's note: Following are edited questions from the audience addressed by Dr. Mark.

Question: I was somewhat surprised at your remarks that compassion should extend to confidentiality. The *Washington Post* recently discussed the case of a physician who is now himself infected with AIDS. This surgeon is not going to divulge to his patients that he has AIDS. Under the State's law, this is a right to privacy. I understand New York State just recently made some changes in this regard so that the doctors can inform the sexual partners of the person who's carrying the virus. When people who would hardly be considered conservative in this area have now begun to question the so-called right of privacy when other people's health is involved, why do you still favor confidentiality?

Dr. Mark: I think we have to be very careful about our definition of confidentiality. I was referring to confidentiality in regard to general public information about someone's infection — so that, for instance, they are thrown out of their housing, and their lives are impacted in a number of very unfavorable ways that have nothing to do with the transmission of the AIDS virus. I think that decisions about what an individual should or could do have to be made by public health officials. It is their job to prevent the transmission of this disease — they have a public and private responsibility.

I'm not in favor of a surgeon who is infectious continuing to operate. There is too much chance of spilling blood inside an abdominal cavity. However, there's no reason he can't do other aspects of medicine, as long as there is no danger that his body fluids will be coming in contact with wounds. There are things that a physician can do which are not going to endanger his patients.

Dr. Broathen, an associate professor of dermatology from Norway, has found that there are cells right underneath the skin — called longevhans cells — which are as susceptible to the AIDS virus as the T-4 lymphosytes in the bloodstream. I'm sure his proposal will be met by a lot of criticism and medical discussion, but he is proposing that it is not necessary to have the invasion of the bloodstream by the AIDS virus in order to produce an infection. Merely an abrasion of the skin or the mucous membrane is enough to produce an infection. He feels that, except for those people who are infected by blood transfusions, or drug abusers with contaminated needles, the usual method of sexual transmission is through macrophages under the skin or mucous membranes and probably not through direct transmission of the virus into the bloodstream.

Consider another factor which is even more important to all of us here — the safety of blood in our blood banks. If, in fact, sero conversion occurs late, this is a problem in terms of our blood banks.

It is not true that the blood bank uses only antibody tests to determine whether an individual should be accepted or rejected as a donor. First of all, there's a certain amount of voluneerism concerned — they ask people who are in high risk groups not to donate their blood. And secondly, they have other tests for related diseases — like Hepatitis B. If they find that those tests are positive they will exclude those donors. But certainly it is not good news that the sero conversion may not occur for a long time after infection.

Dr. Charlie Huggins, head of the blood bank at Massachussetts General, has devised a method of preserving blood (except for the white blood cells), so that it's possible to preserve plasma and even 45% of the platelets for long periods of time — at least a year for plasma and three years for whole blood. He has actually preserved blood for 30 years and given it to patients in the operating room with no ill effects whatsoever. And so there is a possibility that one can take blood, test the donor a year later, or even three years later, and cut down remarkably on the chances that that blood is infected.

Question: From a psychological and sociological point of view, we know from our experiences in this country that we can get into a "group-think" attitude — where we can perpetuate conventional wisdom until we get into a debacle. We're already in this debacle and it is being accented by miseducation. While the present administration is still in office, do you think it might be a good idea to ask for an emergency to be declared so funding is made available?

Dr. Mark: In February, 1987 a group of us went to the Chairman of the Domestic Council asking to be put in contact with people who could donate money to get population sample tests performed, so that we could determine whether or not there is a national emergency.

We were unsuccessful in getting that money. The point that you make is one of the reasons — the "group-think" attitude, which has taken hold of the American Medical Association and the Department of Health and Human Services.

This conventional wisdom of the American Medical Association and the Department of Health and Human Services is not based on scientific evidence. It is not based on medical evidence. It is based on what they think is best. They may be right, but they do not have the evidence at the present time.

The thing that is so disappointing about Dr. Mason and the CDC is that they are not getting this evidence. No one is going to be injured by getting these tests. They can do a tremendous service to the American public.

We have had a fantastic tradition of heroism in our public health service: Walter Reed and the yellow fever; Thomas Parran, surgeon general during the Roosevelt administration, and his book on syphilis (which, incidentally, had many of the same characteristics in the 1930's as AIDS does currently). These men did a tremendous service to the public, and they did it in a situation in which they had no fear. There were no social-political considerations. There were only public health considerations.

I'm afraid that when the present actors on the stage of history are compared to those in the past, their actions may not measure up that well. Their actions do not have the kind of bravery and the kind of single-minded determination to get at the facts that were exhibited by their predecessors. I don't know why; it is a mystery to me. But this "prevailing wisdom" is one of the most devastating things that we've come up against. It's not possible to argue with people that already know in their own mind what is the correct thing to do, because we are not arguing with people using the facts.

Question: The debate in this country seems to be very lopsided. Whenever the subject of AIDS is raised pertaining to the carriers of AIDS, it is a matter of their rights. When it comes to the public's response, it's a matter of public responsibility. The public seems to have very little right to ask questions about costs, and in many states the costs will be staggering.

A large group of AIDS carriers either a) refuse to be tested because they don't want to know; or b) do know that they have AIDS and nevertheless continue to be reckless in their conduct.

How can the public policy debate be shifted to take into account that the rights of the general public might have to curtail the choices of persons who can't act responsibly?

Dr. Mark: AIDS is a state public health problem, and public health officers have the responsibility for preserving public health. If someone is transmitting an infectious and possibly fatal disease, officials have to be responsible to the public for not fulfilling their jobs. They're not immune from lawsuits.

One often gets the response, "If we have AIDS we don't want to know because it is a disease for which there is no treatment." This is false. There is a treatment for AIDS. We do have drugs for the AIDS virus and the AIDS dementia —where people have an infection of their brain and become demented or psychotic. AZT has a remarkable effect in reversing that particular group of symptoms, at least temporarily. The complications of AIDS — the opportunistic infections — are also treatable. There are new drugs which are very effective in some of these opportunistic infections.

AIDS at the present time is no different than a lot of other diseases we've had to deal with. We had syphilis for many years that was treatable but not curable. We have herpes and many forms of cancer and heart disease that are treatable but not curable. If we used that same criteria, we wouldn't diagnose many diseases because they are incurable. So the statement that this is an incurable disease is palpably false, negating the argument that we therefore don't want to know if we have AIDS.

Question: Our school district is developing an AIDS curriculum. The biggest struggle is trying to determine at what age children should receive AIDS information, and how detailed it should be. Do you have any recommendation on this?

Dr. Mark: I think that sex education courses should have a good, clear description of how people get infected and what can happen to them, but I am not in favor of how-to-do-it books on how to achieve orgasm. I see absolutely no purpose in that at all.

There are people who have sexual dysfunctions. That is not a public matter — that is a private matter, requiring treatment by a physician or a counselor, not education in the classroom. We have taken children off the playground and made them concerned about sexual intercourse at a time when they should be riding bicycles or playing football. This is extremely unfortunate. We have not used the single word which is the most effective word in sex education — that word is "no".

In values education, "no" has to be the leading word. We cannot be concerned that psychiatrists are going to say we will produce people who are emotionally stunted or neurotic for the rest of their lives. There is not one scintilla of evidence that they are correct.

Dr. Dobson made the statement that something has happened to change teenagers and society for the worse. What has happened is the drug culture and the sexual revolution. Now I'm not suggesting to you that we wouldn't have AIDS without those things. We would probably still have promiscuity. But what has happened is that the standard-bearers of conduct have become nonjudgmental —teachers, physicians, the legal community, the lawmakers, many in the religious community, and people in telecommunications. They have become nonjudgmental and have allowed the people who are proposing and propounding sexual enjoyment as the be-all and end-all of human behavior to lead us wherever they want to. And they call that freedom.

The freedom to become ill, to contract disease, is not really freedom. Illness and disease are the oldest forms of human slavery. They restrict behavior, they do not expand it. There has been a confusion in terms. We have allowed them to get away with this for a long time.

That is the area that has to be debated. AIDS would still be present, but I don't think it would be nearly as serious if we had the same society we did in the late 1930's before World War II. If we had that society now, we would not have any danger of a national catastrophe with AIDS. There might be some spread of this disease but it would not approach national catastrophe.

We have a lot of people whose habits put them at great risk. How to change those habits is going to be a project of monumental proportions. This is particularly why the population sample statistics are so important. We've got to find out whether there is a compelling national interest.

2

AIDS EDUCATION

William J. Bennett, Ph.D., J.D.
U. S. Secretary of Education

Editor's note: The following is the edited transcript of an oral presentation.

I'd like to begin with a few comments about the Department of Education's book *AIDS and the Education of our Children*. We think the book is accurate; we think it's truthful; we think it's candid; and we think it's responsible. What we say in the book is that AIDS is a behavior-related disease — for most people, AIDS can be avoided by avoiding certain behaviors. AIDS is most often contracted through sexual activity. The book is addressed to teachers and parents, but through them we are urging young people to refrain from sexual activity: to curtail, to abstain, and to save themselves for marriage. This seems to be the obvious thing to say; indeed one could advance many reasons for promoting abstinence. AIDS is only one reason.

But for saying what is truthful and responsible — telling young people to be responsible and to abstain — several critics have scoffed at us. They have suggested that we are moralizing. They have suggested that there is a difference between realism and morality; that one is either "realistic" or one is "moralistic". We do not think we are being moralistic in our book, but we do think we are being morally responsible. If I wanted to describe the book and could choose the term, I would say that it is moral realism. And moral realism is something that we can ill afford to sacrifice in our time.

I am told by some of my critics that I should do a better job of peddling condoms to young people. I am criticized in *Time Magazine* for "not recommending the use of clean needles to young people."

I believe that America does not want a Secretary of Education who begins the school term by saying to America's children, "All right, boys and girls, young men, young ladies, get ready for the school year. Get your books and your pencils and your pads and your calculators, and get your condoms and your packs of clean needles." If someone wants the Secretary of Education to say that, they can get someone else to be Secretary of Education. But I don't think that is what the American people want. Perhaps some of our critics do. What they do not want to do, for whatever reason, is to admit the reality and the power of moral considerations, of values, of what has been called "the internal compass", in terms of its influence on young people's — indeed on all people's — behavior.

Some of you have read the report *Risking the Future* by the National Research Council — a report with which I disagreed in large part. I was glad to see in that report their recognition of the fact that young people's notion of themselves, their "self aspirations", as the author of the report put it — who and what they want to be as human beings — are the things that more than anything else most powerfully determine young people's sexual behavior. It is not the availability of facts, or the presence or absence of a particular course that determines most powerfully their sexual activity and behavior. It is their notion of who they are and who they want to be. That suggests once again the power and reality of moral considerations.

So I would say our book is imbued with realism — moral realism. We do not think that basic values are simply an add-on to personality; they are an essential part of personality. They are, in the area of sexual activity, the rudder of much action. The heart and the mind tend to point the way for all of us, particularly for young people. They give direction and they dictate action.

A friend of mine called education the "architecture of the soul". If it is good education it will form and shape that soul; it will shape that young person in the right way. Saint Augustine, in an earlier time, talked about education in *ordo amoris*, as "education in the order of the loves". To determine education's task is to have young people discover what deserves to be loved and what deserves not to be loved. It is and ought to be a very powerful tool.

In the discussion of AIDS and condoms and the like, I do not think it is particularly courageous to look away, to throw up one's hands as an adult, and to say, "Go ahead, but limit the damage — use condoms." In the end I think that it is more courageous, it is more responsible, to look young people in the eye and say, "This is how you should behave. This is what's responsible. This is the course of action that will not bring you or others harm." I think that is more realistic. I think that is more responsible. And I think that is what we ought to be saying to young people in our time about this and, indeed, about other matters.

I'm very pleased, by the way, with the fact that on a more general level, there is a recognition of the importance of the school's role in the nurture of character. I prefer the term "nurture of character" to "teaching of values". The term "values" seems to have been debased pretty soundly in the late 60's and the early 70's.

We've talked about the nurture of character and we find there is general agreement. I'm glad that the agreement is there. Now we must proceed to the next step, which is to talk about what nurturing character is all about, and how we hope to accomplish that task. I think we're making some progress in the national conversation on that issue.

Editor's Note: Following are edited questions from the audience, which are addressed by Secretary Bennett.

Question: Are there any specific guidelines within the Department of Education that would identify standards in the sex education curricula and the way that sex education should be taught in the nation? Or is that now left up to every individual school system?

Secretary Bennett: It is not necessarily left up to every individual school system, but it is not left up to the federal government, either. These are insufficient options. There are other options — sex education curricula, as with other curricula, are primarily a state and local responsibility. I don't think it would be very difficult, in principle, to devise a sound curriculum for sex education. I expect I could do it over a weekend. It wouldn't be difficult to devise a curriculum in other subjects, as well — math, history, and science.

Kenneth Baker, my counterpart in England, is doing this — he's devising a national curriculum. When I visited with Baker in England the thing that struck me most was how often he used the first person singular pronoun. He would say, "I shall do this, I shall announce a national curriculum." We have decided not to let the Secretary of Education do that in this country. And that's a very good thing. That's because we believe in state and local responsibility.

In a speech I gave on sex education about nine months ago I laid out what I thought ought to be the governing principles of a good course in sex education. My main concern about existing courses was that they tended to be "value-free, value-neutral". The reason the quotes appear is that there is no instruction that is value-free in this area. If you are "value-free" you are simply not being straightforward or you are teaching children to be indifferent to these matters — either of which is a mistake.

In the AIDS book we cite some programs which we think are pretty good, and again we lay out what we think ought to be the governing principles of such courses. But that's as far as we can go. Federal law, in fact, proscribes us from mandating curriculum. However, it does not prevent us from giving our view, or stating what we think ought to be the governing principles.

Question: If you've been investigating values related to public education, can we look for a list of recommended values coming out of the Department?

Secretary Bennett: I'd be glad to send you a speech, but that's about as much as you'll see coming out of the Department —although we will have something coming out in a month or two that may be of interest in the whole area of curriculum (the release of the Department of Education's *James Madison High School: A Curriculum for American Students*).

I don't think there's much disagreement about the kinds of values we ought to teach. *AIDS and the Education of Our Children* talks about matters of sexuality with young people. Most Americans think that sex education courses should emphasize moral considerations — and by moral considerations they mean restraint, abstinence, self control, and the like. The other values which parents would like to see taught are things like courage and integrity and honesty and regard for other people, particularly siblings and friends and parents. It's not a wildly controversial area.

My basic thesis about values education is the same as it was 10-15 years ago when I was writing about this as a philosophy professor. There's no reason that it should change in 15 years. It hasn't changed in 3,000 years — why should it change in 15 years? My basic thesis is that if you want young people to learn the difference between right and wrong you must put them in the presence of people who believe in right and wrong and will make an attempt to live out that difference in their lives. Mary Warnock, an Oxford professor, put it very well: "Young people must be in the presence of people who believe that such notions are serious and ought to be taken seriously in one's life. There is still no power like the quiet power of moral example."

As an ancillary to this kind of teaching, there is the question of course contents. I do not favor, in general, the specialized values courses or moral education courses because I think these considerations should permeate the curriculum, the school, and the school yard. I don't like the idea of isolating values in one 40-minute segment. That suggests an abstractness to the enterprise, which I think is inappropriate.

In terms of material, let me tell you about a survey. When I was at the National Endowment of the Humanities I wrote a letter to 250 people, left/right, Democrat/Republican, male/female, white/black, North/South — right across the board — and asked them what the ten books are that every high school graduate should have read by the time he has completed high school. The columnist George Will, one of the people we wrote, asked if he could reprint my request in his column, and he did. As a result he got about 10,000 responses from around the country. There was very little difference between the 250 we pre-selected and the 10,000 responses that came in at random. The titles that came in were essentially the same. There was not enormous consensus about ten books, but there was very great consensus about five books. This is an example of American people as curriculum specialists.

What are the five books that Americans left, right, and center, Republican and Democrat think that a student should have read by the time he finishes High School? 1) Shakespeare; 2) American documents: the Constitution, Federalist Papers, Declaration of Independence; 3) the Bible (this came from believers and nonbelievers, Jews, Christians and atheists); 4) Huckleberry Finn, the American novel; 5) (and a surprise to me), Homer — *The Odyssey* or *The Iliad.*

Now, think about those five books. They are a very good introduction to the Humanities; a very good introduction to Western Civilization; and not a bad introduction to a course in values and morality. Just the stories, by themselves, in those five books, would constitute a very good introduction to the moral legacy of Western Civilization. The American people as curriculum specialists actually did quite well, I thought. I have not seen too many curriculum specialists come up with a better program for high school seniors. If every high school senior in America had some serious reading in each of those five books, things would be a lot better than they are for a lot of kids. It's almost an education in itself.

Question: Mr. Secretary, you stated your position on communicating moral values. And yet in this booklet, at least two of the programs which are recommended put contraception and abstinence on an equal plane, or they advocate abstinence first and then advise, "Of course, if you can't wait, then please be careful." This seems to really be advocating only one thing, the use of condoms or other birth control methods. I don't know how you resolve that in a pluralistic society, but I'd like to hear your thoughts.

Secretary Bennett: I'd like to take a closer look at some of those programs that you mention and the materials by some of the groups that we talk about. We checked out our recommendations as carefully as we could. We said in the book — addressing this to parents and teachers —"You don't do what the Secretary of Education says just because he's Secretary of Education. This is our best judgment and our best advice." And, in talking about condoms in *AIDS and the Education of Our Children*, we do not say that this is an area that teachers, with parents' approval, may not talk about. It's not our place to say that. What we suggest, however, is that if one decides to talk about condoms, then one must be truthful in so speaking.

I don't shy away from the word "condom". One of the criticisms of us has been that we are talking about morality and thus we are shying away from being brutally frank and realistic. In fact, we are more brutally frank and realistic than a lot of people have been on the debate.

What about condoms? Can they reduce the risk of contracting the AIDS virus? Yes, they can. Are they reliable? Can we regard them as adequate safequards, as was suggested in a recent Public Health Service booklet? No, we cannot, because of their failure rate.

I'm sorry to be graphic, but the subject requires it: If we are talking about certain things, such as anal intercourse, I'm afraid the failure rate of condoms is, as Dr. C. Everett Koop (the U.S. Surgeon General) said recently, extraordinarily high.

So, do you want to talk to your kids about it? That's a local decision, not my decision. All we are saying is that if you do talk about it, be truthful. I don't think much good is done, frankly, by denying the existence of things in the world, such as the existence of AIDS or the existence of condoms. I don't think any good is done with that at all.

At the point where one decides to talk to young people about these matters, one wants the conversation to take place on the part of responsible adults and one wants to be truthful. And that's what we're saying — be truthful. I think there is a kind of self-delusion going on. On the part of some people it is a willed self-delusion — to wish against the tide, to say, "Nothing has changed even though there is AIDS. We should not say that behavior ought to be altered. We'll just carry on as before; we'll just find some new technological way of protecting ourselves, of dealing with it." I think that's denial. I think that is unrealistic and I think we need to be much more straightforward.

Question: I'm from a school district where teachers are very strongly in favor of academic freedom and they want to be able to teach virtually whatever they want regardless of what the community wants. They want to be able to teach in grades 7 through 12 all of the facts about oral and anal sex. And we are struggling as parents; what do we want our children to know; how much information should they have? It's a real struggle.

Secretary Bennett: It is a real struggle. And this is why I think care must be exercised and a great deal of time taken on these issues. This is why some communities may decide (this is my prediction) that whatever education takes place about these matters might not take place in school, but might take place in other settings, because of the kinds of difficulties you suggest. It is simply wrong and imprudent for a school or members of a school staff (teachers or principals) to proceed in an area like this without the green light from parents. They are asking for trouble. They are asking for the kind of explosion and severe disagreement that we see in many communities.

In general, parents want to know what's going on in school, but for most subjects — math, history, science — most parents only need a general sense of what's going on. One doesn't need to go through in a meticulous fashion every exercise of every major unit in an algebra course. But when you're talking about an area like this — whatever one's politics are, whatever one's personal views — simply stipulate that this is very serious business. Parents must approve of the material and what is going to be said at every step of the way or the school is not doing the right thing, and not being very prudent.

Question: In our school district, a parent has the option not to have his child participate in sex education. However, in some cases, AIDS is taught as a communicable disease, rather than as part of a sex education course. Therefore, the parents don't have to approve it. Do you have any comments on that?

Secretary Bennett: No. Again, these things are variously catalogued by the schools. If it is a matter of engaging in subterfuge, and thus somehow trying to limit parents' ability to act, then obviously it's wrong. This is the advice we give the schools: "It will backfire on you, school people, if you're trying to do this. Be candid and be up front."

Let's talk about the positive side — where it works. I've seen courses on values and courses on sex education work essentially where there is a large degree of trust between parents, the principal and the teachers. They know each other, they trust each other, and the parents believe that the schools will tend to support and back up what parents believe and what parents are trying to teach, and will not try to sabotage the beliefs that parents are providing the children. Where that's the situation, parents are prepared to provide a lot more leeway to the schools to talk.

Where there isn't that basic trust, where there is suspicion, where there is worry, there is heightened concern in controversial areas. But if the school does something in this area — and I'm not making the conclusion that that's what the school district is doing in what you describe — but if the school is doing something to get around parental supervision, or parental oversight, it simply adds to the destruction of that bond of trust, which has to exist for schools to work.

Question: We found that in almost every state well-informed legislators are very supportive of positive family action. What would you suggest that we as supporters of the family can do to face off with the NEA, NOW, and other organizations who are so well-funded and so well-organized?

Secretary Bennett: Well, I think that where you have disagreement you need to get involved and you need to act. I don't know that I can be much more helpful or specific than that, except to tell you that I'm beginning to develop a thesis about an old notion that is familiar to all of you — "quality time". "Quality time" is the idea that all you need to do is spend a little quality time with kids and this would make up for not spending "quantity" time, or a lot of time.

As a parent, one discovers a lot of things. For instance, if you're dedicated to this notion of quality time, there's no guarantee that your child will be interested in the same quality time that you are. You may decide, "Here's our 20 minutes, let's sit and read *The New Yorker* together." But your child may have other plans. It's logging time that matters — simply logging time together. And, interestingly, I discovered as a parent (and I find out the research supports me) that the quality of that time doesn't have to be great. You don't have to be doing a lot of interesting or stimulating things. Just being together matters.

Why am I talking about that in response to your question? Because it carries over into other contexts. I've been in 46 states now; I've been back and forth and up and down the United States talking to everybody who's willing to listen about a whole range of issues. You sometimes wonder as you're travelling from one place to another, "Is this doing any good? Is this having any effect?" And you find out sometimes that it is having an effect. You get a little echo here and there. You find out that something you said somewhere made a difference. Maybe it wasn't a big speech — maybe it was the talk before or afterwards that made a difference.

That supports what one of my favorite writers, William Butler Yeats, wrote in one of his great poems:

> All the drop scenes drop at once
> Upon a hundred thousand stages.

This reflects the particularity of life, that there are a hundred thousand stages out there, a hundred thousand debates and arguments and disagreements, and that it really does matter what individuals do in very particular circumstances: attending school board meetings; deciding who should be the principal of a school; opposing a certain curriculum, or favoring a certain curriculum; working with the state legislature. These things really do matter and they have a ripple effect.

I think it's best to be involved locally, with one's friends, one's colleagues, and one's neighbors, and not to look for enormous successes, or great changes, but to persevere. The interesting thing is that after slogging around in particularities and particular struggles for years one can look back and perhaps gain some satisfaction.

In the area we are talking about, a lot of battles have been won and we should not forget that. The debate about education and values has changed rather dramatically in 10 or 15 years. That has been due, in part, to national and world historical events, but it's been due much more, I think, to the accumulation of lots of little battles, lots of small and particular fights.

Concerning the issue we started with — AIDS and how to teach young people about AIDS — you find very few anymore who are not willing to stipulate that, yes, the first thing we ought to do is teach abstinence and restraint. The argument now is on a second level: supposing the kids aren't restraining, supposing they're sexually active, then what do we say to them? It is hard to find too many people in our time who will say in public anything different from what we've said in public in this book. That's a victory for the American people, and for the common sense of the American people. Go back and look at books in the early 1970's in sex education and I think you'd find very different things.

The world has changed in part for the good. These little battles are worth it, plus they're kind of fun. There's nothing quite like being in a good fight. If the fight is worthy, it's a good place to be.

PART II

ISSUES IN

BIOMEDICAL ETHICS

3

SURROGATE MOTHERS: THE NEW BONDSWOMEN

Abigail Rian Evans, M. Div., Ph.D.
Director of New Programs, Kennedy Institute of Ethics
Director of Health Ministries, National Capital Presbytery

INTRODUCTION

The good that men (women) do is only right in proportion to what they refuse to do. [1]

We live in an age where we are losing the distinction between having knowledge and using it. The trend is that if we know a technique or procedure, we feel obligated to use it. Nowhere is this more apparent than in the area of surrogate motherhood. It seems as if only now, with broken lives and legal suits, are we asking what our ethical responsibilities are. Should the only limits to our actions be technical possibilities and financial resources? Are there some areas where moral prohibitions should exist?

We want to be careful in condemning surrogate motherhood that this not appear as resistance or fear of innovation. We want to form conclusions based on moral principles. The new is often frightening, as has been reflected by past denials that the world was round, not flat; that germs, not evil spirits, caused sickness; and that man could conquer space without replacing God. Hence, it is with hesitancy that one opposes surrogacy, which to some appears as yet one more way of assisting an imperfect nature in her job of providing couples with children. There are 10 million infertile couples in the U.S. today. [2] Is

---

1. Paul Ramsey, *Fabricated Man: The Ethics of Genetic Control* (New Haven: Yale Univ. Press, 1970).
2. Beth Spring, "What Is the Future for Surrogate Motherhood?", *Christianity Today* (1987): 42.

resistance simply based on some romantic notion of parenthood and opposition to technology per se, or is it rooted in justified moral and religious reservations which cut at the very core of what it means to be human, and undermine the created order of our world?

For some people, surrogate motherhood is seen as a viable solution to the age-old problem of infertility. There have been 600 surrogate contracts to date in the U.S.A. There are different types of surrogacy —a wet nurse who cares for an infant, a woman whose womb is used but who has no biological connection with the child, or a woman who contributes her egg and womb. There is certainly a difference between the surrogate whose sole desire is to help a couple, such as a mother assisting her infertile daughter, and a total stranger who does it solely for pay; in other words, the motivation may be service or pay. One working definition is, "A surrogate mother is a woman, married or unmarried, who agrees to have a child for a person who is incapable of giving birth." [3] In this paper I will examine primarily *standard* surrogacy. It is ironic that the term "surrogate" is applied to the woman who carries and gives birth to the child (and in most cases furnishes the egg), rather than to the adoptive mother. "Host mother", the early designation, may be more accurate, though pejorative in its own way.

At the outset, let us acknowledge that some good may result from surrogate motherhood. First, it represents an unselfish act of suffering and pain, to a greater or lesser degree, for someone else's gain; however, payment for surrogate services undermines this to a large degree. Second, it provides the childless couple with a baby that in most cases carries the genetic make-up of the father.

The motivation — providing a child for an infertile couple — may seem noble, since having a child is generally perceived to be a moral good. However, the morality of an act does not rest solely on its motivation, but also on the means and the outcome. Motivation may be for noble reasons or it may be for economic gain. I am suggesting that the means used to achieve the birth (surrogacy) is morally wrong, though good (a child) may result.

We are fast approaching a point where any and all means of reproducing the human race are accepted. One of the underlying issues of surrogacy is the question of technical assistance in procreation. If we take the Roman Catholic position that almost all technical intervention is prohibited, including homologous AID (the GIFT procedure is still

---

3. Margaret D. Townsend, "Surrogate mother agreements: Contemporary legal aspects of a biblical notion," *University of Richmond Law Review* 6(2) (1987): 467.

being debated, but very limited procedures are allowed as an extension of the conjugal act) or the orthodox Jewish perspective that AID is adultery, then surrogate motherhood becomes a moot question. Even if we do not agree with the Roman Catholic Church, there are many people who have a growing concern about our attitudes toward procreation.

Leon Kass has captured the whole shift in our view of the procreation of life:

> Consider the views of life and the world reflected in the following different expressions to describe the process of generating new life. Ancient Israel, impressed with the phenomenon of transmission of life from father to son, used a word we translate as "begetting" or "siring". The Greeks, impressed with the springing forth of new life in the cyclical processes of generation and decay, called it *genesis*, from a root meaning "to come into being". (It was the Greek translators who gave this name to the first book of the Hebrew Bible.) The premodern Christian English-speaking world, impressed with the world as given by a Creator, used the term "pro-creation". We, impressed with the machine and the gross national product (our own work of creation), employ a metaphor of the factory, "reproduction". And Aldous Huxley has provided "decantation" for that technology-worshipping Brave New World of tomorrow. [4]

The thesis of this paper is that surrogate motherhood is a new form of slavery which undermines the nature of woman as related to man, especially the unique husband/wife relationship; forces a separation between the biological and nurturing aspects of motherhood; destroys the parent/child covenant; and creates moral and legal problems which disregard persons' dignity and rights, cutting at the heart of the family.

SURROGATE MOTHERHOOD UNDERMINES THE NATURE OF WOMAN AS RELATED TO MAN, ESPECIALLY THE UNIQUE HUSBAND/WIFE RELATIONSHIP

Any discussions of surrogacy should first examine the nature of woman and how our understanding of womanhood affects surrogacy's morality and practicality. I will analyze the nature of woman from a

---

4. Leon Kass, *Toward a More Natural Science: Biology and Human Affairs* (New York: Free Press, 1985), p.48.

Judeo-Christian perspective and how this relates to our views toward this issue. The first important insight from the Scriptures concerning the nature of woman is her relationship to man, both in general and specifically to her husband.

Woman As Complementary to Man

According to the Hebrew/Christian Scriptures, male and female were created in the image of God. Hence, women shared equally in the spiritual nature of God, embodied in the soul which consists of spirit and mind. Woman is not made in man's image, but God's image (Gen. 1:27 and Gen. 2:21-23). Male and female are not identical, but are complementary and equal in terms of their dignity and worth.

It is important to establish the complementary nature of the two sexes. We understand who we are as women by our relationship to men. The Genesis story explains the creation of woman, not for the purpose of propagating the human race, but rather because "It is not good for man to be alone; I will make him a helper (Ezer) fit for him." (2:18) Part of understanding woman's nature is based on understanding her relationship to man. If we look only at the male or only at the female, we have a partial picture of what it means to be human.

We should *not* attempt to reach a "higher" form of humanity, as Simone de Beauvoir suggests, to overcome masculinity and femininity, to transcend male and female as if to improve on God's creation of sexuality. This would be a flight into *in*humanity rather than fuller humanity. It would sometimes appear that we wish to correct what God did at creation by either blurring or eliminating the distinction between the sexes. There are many types of differentiations and relationships between men, e.g., father/son, boss/worker, but there is a structural and functional difference between male and female.

Male and female complete and transcend each other. God created a helpmate for man within the human species who is nonetheless different from him. As Martin Buber expressed it, man's existence as "I" would not be complete without the "Thou". In the Genesis creation story, the mutual relationship as male and female was no cause for mutual reproach; there was no need to envy their respective advantages. The man in himself was a question without an answer; and the woman, the answer to his question. They were not against each other, but with each other — together without embarrassment or disquiet.

The Genesis account of creation gives us some important clues to the purpose of woman. It portrays her as more than a "mother machine", to borrow a phrase from Gena Corea. First, she was created for companionship, as previously outlined, and so woman belongs with man. Second, for self-illumination: "This at last is bone of my bones and flesh of my flesh." (Genesis 2:23) Woman enables man to understand who he is. Third, for fulfillment. "And they became one flesh." (Genesis 2:24) Man alone was incomplete, and woman completes what it means to be man, as well as what it means to be human.

The symbolism of woman's creation from man's rib is reflective of their closeness and on-going interdependence. The New Testament picks up this theme:
"Nevertheless, in the Lord woman is not independent of man nor man of woman; for as woman was made from man, so man is now born of woman." (I Corinthians 11:11-12)

> Woman was created from the rib of man
> She was not made from his head to top him
> Nor from his feet to be trampled on
> She was made from his side to be equal to him
> From under his arm to be protected by him;
> From near his heart to be loved by him.

Husband/Wife Relationship

This generic male/female relationship is intensified and particularized in marriage. Here a unique bond is created between one man and one woman sealed by mutual commitment and fidelity. It is evident that surrogacy strikes at the very heart of the unique relationship of the husband and wife; first, that of the surrogate and her husband (when the surrogate is married), and second, that of the recipient couple.

Not only the initiating couple's relationship, but also that of the surrogate mother and her husband is profoundly affected. The husband of the surrogate mother must sign a contract waiving all his rights to the child. What feelings does this generate, since his wife is carrying another man's child? How will he relate to her during this time of pregnancy? Will he feel that she is no better than a machine? If, for example, the woman experiences discomfort or even pain and sickness during her pregnancy, how will her husband respond? He may feel she has brought this on herself, and that certainly if she is being paid for it, she should expect a certain amount of discomfort; she may not receive the kind of sympathy which ordinarily might be forthcoming during a pregnancy.

And what about the couple who adopts the child? The wife who was unable to be a biological mother is already dealing with a sense of failure and guilt. How will she feel toward this other woman? The Old

Testament story of Sarah and Hagar is instructive at this point. Sarah asked her maid to give a child to her husband, Abraham. Hagar apparently consented to this, but once Hagar became pregnant and Ishmael was born, Sarah resented the maid and had them both banished. This says something about the inability to predict emotion in such situations. At the outset it may appear to be a good solution to a sad situation, but once the repercussions of that "solution" begin to take place, we may change our minds.

Surrogacy Undermines Procreation As the Fruit of the Conjugal Act

Most of the new reproductive technologies separate love, the conjugal act, parenting and family. Surrogate motherhood carries this separation one step further by introducing a third person; not only the products of another person, but a person *in her totality*. Somehow, disembodied elements such as impersonally donated sperm and eggs are *less intrusive emotionally* to the unique relationship between one man and one woman. I am not necessarily objecting to all technical assistance in reproduction, nor are my arguments against surrogate motherhood contingent upon opposition to *in vitro* fertilization (IVF) per se. I do not believe that all technical assistance for birthing is immoral, nor is it necessary to categorically eliminate all IVF, but to use it only within marriage under very stringent standards as a measure of last resort.

The Vatican paper, "Instruction on Respect for Human Life in Its Origin and on the Dignity of Procreation", bases its primary objection to surrogacy on its opposition to IVF and other reproductive interventions. These are seen as undermining maternal love and breaking the conjugal act, as well as reflecting a basic hostility against life. Curiously, the Roman Catholic Church seems more interested in maintaining the unitive and procreative dimension of intercourse than the exclusivity of one man and one woman. This very helpful paper hopefully will lead to subsequent studies which explore additional moral problems generated particularly by surrogate motherhood. Surrogacy certainly undermines the exclusive nature of one man and one woman. This variation of a *menage a trois* brings another woman, however briefly, into the midst of the intimate experience of a man and a woman, i.e. having a child. Tensions will surely develop between these three in all sorts of combinations of jealousy, feelings of inadequacy at not being able to bear a child, or feelings of exploitation in bearing one for someone else.

SURROGATE MOTHERHOOD FORCES A SEPARATION BETWEEN THE BIOLOGICAL AND NURTURING ASPECTS OF MOTHERHOOD

The Judeo-Christian perspective not only illuminates the complimentarity of male and female, but the uniqueness of woman as mother. The first three words to describe the second sex are relational words — helper, woman, wife; the fourth word, "Eve", establishes her uniqueness. These words establish what we previously discussed as woman's companionship and self-illumination vis-a-vis man. First, she is called "helper" (*ezer*). This same word in other contexts refers to God (Exodus 18:4, Psalm 33:20, Psalm 121). It means "help in the presence of" and contains the notion of similarity as well as supplementation. Some rabbinical scholars, such as Rabbi Hertz, comment that the description of woman as *ezer* shows she is not a shadow or subordinate of man, but man's other self.

Second, the name "woman" (*eeshah*) means "from man". This name is given to the female by Adam, reflecting her interdependence with man. Third, woman is called "wife". Actually the same word, *eeshah*, is used in the Hebrew, but is translated "wife" in English, German, and French in order to establish monogamous marriage as part of the order of creation.

Fourth, woman is called "Eve" (*havah*), mother of all living. Woman is creative, nurturing, giving. Carrying a child becomes an act of sharing one's body in the most intimate way possible. The presence of a guest in her body, albeit sometimes uninvited, is the ultimate act of sharing. Carrying, bearing, and bringing up a child can be deeply satisfying, but is not the only way of reflecting these feminine characteristics of motherhood. However, the potentiality of being a biological mother says something as well about what it means psychologically to be a woman. The life-giving, life-bearing aspect of woman is an innate part of her being. It might be more accurate psychologically to say that to be a woman is to reflect these maternal characteristics of nurture and caring. The characteristics may be reflected whether a woman is a biological mother or not, as women have shown in their choice of service occupations such as nursing, teaching, etc. Now more than ever before, women may choose to be biological mothers, but if this is severed from the nurturing and caring side of mothering, it divides a woman's nature.

Surrogacy separates the biological and nurturing dimensions of motherhood. It separates a woman from the fruit of her womb. It attempts to change the legal definition of "mother". Traditionally, she was the one from whose womb the child came; now a mother may be the one who purchases, not carries, a baby. A woman is chosen to be a surrogate based on her proven child-bearing capacities as well as her "psychological soundness or mental health". Mental health is here defined in terms of her willingness to render her baby upon its birth to another person; certainly a strange way of describing psychological stability. Scientific studies such as those by Klaus and Kennel have established maternal/infant bonding in utero and the deep physical and emotional ties which are created. [5] The decision to bear a child for someone else, in itself, is bound to create severe emotional and mental problems. As Anne Fleming has expressed it, "... the one thing — maybe the only thing — that is clear is that surrogacy is no business for women who are going to go around falling in love with their own babies, no business at all." [6]

To some this image of woman may appear a romanticized notion of a long-gone era and have little to say about today's professional women. However, most studies reflect that the majority of women still prize marriage and children as worthy goals which enrich and fulfill who they are, even if not completely defining it. The feminists of the '70s, who criticized the homemaker role, are now in the '80s proclaiming it is equally important as the professional role. Betty Friedan in *The Second Stage* declared that the problem that currently has no name is how to juggle work, love, home, and children. Erica Jong, in a *Saturday Review* article several years ago, said feminists were beating their heads against a wall by trying to deny the importance to most women of nurturing, childbearing, and warm familial relationships. Certainly surrogacy robs a woman of that dimension of her life by taking away the child she carries and births.

With surrogate motherhood, we seem to be entering an era where women will consider motherhood not a role, but a profession — a job to be paid for services rendered. This approach collapses what were two distinct aspects of a modern woman's life — a career and motherhood — so she becomes a professional mother.

Feminist writers such as Gena Corea have captured one of the problems with the new reproductive technologies by its relegation of women to "mother machines". This type of dehumanization which Judge Sorkow highlighted by his reference to surrogate mothers as

---

5. Marshall H. Klaus and John H. Kennell, *Maternal-Infant Bonding: The Impact of Early Separation or Loss on Family Developement* (St. Louis: Mosby, 1976).
6. Anne Taylor Fleming, "Our fascination with Baby M", *New York Times Magazine* (March 29, 1987): 87.

"Alternative Reproductive Vehicles" (ARV) is a form of discrimination far harsher than any salary differentials or employment prejudices. In some ways the use of surrogacy instead of adoption may reflect a male *hubris* for a biological child no matter what the emotional cost to the women involved. It strikes at the core of what it means to be a woman and tears apart her inner self. She is used as an object to satisfy someone else's needs and desires.

I wish to raise one word of caution here that by describing woman in the more traditional roles, I am not suggesting that she is only suited to be a wife and mother. *Au contraire*. There are no roles, in the sense of jobs, careers, or relationships, that are inappropriate for a woman. The number of women entering the labor force, which has increased by 13% in the last two decades, testifies not only to economic necessity, but to the changing roles of women. The number of women in professions such as law, medicine, and religion have doubled in the past decade. However, surrogacy will set back the strides women have made for equality. Surrogate mothers will become bondswomen.

SURROGATE MOTHERHOOD DESTROYS THE PARENT/CHILD COVENANT

Surrogate motherhood, more than any other of the new reproductive technologies, confuses and destroys the parent/child relationship. Who are the parents — the biological or adoptive ones? With adopted children attempting to locate their biological parents, how much will this natural instinct be compounded by surrogacy? Will a child be told about his manner of birth? Who are the parents? Here parenthood appears to result from negotiation rather than love. One of the central questions that surrogacy raises is whether there is a right to be a parent. There is a tendency to view infertility as a disease with any cure acceptable, but these "cures" are almost exclusively available to the wealthy, as they come with a price tag of $25,000. We believe that parenthood is not a contract but a covenant, an obligation and responsibility rather than a right. For this reason surrogacy, by relying on the contract model, undermines parenthood as a covenant.

The contrast between contract and covenant is an instructive one and has been well delineated in the writings of Robert Veatch, Paul Ramsey, and William F. May. In essence, a contract relies on closely-defined parameters and obligations. The difficulty with contracts in terms of parenthood is that they do not allow for changing relations and the emotional side of human nature. Contracts are too rigid in their formulation because it is not possible to anticipate all circumstances in the parent/child relationship. Judge Sorkow ruled in favor of the Sterns over Mary Beth Whitehead on the basis of honoring contracts and the child's best interest, but left vast areas of related issues about parenthood unaddressed. Roger Rosenblatt points out how human dimensions can creep into such contracts:

Picture Stern at the outset of the bargain. He and his wife want a baby, and here is the clean, modern, technologically miraculous way to get one. What he does not take into account is that he is engaging someone to feel sensations on behalf of him and his wife that properly belong only to him and his wife. What seems so easy mechanically turns out to be an impossibility, yet the sanctioning by contract obfuscates the reality. Instead of a simple deal, he has swung a deal whose complications are infinite, and infinitely surprising; they are not in anyone's control. For a deal like that, no terms make sense. They are bound to be violated (as Whitehead wound up violating them) because they apply to a realm of human conduct that is biological, erratic and deeply mysterious. If Whitehead had volunteered her pregnancy as an act of generosity to the Sterns, the matter would have involved the same ambiguities, puzzlement and pain. Money made matters considerably more difficult, since money imposed a legal cast on a service not reasonably regulated by laws, not reasonably regulated at all; but all such bargains are unwise, and when they work, more is owed to luck than contracts. [7]

Two bioethicists who describe and embrace the contract model are H. Tristam Engelhardt and Robert Veatch. They are primarily discussing it in relation to the patient/physician relationship, but their definitions are instructive for insights into surrogate contracts. For Engelhardt, the central piece of a contract is a strong emphasis on contractual rights and duties. A patient's rights are developed out of civil or political interests and not out of the relationship itself; hence, they must be legally assured rather than being grounded in natural law or general ethical theory. The contract model for him best avoids the paternalistic tendencies in health care delivery as well as guaranteeing patients' rights.

Veatch uses the term "contract" in a symbolic, not a legal sense, and relies on the moral images of the marriage contract and the philosophical

---

7. Roger Rosenblatt, "Baby M — Emotions for sale", *Time* (April 6, 1987), p.88.

roots of Locke and Rousseau's social contract and the Rawlsian analysis of justice. The characteristics of the contract model for him are as follows:
1. Obligations and benefits must exist for both parties (Note here the use of the word "parties" rather than "persons");
2. The essential norms for the relationship are freedom, dignity, truth-telling, promise-keeping and justice;
3. The relationship is based on the premises of trust and confidence;
4. There is a sharing of ethical authority and responsibility; and
5. The medical decisions are made within the framework of the patient's own value system.

For Veatch, a contract is generated from mutual promises and pledging; it is a binding agreement except on grounds of conscience. In most situations, however, conflicts of conscience would not arise, since desired services would be negotiated ahead of time. Since a contract is voluntarily entered into, it can be as inclusive or as exclusive as the parties involved desire. Contract, as Veatch describes it, is certainly on a higher plane than that which is currently being written in surrogate motherhood cases. [8]

The introduction of the theological concept of covenant is an underlying theme of Paul Ramsey's medical ethics. The canon of loyalty, fidelity, respect for persons, and the binding nature of relationships is based on the Old Testament understanding of the faithful YHWH and His chosen people, Israel. The covenant relationship is marked by trust, commitment, honesty, vulnerability, empathy, a steadfastness, a sense of one's being there. [9] William May takes a slightly different approach from Ramsey to the covenant model, though he acknowledges the similar roots of Old Testament theology. His image of the covenant owes much to Faulkner (especially *Go Down Moses, Delta Autumn, The Old People,* and *Intruder in the Dust*). The emphasis is on the growing edge, the vitality of the relationship as shown, e.g., by Faulkner in white and black relationships in the South. In order to show more clearly the nature of the covenant model, May contrasts it with code and contract.

The distinguishing features of a code are as follows: (1) an emphasis on technical proficiency where those who do not measure up may be

---

8. Robert Veatch, *A Theory of Medical Ethics* (New York: Basic Books, 1981).
9. Paul Ramsey, *The Patient As Person: Explorations in Medical Ethics* (New Haven: Yale University Press, 1970).

ostracized; and (2) the giving of directions for behavior which are categorized and universal for particular groups and societies. The code includes form as well as content, so that style and decorum become almost a technique, as in Hemingway's description of the ritual killing of the bull.

The contract model for May is characterized by the following attributes:

1. an exchange of goods and services;
2. a basis in self-interest rather than the condescension of charity;
3. the provision of legal enforcement of its terms;
4. a limitation of obligations only to what the contract calls for, suppressing the element of gift;
5. a tit-for-tat approach; and
6. an external relationship rather than internal to the parties involved.

With these two models delineated, May returns to the concept of *covenant*. For May, the concept of covenant has aesthetic as well as theological elements. It is characterized as follows:

1. roots in specific historical events which determine much of the future relationship of the persons involved;
2. an exchange of gifts between the soon-to-be covenanted partners;
3. a promise based on the anticipated exchange of gifts;
4. the shaping of the subsequent life of each partner with mutual indebtedness; and
5. an ongoing commitment which is internal. [10]

The covenant model injects the donative element, highlighting the binding nature of the relationship and broadening accountability. In the parent/child covenant there is a mutual accountability which is important. The relationship is almost totally one-sided when the child is a newborn; but as she grows, wider responsibility is also expected from her, providing more of a symmetry. The central features of the covenant are its bonding nature and all-timeness. This is not a limited obligation, but one that continues for the lifetime of the persons.

A contrast between covenant and contract, respectively, may help in understanding how parenthood is more appropriately referred to as a covenant: (1) two persons in relation vs. two parties in legally agreed

10. William May, "Code and covenant or contract and philanthropy; Alternative bases for professional ethics", in *Ethics in Medicine; Historical Perspectives and Contemporary concerns* (Cambridge, MA: MIT Press, 1977).

upon roles; (2) care, cure, commitments vs. goods, services, negotiations; (3) response to ongoing changing needs vs. response only to what is negotiated ahead of time; (4) characterized by paternalism vs. characterized by autonomy; (5) values of patient respected and protected vs. values of patient unknown; (6) internal vs. external obligations; (7) based on codes and ethics vs. based on laws and regulations; (8) binding vs. limited obligations, minimalism; (9) donative element, beyond self-interest vs. mutual self-interest; (10) deontological vs. utilitarian and consequentialist; (11) first beneficence vs. first non-maleficence. The contrasting value as described here reflects the nature of contract as concerned with specifically defined rights, whereas covenant is concerned with the changing needs of persons.

SURROGATE MOTHERHOOD DISREGARDS THE DIGNITY OF PERSONS AND CREATES IRRESOLVABLE CONFLICTS OF RIGHTS

There are numerous moral problems which are generated by surrogate motherhood. The primary problems which underly our discussions of the nature of woman and parent/child covenant are the disregard for persons and the difficulty of honoring everyone's rights and dignity.

Persons Are Treated as Means, Not Ends

Immanuel Kant made famous the categorical imperative which described universality as determining both the morality of acts and their necessary goal of treating persons as ends in themselves, rather than merely as means. The moral dimension of judging an act by its universality is an important criterion in assessing surrogate motherhood. Even its strongest advocates would not recognize this as a desirable universal method of parenting; hence it fails on Kant's first criterion. The second part of his moral position is grounded in the belief of the inherent dignity and worth of each person. Respect for persons is not based on age, sex, physical or mental qualities, or quality of life or achievements.

The surrogate mother becomes the means by which someone else becomes a parent, and her needs, feelings and womanhood are not valued in and of themselves. In a very limited sense, a parallel may be drawn with pregnancy by rape; here a child results from an evil act, but the child himself is not evil. The method is a violation of the woman's body. Now, one could reply that the primary difference between surrogacy and rape is the free choice of the woman in the former act. However, the woman in both instances is treated as an object — a means to an end — sexual pleasure/rage or producing a baby. Perhaps one could even extend this logic to say that the woman is psychologically forced or economically coerced into being a surrogate mother. In the majority of cases, these women are from a lower socio-economic group than that of the adoptive parents.

Not only is the surrogate mother treated as a means, but so is the baby. The child becomes a possession to be bought and sold — an object of a contract. If "service", rather than the baby, is what is being bought, then the host mother should have the option to keep the child. It is hard to distinguish this from baby-selling. Furthermore, how can you sell something you do not own?

There is bound to be a psychological impact on those babies who are birthed by technology. A cartoon in the *Washington Post* captured this with a drawing of "Pandora's Womb". Here were pictured dozens of babies talking to one another: "Yeah, the deal's off. They say I'm handicapped."; "Where were you born?"; "Ten Grand?!!? Mine only got $3,750."; "I figure by second grade the courts will decide who my legal parents are."; "You mean, where was I brokered ... "; "My mom's a career woman, so she couldn't make it for the birth ..."; "Who's your agent?"; "I'm going to a single parent."; "You think that's bad, I've got two, but they're both gay ... " [11]

Another problem is the "defective" baby. The "defective" baby has no rights. Current surrogate contracts give the biological father the right to request an abortion if amniocentesis reveals congenital abnormalities. The Whitehead contract, for example, stipulated that,

> MARY BETH WHITEHEAD, Surrogate, agrees...upon the request of said physician to undergo amniocentesis or similar tests to detect genetic and congenital defects. In the event said test reveals that the fetus is genetically or congenitally abnormal, MARY BETH WHITEHEAD, Surrogate, agrees to abort the fetus upon demand of WILLIAM STERN, Natural Father...[12]

Depending on one's view on abortion, this can already violate the unborn child. What "defects" warrant abortion? Would the wrong sex or certain physical characteristics become sufficient grounds? Furthermore, there are some abnormalities which cannot be or are not being

---

11. Benson cartoon, "Pandora's Womb," *Washington Times*, 3D, (September 4, 1987).
12. "Surrogate Parenting Agreement", from the firm of Cassidy, Despo, Foss & San Filippo (Red Bank, NJ, February 5, 1985).

detected in utero; these babies become pawns in debates about duties and obligations. There have already been cases where paternity was disputed and none of the parents wanted the handicapped baby.

A further complication of this act is its effect on the other children of the surrogate mother. If the host mother has other children (required currently to prove her child-bearing capacity), certainly they would experience anxiety that perhaps they would be sold as well. Even if this ultimate fear is ungrounded, certainly their view of motherhood would be distorted.

Conflict of Rights

One problem related to respect of persons is the conflict of rights. For example, during a surrogate mother's pregnancy there is a tension between the privacy and freedom of the mother and the rights of the fetus. Should a surrogate have to conform to a certain lifestyle, for example abstaining from cigarettes or following specific diet and exercise regimens? How will this be monitored? How can privacy be assured? Some legal opinions on these issues favor the protection of the surrogate's rights, since the initiating couple cannot be promised a perfect child any more than they would be if they had a baby by normal means. "In essence, the initiating parents must contend with a situation of 'reverse' product liability. They, as consumers, must bear the major risk, rather than the surrogate mother as producer." [13] One notes, by the use of this very language, how metaphors of the factory have taken control. However, there are other legal perspectives as reflected in the Mary Beth Whitehead/William Stern contract; here it seems that the Sterns did have the right to a "perfect" child, since abortion was required if an abnormality was detected.

Another aspect of the struggle of rights is who has the right to the baby. An attachment may develop between the surrogate and the baby, in which case opinion is divided as to whose rights triumph. One alternative would be for the surrogate to make a decision before birth. In most cases to date, the best interests of the child have not been considered. This concern introduces another set of rights — the child's rights to the best parents. Of course, this raises all sorts of problems since in the past the biological mother almost always had first "claim" to a child.

As was suggested in discussions about the parent/child covenant, it is

13. Andrea E. Stumpf, "Redefining mother: A legal matrix for new reproductive technologies", *Yale Law Journal* 96(1) (1986): 204.

doubtful that "rights" are even appropriate language for discussing family responsibility. As Carol Gilligan has rightly pointed out, care-based claims should outweigh rights-based claims.

The above review has attempted to clarify the fundamental moral issues associated with surrogate motherhood. The focus of the discussion has been on the departures from a woman's right relationship to herself, her husband, and her child that are introduced by this practice. It is of little surprise that legal systems attempting to grapple with such fundamentally charged issues have but produced a patchwork of unsatisfactory conclusions. The following section attempts to summarize some of these from the perspective of the moral issues.

SURROGATE MOTHERHOOD CREATES LEGAL QUAGMIRES WHICH CONTRADICT MANY OF THE PAST LAWS PROTECTING THE FAMILY

Both legal and financial problems which stem from the practice of surrogate motherhood are further illustration of its moral questionableness. There are five primary activities in surrogate parenting, all of which can create legal problems: (1) artificial insemination by donor; (2) payment of fees to the genetic and gestational surrogate; (3) agreement by the biological mother to relinquish her parental rights; (4) legitimation of the baby by the biological father; (5) adoption of the baby by his wife. The law needs to focus on the unique combination of these factors.

The Nature of Legal Dilemmas

Surrogate motherhood is a legal quagmire of contracts, suits, fees, and unapplicable precedents. "Contract law is more at home in the business world than in the nursery; artificial insemination statutes were designed to legitimize, not bastardize a child; and adoption procedures were established to facilitate giving up an unwanted child rather than to orchestrate its conception." [14] Many in the legal profession believe that current surrogate motherhood contracts may be unenforceable. With only limited case law and no statutory guidance available on surrogate transactions, legal questions are emerging weekly without definitive answers. Even physicians have reservations about this procedure. The American Medical Association's Judicial Council, for example,

---

14. Margaret D. Townsend, "Surrogate mother agreements: Contemporary legal aspects of a biblical notion", *University of Richmond Law Review* 16(2) (Winter 1982): 468.

prepared a report expressing "considerable concern about 'the potential legal and ethical jeopardy that physicians who participate in such arrangements face. When all considerations are brought together, these arrangements do not appear to serve societal interest.' " [15]

The legal difficulties stem not only from the lack of precedent, but the validity and enforceability of such contracts once they are drawn up. These contracts require deciding on terms of agreement months in advance without allowing for changed circumstances of either a psychological, economic, physical, or emotional nature. For example, the prospective adoptive parents may divorce, the surrogate may become ill or change her mind, the baby may become unwanted — just to name a few of the unanticipated problems. A court may find a surrogate contract null because it does not serve everyone's best interests, including the public at large. As Rabbi David Bleich pointed out, a contract is an anomaly in this situation as it is for something that does not exist. The custody of a child cannot be conveyed by law as it is an obligation, not a right. Current laws may prove to be an impediment rather than an improvement.

Public opinion polls about surrogate motherhood reflect our ambiguity towards this procedure.

A January 1987 Gallup poll found that 63 percent of the people surveyed approved of surrogate motherhood when the wife was unable to bear a child, and 52 percent favored it when birth defects were likely due to the wife's genetic makeup. Eighty-one percent of the women polled said they would not consider becoming a surrogate mother. [16]

There are now over one hundred state bills under discussion regulating or banning surrogacy. The Warnock Commission in Great Britain opposed surrogacy. The United Kingdom, France and Australia have recently banned the practice. Only the Ontario Law Reform Commission statement, the report of the American Fertility Society Ethics Committee and Dutch Health Council Committee found fee-based surrogacy acceptable. [17]

The convoluted legal steps which are necessary to assure the legality

---

15. "AMA raps surrogate motherhood as ethical and legal quagmire", *Medical World News* (January 9, 1984): 24.
16. LeRoy Walters, "Ethics and new reproductive technologies: An international review of committee statements", *Hastings Center Report* 17(3) (1987): 3-9. With additional statistics from an unpublished study, "Public opinion on indications for surrogate motherhood," 1987.
17. *Ibid.*, p. 8.

of surrogacy are evidence enough of its unnaturalness. The initiating parents have to establish the legitimacy of the child and assure adoption procedures are followed. The legal rights of the child must be completely vested in the natural father and his wife. [18] The two presumptions by which the law perpetuates the nuclear family (father, mother, child) — the presumption of biology and the presumption of legitimacy — have to be stretched into bizarre focus in surrogate contracts. For example, the natural father has to adopt his own child. The question of parenting also relates to the non-technical procedures involved in these contracts. The precedent situations closest to surrogacy are AID laws, which in 29 states consider the husband of a woman who is inseminated the legal father. In contrast with surrogate contracts, the opposite holds true, as the man who inseminates is considered the father and his wife the mother.

Because we are examining the nature of parenthood, it may be important to contrast surrogacy and adoption as the route to becoming a parent. Since adoption has been legal for decades and not generally judged to be morally questionable, why doesn't it fall under the same condemnation as surrogacy? The moral differences between adoption and surrogate motherhood are, respectively: (1) Adoption takes tragic circumstances already past and attempts to bring something good out of them, while surrogacy creates tragic circumstances by using one person's body for another's pleasure or gain. One could label this a form of slavery. (2) Adoption gives an existent child a home, while surrogacy takes a child away from a home. (3) Adoptive mothers who give away a child for adoption are *not able* to care for the child, while surrogate mothers do not *want* to care for the child. (4) In adoption the original design in conceiving is not to give a child away, while in surrogacy the original plan is to give the child away. (5) In adoption, the biological parents have the option to keep the child, while surrogate parents from the outset agree to waive any rights to the child.

Due to all these factors, I believe adoption does not necessarily break the parent/child covenant because the desire is to give the child a better home, whereas surrogacy allows contract to trump covenant.

In addition to the legal problems is the whole matter of lawyers' ethics. Are fees appropriate when they surpass what the surrogate mother receives? If surrogates were not paid at all and only lawyers

---

18. Andrea E. Stumpf, "Redefining mother: A legal matrix for new reproductive technologies", *Yale Law Journal* 96(1) (1986): 190.

were paid, this would appear even more questionable. What about lawyers who advertise for interviews and match up surrogate and initiating parents? How far do their moral and legal liabilities extend to providing the perfect match?

Law is attempting now to recognize the psychological dimension to parenting and to build that into the process covering rights and obligations. This distinction, however, appears weighted on the side of the initiating parents rather than the biological mother. Phrases such as "understanding the infertile wife's role as mother" make clear that surrogate arrangements render the biological link obsolete as the legal determinant of "mother". [19] The trend here is to presuppose that child bearing and child rearing can be divided between two women; motherhood then becomes an option or a choice. Terms such as "mental" conception of a child are employed to refer to the initiating parents' role. Here we have two mothers but one child. However, the birthing in these instances is assisted by a lawyer and physician so what was once a family affair becomes a community happening — a public event.

Further complications arise from the possibility of a baby's being born with disabilities. Clauses such as required abortion in the case of "defective" fetuses determined in utero reflect these situations but do not cover undetected cases. Whose responsibility are decisions about treatment/non-treatment of these babies? Is the Ontario Commission's Report to be followed, if neither the adoptive parents nor the biological mother desire the child, by applying child protection laws? Who is culpable for child neglect if non-treatment is advocated by all parties? Who pays for treatment? What if the child dies while legal questions are being sorted? Another related issue is one of inheritance; in contested cases if one set of parents dies, does the baby inherit their estate?

Financial Considerations

Currently there is considerable debate concerning the payment of fees to surrogate mothers. (The total costs average $25,000 which includes lawyer's fees, tests, and payment to the surrogate mother. This cost compares with an average of $10,000 for an adoption.) The problem is whether morality mandates payment as just compensation or no payment because of reservations about baby selling. A number of judges (e.g. Attorney General of Louisiana) limit payment to prenatal expenses, whereas others, (e.g. Katie Beoply) argue that in recognition

19. *Ibid.*, 197.

of the value of gestation as well as the value of domestic work of the woman who is babysitting or renting her womb, payment should be made. I would question whether "valuing" can even be applied to the law's whole attitude toward surrogate mothers. The surrogate becomes a baby machine where her entire body is not valued, but only one part of her — her womb.

Paying women to have babies raises a whole set of related economic issues. For example, a new law in California allows up to four months unpaid leave for pregnant women, who must be given the same or a comparable job after pregnancy. Will this apply to surrogates?

CONCLUSION

In reviewing the various legal and moral problems inherent in surrogate motherhood, we have tried to show that surrogate motherhood is an unacceptable form of solving the problem of infertility. We recognize the anguish and grief of not having a child and the growing difficulty of adoption. We recommend investigation of other approaches for infertile couples that scientific medicine might offer, such as GIFT, which avoid the resultant tragedies of surrogacy.

We believe that simply fixing the legal problems of loopholes and unanticipated exigencies, or even diminishing the conflict of rights, will not ameliorate the wrongs perpetrated by this practice. Undermining the very heart of what it means to be a woman, a parent, and a family where mutual respect, obligations, and covenanting exist between its members, our society as a whole will suffer if surrogate motherhood continues. We are not suggesting that all surrogate mothers have the wrong motivations, even though 89% of them wanted to be paid for their services. They were also concerned about helping an infertile couple and experiencing the satisfaction of pregnancy. [20] Rather, this practice will create a class of bondswomen where women are denigrated and motherhood is a contract and service rather than a covenant with the child from conception to death.

20. Phillip J. Parker, M.D., "Motivation of surrogate mothers: Initial findings", *AM J. Psychiatry* 140(1) (January 1983): 117-118.

4

THE CHANGING CONCEPTS OF PARENTHOOD AND PERSONHOOD

Rita L. Marker
Human Life Center
University of Steubenville

Under these conditions, whose baby am I? Who is my mother, my father...? Indeed, if babies are bought and sold as consumer products, will I be rejected if I don't measure up? [1]

Parenthood and personhood were, at one time, terms used without question. So deep was the understanding of their significance that one did not ask for definition when discussing parents or persons. This is no longer the case.

In the past two decades, incredible changes have taken place. Abortion and contraceptives for teenage children, once considered unthinkable, have become commonplace. Death as a solution to the problem of unwanted pregnancy and medical manipulation to prevent teen pregnancy are touted as advances of modern society.

And now, two additional advances are being set forth as new solutions to current problems. Euthanasia and reproductive technology have entered the scene, offering the same options. Death as a solution to the problem of dependency or disability and laboratory manufacturing to alleviate childlessness have joined the list of "choices" to which all, some say, should have a right.

The promotion and acceptance of each new "right" — to abortion; to birth control for unmarried teens; to reproductive technology; to euthanasia — further attacks parenthood and personhood, both of which form the foundation of the family.

---

[1] Sidney Callahan, "No child wants to live in a womb for hire," *National Catholic Reporter*, October 11, 1985.

Parenthood and its accompanying responsibility to protect, nurture, guide and unconditionally love the child is increasingly portrayed as a means of self-fulfillment for the adult wishing to have a child. The child's importance is based on the ability to fulfill a need — much as any consumer product.

Respect for personhood and the recognition of the value of every person's life is being replaced by a calculation of the individual's ability to contribute to society. Persons perceived to be burdens to others are portrayed as less than human and, in many cases, better off dead than dependent.

Sexual intimacy, once acknowledged as belonging only within the context of marriage, has been trivialized, often seen as just another pleasurable activity which should not result in an "unwanted child" and as unnecessary to obtaining a "wanted child".

MILESTONES IN THE ROAD TO CHANGE

Much has been written and discussed in recent years about a consistent ethic of life. While there is some disagreement about priorities and methodology, a consistent ethic of life — often called the "seamless garment" — does exist, characterized by a connecting thread expressed in respect for the sanctity of innocent human life, the gift of sexuality, and the family as the basic unit of society.

So, too, there is a consistent ethic of death which could be called the "seamless shroud", characterized by an emphasis on the quality of life, a trivialization of sexuality and a devaluation of the importance of the family unit. It is this consistent ethic of death that has led to the current atmosphere in which personhood and parenthood are being questioned, demeaned, and finally discarded as remnants of a quaint, outmoded value system.

Creating a "right" out of that which was once considered wrong does not come about by chance. Nor does it emanate from the wishes of the general public or the majority of practicing health professionals. Rather, the attitude changes are carefully shaped by relatively small groups of opinion molders, "experts" and policy makers.

Careful examination of the framing of new "rights" unsurfaces a progression:

>...Emphasis on the "hard case" and statistics, creating a general problem or need.
>...Promotion of a new solution to meet the need or solve the problem.

...Advancement of the solution as a "choice".
...Elevation of the "choice" to the level of a "right".
...Support of the "right" with public funding or legal protection.
...Portrayal of the subsidized or protected right as a responsibility.
...Establishment of the exercise of the right as a new norm for behavior.

ABORTION AND SBC'S AS FORERUNNERS

Concern about problems faced by some women during pregnancy and growing alarm about teen pregnancy rates set the stage for accepting abortion and teen birth control as necessary elements of societal well-being.

Preceded by flurries of statistics and widely reported "hard cases", abortion advocates advanced under the banner of "the right to choose". No matter that the hard cases were sometimes pure fiction or that the statistics had been plucked from thin air. By the time the falsehoods were brought to light, public opinion and policy had been changed.

Such was the case of Norma McCorvey, the woman whose case prompted the *Roe v. Wade* decision. Portrayed as the victim of gang rape, thus solidifying public opinion behind the "rightness" of the court decision for such a "hard case", McCorvey revealed fourteen years later that she had become pregnant through what she had thought was love, *not* as a result of rape. [2]

The "hard-case" of the pregnant teen and the misuse of statistics have bolstered support for the provision of contraceptives to school children. One vehicle for this is the school based clinic (SBC). The statistics game has become so much a part of the SBC organizational scenario that the Center for Population Options (CPO), a national leader in the SBC movement, has developed a special handbook and software package "to help you compute the cost of teenage childbearing in *your* community". [3] Note, however, that the statistics do not deal with the crucial point of the effectiveness of SBC's in preventing teen pregnancy.

In mid-1986 a flurry of articles appeared in newspapers and magazines citing a study which purported to prove the effectiveness of SBC's. However, the study, conducted by Zabin, Smith and Hirsch, did

---

[2] Tony Mauro, " 'Roe v. Wade' case: A 14-yr. secret revealed," *U.S.A. Today*, September 9, 1987

[3] Center for Population Options "Dear Colleague" letter signed by Katia Segre, Resource Center Coordinator. Received October, 1986.

nothing of the kind. In fact, the only concrete "finding" was that the study had proven nothing.

Even the authors of the study, in an article outlining its methodology and results, noted that the problems encountered in making the study rendered it useless. [4] This recognition did not receive national coverage. The erroneous reports of SBC effectiveness remained in the public's mind.

From the hard cases and statistical manipulations on which the "right" to abortions and teen contraceptive clinics were based grew public and foundation funding and legal protection of the "right to choose". Well-known and well-financed organizations promoted and lent support — sometimes blatant, sometimes subtle — to the belief that these "rights" not only could, but also *should*, be chosen.

Those who have followed the abortion and SBC movements know it was not long before the right to abortion turned into pressure on every pregnant woman to kill her unborn child unless she had good reason for not doing so. Women of all ages face pressure to explain why they have not chosen the "option" of abortion.

Teens, by being told that the "choice" is theirs to make, are being pressured to choose sexual activity. Today, in some professional circles, sexual activity among teens is held up as the model. According to a recent article in *Ob-Gyn News*, "Health professionals and counselors can gain a greater understanding of teenage pregnancy by acknowledging that sexual activity among American and many European teenagers is now the norm, not an indication of social deviance." [5]

In practice, "choices" of abortion for pregnant women and birth control for teens have been raised to the level of expected behavior. For all practical purposes, those who disagree with abortion and teen contraception are seen as going against the tide.

The erosion of the meanings of parenthood and personhood is thus well underway; the abortion mentality assaults the role of parents to protect, not destroy, their children and obliterates the recognition of the unborn child as a person; the teen contraceptive movement likewise fosters a disregard for parental rights to protect and guide teenage children in important life decisions at the same time that it fosters a perception among teens that parenthood is a bad "side effect" of sexual activity.

---

4 Rita L. Marker, "School Based Clinics: A Movement to Create a New Society," *International Review of Natural Family Planning*, vol. X, no. 4, (Winter, 1986), pp. 281-282.

5 "Encourages physicians to accept teenage sexual activity as norm," *Ob-Gyn News*, August 1-14, 1986, p. 18.

HUMAN "NON-PERSONS"

With eleven words, "We need not resolve the difficult question of when life begins", [6] the United States Supreme Court called into question the personhood of unborn children and set in place a mindset that tiny dependent human beings are not persons but products — "products of conception".

Such studied uncertainty was so effective in removing the underpinnings of a respect for unborn life that it is now being used in an attack upon the lives of the disabled, the elderly and the dying. It is no small coincidence that, as the euthanasia movement gains momentum, questions about the personhood of the medically vulnerable are being introduced within the context of scholarly debate.

In his keynote address to the Second International Congress on Ethics in Medicine, Morris B. Abram, who served as chairman of the President's Commission for the Study of Ethical Problems in Medicine and Biomedical and Behavioral Research, expressed the view that we will grapple soon with deciding whether or not the brain damaged person who is breathing unaided is, nevertheless, "dead".

"We may well come to that conclusion," he said. However, he further explained that this may take some time, since old "myths die very hard." [7]

As the denigration of personhood progresses, the concept of parenthood is further called into question.

QUALITY CONTROL IN "MANUFACTURING"

Surrogate motherhood — the newest cottage industry — has identified the child as the "product" of the industry and the rented womb as the location of the "manufacturing" process. Quality control of the product is important to the industry as is fulfillment of the contract conditions agreed upon prior to manufacture.

The broad range of reproductive technologies raises questions of both parenthood and personhood, although the questions seem to be given little priority by the technicians themselves. Techniques such as artificial insemination using frozen sperm, *in vitro* fertilization, frozen

---

6 *Roe v. Wade* 193 S.Ct. 705,730, 410 U.S. 113, 159 (1973).

7 Second International Congress on Ethics and Medicine sponsored by Beth Israel Medical Center, New York; Ben-Gurion University of the Negev, Beersheva, Israel; and the Karolinska Institute, Stockholm, Sweden; New York, New York; June 9-12, 1987; "The Boundaries of Life," keynote address by Morris B. Abram, Esq., June 9, 1987.

embryos, genetic manipulation and surrogate motherhood are seen by their pioneers and entrepreneurs as positive scientific advances. As Gary Hodgen, scientific director of the Jones Institute for Reproductive Medicine (the first U.S. *in vitro* clinic) has said, "We're no longer talking about whether it [*in vitro* fertilization] can be done, but about how to do it better." [8] Whether it *should* be done seems to be a non-issue.

Lack of interest in the morality of reproductive technological procedures was exemplified at the Fifth World Congress on In Vitro Fertilization and Embryo Transfer, held last Spring in Norfolk, Virginia. Although the Congress drew 1,700 researchers and clinicians who packed sessions for discussions about inserting one sperm into an egg; cracking one cell of a four-celled embryo; and freezing, thawing, growing and transplanting embryos, only 300 conference attendees bothered to attend the one panel on ethics. (Scheduling of the ethics panel conflicted with a field trip to Colonial Williamsburg.)

The conference, which opened with Dr. Patrick Steptoe — often referred to as the "father" of Louise Brown, the world's first test-tube baby — on stage, playing his original piano composition, "Tribute to a Dying Embryo", was described by one reporter as a week-long discussion of desexed, disembodied and dehumanized reproduction. [9]

Yet the disintegration of the importance of childbearing within the context of marriage and family has precedent. Lest it be thought that such a depersonalization of human reproduction is uniquely current, it may be wise to recall that the Germany of the thirties and forties had a similar outlook on life. Positive eugenics known as *Lebensborn* was part of the plan to "breed" a biological elite with those children judged to be beneath the required program quality shipped off to concentration camps. [10]

Positive eugenics played an important and inseparable role in the biomedical vision of Germany. This role in allowing births for only the acceptable was inseparable from the negative eugenics responsible for forced sterilization and, eventually, euthanasia. The medical profession played the role of protecting and revitalizing the genetic health of the *Volk* in Germany's experience. [11]

---

8. Andrea Boroff Eagan, "Baby roulette: The selling of In Vitro fertilization," *Village Voice*, August 25, 1987, pp. 16-20.
9. Ibid.
10. Robert Lifton, *The Nazi Doctors: Medical Killing and the Psychology of Genocide* (New York: Basic Books, 1986), p. 43.
11. Ibid., p. 42.

COERCING HEALTH PROFESSIONALS

Current day American medical practices are rooted in the myth that a solitary absolute exists. That singular absolute is that there are *no* absolutes. One belief (a living human being is not a person) is said to be as valid and worthy of support and protection as its opposite (a living human being is a person).

The fact that providing support for each viewpoint directly attacks the other is conveniently overlooked. Thus such statements as, "I'm against abortion (euthanasia, contraceptives for teens, freezing embryos), but I support the right of others to choose it" are looked upon as enlightened and magnanimous.

"I'm personally opposed but..." has, in many quarters, become the politically acceptable, intellectually dishonest preface to tacit approval of everything from killing innocent persons to championing promiscuity.

Such deceptive word games run headlong into reality, however, when put into the concrete world of medical practice. Upholding a respect for the lives of all human beings is given lip service but, increasingly, health professionals find themselves in positions where they are required to carry out the requests and orders of those who consider some human beings dispensable. This has led some health professionals to take their plight to the public.

A California physician who defied a court order to remove feeding apparatus from an elderly patient, thus risking jail for his moral and ethical convictions, later described the incident in an article descriptively titled, "The Judge Ordered Me to Kill My Patient". [12]

A New Jersey nursing home was ordered to carry out the starvation and dehydration death of a young brain damaged woman, although nursing home officials had stated that to do so would "set precedent placing many patients in danger of loss of their lives by active euthanasia. Long-standing medical and nursing principles and sentiments — to heal, to comfort and sustain life through common medical procedures and care — would be jeopardized". [13] (The woman's family later transferred her to another health care facility where she died following the removal of her food and fluids. The decision, however, still stands.)

---

12. Allen Jay, M.D., "The Judge ordered me to kill my patient," *Medical Economics*, August 10, 1987, pp. 120-124.

13. Press Advisory regarding the Matter of Nancy Ellen Jobes, released October 17, 1985 by Lincoln Park Nursing and Convalescent Home; Lincoln Park, New Jersey. Hereafter cited as Lincoln Park Press Advisory.

In addition to physicians and health care facilities, nurses also face the prospect of being forced to carry out orders to kill, rather than care for, patients. Although an individual nurse technically has the right to refuse to participate in carrying out such orders, in practice, nurses receive little or no protection from coercion. Since they serve as "at will" employees who can be dismissed without cause, some nurses have expressed fear that they will be forced to go along with actions intended to kill patients or lose their jobs. [14]

How did medical ethics in the care of the vulnerable reach this stage? In large part, the status quo resulted from default. Physicians, nurses and other health professionals — with the exception of those in the forefront of the movements for change — were unaware that any changes were occurring until faced with the new ethics already in place.

FRAMERS OF THE NEW ETHICS

According to Robyn Rowland, Ph.D., the process of accepting changes in bio-medical ethics is gradual in its presentation. In this way, when a new technology or policy is introduced, "many people see it as just a natural progression in the advances of science without considering wider repercussions or values", and any who may express concern are "told by startled researchers that they had mentioned their intentions months ago". [15] Thus any disagreement is stifled.

Sensitive and crucial as the field of bio-medical ethics is, training of health professionals has neglected to address even the most basic understanding of the issues. According to Marsha Fowler, R.N., Chairperson of the American Nurses' Association (ANA) Committee on Ethics, "There are not enough nurses prepared in ethics. Only a dozen or so nurses deal consistently in ethics in the United States." Of these, only two have earned doctorates in ethics. [16]

Physicians also receive little or no training in ethics and find themselves increasingly dependent upon a new type of professional called the "ethicist". Unfortunately, the ethicist, unlike the physician, lawyer, nurse or even the beautician or electrician, is not required to pass any specific qualifying examination. The local ethicist on call to resolve conflict situations at a health care facility may be a clergyman,

---

14. Rita L. Marker, "To care or to kill: Nurses face tough decisions," *Detroit News*, September 10, 1987, p. 18A. Hereafter cited as "Tough Decisions."
15. Robyn Rowland, Ph.D., "Social Implications of Reproductive Technology," *International Review of Natural Family Planning*, vol. VIII, no. 3, (Fall, 1984), p. 191. Hereafter cited as Rowland.
16. Telephone interview with Marsha Fowler, R.N., August 8, 1987.

lawyer or philosophy professor. "An ethicist," wrote one physician, "is almost anyone who identifies himself as such." [17]

Lack of training in ethics is matched by lack of information sources related to controversial issues in medical ethics. Certainly one of the most heated debates concerning death and dying has centered around the "living will".

Even more disconcerting is the finding that, of those who listed the newspaper as their primary information source in a recent study, "Dear Abby" 's column was the primary information source related to the subject. [18] (It is highly doubtful that those respondents were aware that "Dear Abby" — Abigail Van Buren — was for years a member of the advisory board of the Euthanasia Education Council, the organization that originated the living will as a tool to promote acceptance of euthanasia. [19])

Recognizing that the information upon which medical decisions are based may be derived from the popular press with, perhaps, the assistance of an ethicist whose credentials are of unknown origin, it appears that medical professionals receive and are influenced by the same sources as the general public, i.e. newspapers and television.

MEDIA DISTORTIONS

Media handling of the personhood of the unborn child is well known. What, though, of the personhood of the medically vulnerable adult?

A classic case is that of Nancy Ellen Jobes. Jobes was a 32-year-old New Jersey woman who had suffered severe brain damage due to an anesthesia accident during surgery.

Shortly after a $900,000 malpractice settlement was reached, Jobes' husband and family requested that the young woman's feeding be stopped. Superior Court Judge Arnold Stein, in granting the request, wrote, "If the feeding tube is removed, dehydration and starvation will follow and Ms. Jobes will die. If feeding continues, she will live indefinitely". [20]

---

17. Joseph D. Wasserug, M.D., "Medical ethics is — and must remain — a practicing art," *American Medical News*, June 12, 1987, p. 42.
18. Gene Cranston Anderson, Mary Ann Heromin Walker, Patricia M. Pierce and Cynthia Mace Mills, "Living wills: Do nurses and physicians have them?" *American Journal of Nursing*, vol. 86, no. 3, (March, 1986), p. 271.
19. Rita L. Marker, "The Living Will: Just a Simple Declaration?" Human Life Center, University of Steubenville; Steubenville, Ohio; 1986.
20. "Tough Decisions."

Lincoln Park Nursing Home, where Jobes was a resident, appealed Stein's decision. The case went to the New Jersey Supreme Court, where in a 6-1 decision in June 1987 the court upheld the Stein decision, although the court acknowledged there was no "clear and convincing evidence" that Jobes would have wished her life ended. [21]

Throughout the judicial process, Lincoln Park Nursing Home strongly opposed removing Jobes' food and fluids. "She is not terminally ill," nursing home administrators said. "She occupies a resident room with no special equipment or facilities. She responds to touch and sound... She follows the movements of a person with her eyes..." [22]

Nancy Ellen Jobes was living in a stable, comfortable condition. Her medical expenses were covered by insurance.

Yet, in news article after news article about Nancy Ellen Jobes, the young woman was portrayed inaccurately. Most articles referred to her as being in a coma. However, "*coma* is a state of profound unconsciousness, characterized by the absence of spontaneous eye movements, response to painful stimuli and vocalization. The comatose person cannot be aroused." [23] Clearly, such a state was not that of Nancy Ellen Jobes.

On the day following the filing of legal papers to remove her food and fluids, however, the newspaper headline stated, "Right-to-Die Decision Sought: Boonton Man Asks Ruling on *Comatose Wife*" [24] (Emphasis added).

Subsequent articles contained headlines or quotations supporting the misleading description:

"Nursing Home Opposes Removal of *Comatose* Woman's Life Support" [25] (Emphasis added).

"A New Jersey nursing home filed court papers yesterday to block efforts to remove a life-sustaining feed tube from a 30-year-old woman who is in a *permanent coma*" [26] (Emphasis added).

21. Ibid.
22. Lincoln Park Press Advisory.
23. *Mosby's Medical and Nursing Dictionary*, (St. Louis, Toronto, London: The C.V. Mosby Company, 1983), p. 251.
24. Robin Lally, "Right-to-die decision sought: Boonton man asks ruling on comatose wife," *Daily Record*, New Jersey, October 3, 1985, p. 1.
25. Lawrence Ragonese, "Nursing home opposed removal of comatose woman's life support," *The Star Ledger*, New Jersey, October, 17, 1985, p. 43.
26. Randy Diamond and Kathleen Kerr, "We won't pull plug on her, home says," *Daily News*, New York, October 18, 1985.

"Although 30-year-old Nancy Ellen Jobes, *comatose* for nearly five years, may no longer feel pain, her family suffers" [27] (Emphasis added).

"*Comatose* Woman's Husband: 'Let Her Rest.'" [28] (Emphasis added).

"Jersey Judge Permits Denial of Food to Paitent [sic] in *Coma*" [29] (Emphasis added).

Inaccurate depiction of Nancy Ellen Jobes was not limited to labeling her as comatose. She was, throughout the court process, referred to as non-human or even dead. According to her father, "The person in the nursing home bed is a shell" of her former self. [30] Eleanor Laird, Ms. Jobes' mother, contended that her daughter had "died on that fateful day in April" (the day on which she had suffered the anesthesia accident which caused her brain damage) and the time since then had been "like a five-year wake". [31]

Perhaps the most obvious attempt to evoke feelings of repugnance and distaste for the disabled young woman was made by an expert witness in the case. Dr. Henry Liss, a Chatham neurologist, was reported as saying Nancy Ellen Jobes was "a 'monstrosity' created by medical science, which has not developed a method to terminate its 'creations.'" [32] (All this about a young woman whose only "life support" was a feeding tube.)

Liss further explained, "...she's not really living.. she's not a human entity." [33]

News accounts in the two days following the Liss testimony reinforced the image of Nancy Ellen Jobes as a non-person, stating, "all that remains is a physical shell", [34] "... there is no life there" [35] and

---

27. Sandra Gardner, "3d Right-to-die case is scheduled," *The New York Times*, January 26, 1986. Hereafter cited as Gardner.
28. "Comatose woman's husband: 'Let her rest'," *Courier*, New Jersey, March 26, 1986.
29. Ronald Sullivan, "Jersey judge permits denial of food to paitent [sic] in coma," *The New York Times*, April 24, 1986.
30. Paul Grzella, "Request to pull food tube an act of love, kin say," *Courier-News*, New Jersey, October 16, 1985.
31. Gardner.
32. Lawrence Ragonese, "Neurologist at Morris trial argues, 'right to die': Brain-damaged woman called 'monstrosity' of medical science," *The Star-Ledger*, New Jersey, March 25, 1986, p. 16.
33. Ibid.
34. Lawrence Ragonese, "Husband of comatose woman testifies she opposed artificial life support," *The Star-Ledger*, New Jersey, March 26, 1986, p. 32.
35. Ibid.

"prolonging the shell is the essence of futility". [36]

Nancy Ellen Jobes died at Morristown Memorial Hospital, Morristown, New Jersey on August 7, 1987. Commenting on her death, Rev. George Vorsheem, pastor of the Presbyterian Church of Morris Plains, New Jersey, and a close family friend, said, "...they [her family] realized she was just not there. They said goodbye a number of years ago." [37]

In the minds of the general public — after reading news accounts of her condition — Nancy Ellen Jobes had ceased to be a person once she had become severely disabled.

PUBLIC POLICY TREND SETTERS

Media also plays a key role in bringing pronouncements and positions of "experts" to public attention. Such expert opinion, emanating from public policy organizations and professional societies, often precipitates the move into new frontiers of practice and policy. And, inevitably, public attitude shifts, accepting the newly legal as the certainly moral.

On March 15, 1986, the AMA's Council on Ethical and Judicial Affairs (a seven-person committee) released a "clarification and expansion" of its Opinion 2.15 which addresses withholding and withdrawal of life support or prolonging treatment. The clarification stated in part:

Even if death is not imminent, but a patient's coma is beyond doubt irreversible and there are adequate safeguards to confirm the accuracy of the diagnosis, and with the concurrence of those who have responsibility for the care of the patient, it is not unethical to discontinue all means of life-prolonging medical treatment. *Life-prolonging medical treatment includes* medication and artificially or technologically supplied respiration, *nutrition or hydration*. [38] (Emphasis added.)

No reference was made regarding what may constitute "adequate safeguards to confirm the accuracy of the diagnosis" of irreversible coma.

---

36. Lawrence Ragonese, "Friends, family recount comatose woman's 'death with dignity' remarks," *The Star-Ledger*, New Jersey, March 27, 1986, p. 28.
37. Joseph F. Sullivan, "Woman in right-to-die case dies after tube is removed," *The New York Times*, August 8, 1987, p. 1.
38. Jane D. Hoyt, "A 'new ethic' for the 'New Medicine,'" *Human Life Issues*, vol. 12, no. 1, (Spring, 1986), p. 9.

Release of the clarification took place at a conference titled, "A New Ethic for the New Medicine" co-sponsored by the AMA Council on Ethical and Judicial Affairs and the Hastings Center in New Orleans, Louisiana.

The AMA opinion was cited several weeks later by New Jersey Superior Court Judge Stein in his ruling that food and fluids could be removed from Nancy Ellen Jobes.[39] Although the AMA statement had made reference to patients who were comatose, it was applied almost immediately to the noncomatose Jobes.

The Hastings Center — the organization that, with the AMA Council on Ethical and Judicial Affairs sponsored the "New Ethics for the New Medicine" conference — was founded in 1969 to fill the need for sustained professional investigation of the ethical impact of the biological revolution. Among the issues addressed by the Center are death and dying, population control, genetic engineering and behavior control.

A recently released Hastings Center report setting forth "Guidelines on the Treatment and Care of the Dying" notes that designated surrogates should have the right to refuse life-sustaining treatment not only for the terminally ill and dying patient, but also for the gravely impaired and others "not necessarily in danger of imminent death..."[40]

Among the members of the board of directors of the influential organization is Richard Lamm, former Governor of Colorado. Lamm's not so subtle, well-publicized comments related to particularly vulnerable groups of people leave little doubt about his view of the personhood and value of those dependent upon others for care and support.

In widely quoted remarks, Lamm stated that elderly people who are terminally ill have a "duty to die and get out of the way".[41] He has, in addition, questioned the value of costs for educating mentally retarded children, since "after four or five years all they do is roll over".[42]

Daniel Callahan, director of the Hastings Center, was one of the drafters of the new guidelines. In a now famous article, Callahan reflected upon provision of food and fluids, stating, "...denial of

39. Mark Rust, "Cessation of feeding approved by two courts," *American Medical News*, May 2, 1986, p. 10.
40. Alan L. Otten, "Patients should have the right to refuse life-sustaining treatment, panel says," *Wall Street Journal*, September 11, 1987, p. 46.
41. Haynes Johnson, "Duty-to-die flap obscures important national issue," *Minneapolis Star & Tribune*, April 3, 1984.
42. Wayne Slater, "Colorado's Governor Lamm praised, blasted for death remarks," *Minneapolis Star & Tribune*, April 3, 1984.

nutrition may in the long run become the only effective way to make certain that a large number of biologically tenacious patients actually die". [43]

While not specifically labeling the elderly, the senile or the otherwise medically vulnerable as "non-persons", references denoting them as "biologically tenacious" or capable only of "rolling over" does carry such an implication.

It is probable that the stage is now being set for a formalized shrinking of the population deemed to have the quality of life sufficient to receive protection under the law. Indications are that such a move is on the horizon.

The American Society of Law and Medicine (ASLM), an organization founded in 1972 to provide a forum for interdisciplinary discussion of the complex issues at the interface of law, medicine and health care, at its October 1987 conference, tackled the subject, *"Consciousness as the Critical Moral (Constitutional) Threshold* for Life" (Emphasis added). Addressing the topic was Dr. Ronald Cranford, ASLM president-elect. Cranford — who also participated in drafting the Hastings Center guidelines — was among the authors who, in 1984, proposed easing the burdensome elderly out of life with suggestions for limiting care, including food, for those who, although not terminally ill, are "pleasantly senile". [44]

UNIFORM LAW COMMISSION

Perhaps one of the least known but most influential public policy organizations is the National Conference of Commissioners on Uniform State Laws, also known as the Uniform Law Commission (ULC). The organization was designed to prevent problems which arise from differences in state laws — differences which create specific interstate and national problems. The ULC has drafted and approved more than two hundred and twenty-five acts ranging from those which would eliminate jurisdictional child custody disputes to laws which address the legalities of electronic transfer of stock ownership. Among the better known laws drafted by the ULC are the Uniform Anatomical Gifts Act and the Uniform Commercial Code.

More than 300 members, called Commissioners, represent every

---

43. Daniel Callahan, "On Feeding the Dying," *The Hastings Center Report*, (October, 1983), p. 22.
44. Sidney H. Wanzer, M.D., et al, "The physician's responsibility toward hopelessly ill patients," *New England Journal of Medicine*, vol. 310, no. 15, (April 12, 1984), p. 955.

state, the District of Columbia and Puerto Rico. Generally appointed by the governors of each state, Commissioners are practicing attorneys, judges, law school deans and professors. Proposals for uniform laws generally come from Commissioners or from the American Bar Association, but can be suggested by outside organizations.

Once a decision is made to take up a particular topic, a special committee is formed to draft an act. Tentative drafts go through a review process and require consideration at two annual meetings prior to passage. Once an act is approved, ULC Commissioners are obligated to return to their respective states and work for adoption of the act.

One of the most controversial acts passed in recent years by the ULC was the "Uniform Rights of the Terminally Ill Act", a uniform living will law. One Commissioner who had opposed its passage described the practices which will be allowed if the uniform act becomes law, saying, "This is a more refined, less ugly method of killing another human being, but I don't see that it's any different than shooting a suffering spouse". [45]

Passage of the "Uniform Rights of the Terminally Ill Act" by the ULC was considered a significant victory for euthanasia advocates. It was at the urging of groups which included the Society for the Right to Die (known until 1975 as the Euthanasia Society of America) that the ULC finally decided the time was right to draft "right-to-die" legislation.

Throughout the course of the Act's two-year process of consideration, Sidney Rosoff, chairman of the Society for the Right to Die and immediate past president of the World Federation of Right to Die Societies, worked closely with the Drafting Committee. [46]

Invited as the medical expert to advise the Commissioners during floor debate, Dr. Ronald Cranford (mentioned above as participating in drafting of the Hastings Center Guidelines and as the president-elect of ASLM) was one of only three non-Commissioners given privileges of the floor during consideration of the uniform living will act. [47]

FROM TERMINATING LIFE TO CREATING LIFE

The ULC, at the meeting in which the uniform living will law was approved, designated a committee to draft proposed legislation on

45. Rita L. Marker, "The Right to Death," *Human Life Issues* supplement to Fall, 1985 edition, p. 1.
46. Ibid.
47. Ibid., p. 5.

reproductive technology, thus entering into the realm of defining "parenthood".

The draft legislation title, "Status of Children of the New Biology", received the first of its two required annual readings at the Summer 1987, ULC meeting held in Newport Beach, California. Among the stated reasons for formulating the new legislation is that of "considering and balancing the rights and needs of adult actors who participate in the new conception and birth processes". [48]

Among the "adult actors" described in the first draft of the legislation are the "donor," who is "the person (other than a surrogate mother) who provides sperm or egg for the benefit of another person through aided conception, whether or not a payment is made for this"; the "genetic parent", who is "the person who contributed the sperm or egg that resulted in biological conception of the child"; [49] the "surrogate mother" who is "a person who bears a child conceived through aided conception for another person pursuant to an agreement..."; [50] and the "contracting parents" who are a "husband and wife, married to each other, who enter into an agreement with a surrogate mother in which they assume all parental rights and duties with regard to a child born to a surrogate mother..." [51]

The surrogate agreement prescribed in the draft requires that the contract be in writing and be approved by the court. Interestingly enough, the court, in its approval process, must determine that "adequate genetic testing has been undertaken to avoid 'mismatches' ".[52] Presumably, this ensures a better "product".

The agreement, according to the draft, "will become effective upon conception of the child. From that time *all parental rights and duties*, and all legal rights such as inheritance that might be accorded a child on birth, will be determined on the basis that the contracting parties *are the child's legal parents*. However, the agreement will not affect the surrogate mother's legal right to control over her body, *including the decision whether to terminate pregnancy*." [53], [54]

In effect, the proposed legislation would deny the parenthood of the

49. Ibid.
50. Ibid., pp. 3-4.
51. Ibid., p. 4.
52. Ibid., p. 9.
53. Ibid.
54. The text of the proposed legislation quoted in this chapter is based on the draft presented at the ULC's meeting in the Summer of 1987. A subsequent draft, taking into consideration the ideas posed in debate at the meeting, is available from the National Conference of Commissioners on Uniform State Laws; 645 North Michigan Avenue, Suite 510; Chicago, Illinois 60611.

pregnant woman and the personhood of the new life from the moment of conception. Parenthood, under the law, would belong to the contracting parents. However, the new "parents" who purportedly would assume all parental rights and duties from the moment of conception would be unable to perform the most fundamental parental task — that of protecting their child from harm — since the surrogate, who is no longer viewed as a parent, may, under the guise of controlling her own body, kill the unborn child by abortion.

The pregnant woman has become a manufacturer, bound to turn over the product upon completion.

END RESULTS OF PERSONS AS PRODUCTS

Initially reproductive technology arrived on the scene ostensibly to meet the needs of infertile married couples, now estimated to be over 16% of U.S. couples of childbearing age. [55] However, assistance to married infertile couples and their "choice" to conceive with technological assistance soon led to discussions that this choice belonged to others as well. Any restriction, it was argued, would be unfair and arbitrary.

In the celebrated "Baby M" case, Elizabeth Stern, wife of the father of Baby M, contended she was infertile. It was not until later that it was learned that the 41-year-old Stern, who had put off child-rearing to study for a medical degree was not infertile but rather "feared pregnancy would jeopardize her health". [56]

A recent article in a scholarly journal maintains that limiting the "right" of artificial reproduction to only the married is unwarranted, contending that fatherless or lesbian households should have the opportunity to have children. [57] Such sentiments have been carried further, enshrining the "choice" of reproductive technology as a protected right.

In his "Baby M" decision, Judge Harvey R. Sorkow stated:

It must be reasoned that if one has a right to procreate coitally, then one has the right to reproduce noncoitally... This court holds

---

48. "Status of the Children of the New Biology." Draft presented at the 96th annual meeting of the National Conference of Commissioners on Uniform State Laws, July 31-August 7, 1987, Newport Beach, California, p. 3.
55. "Desperately seeking baby," *U.S. News and World Report*, October 5, 1987, p. 59.
56. "Who's who in the fight for Baby M," *The New York Times*, April 1, 1987, p.13.
57. "Limitation on artificial reproduction?" *Bio-Law*, (University Publications of America, 1987) p. U:319 summarizing article by Susan Golombok and John Rust, "The Warnock Report and single women: What about the children?" *Journal of Medical Ethics*, 12 (1986), pp. 182-186.

that the protected means extends to the use of surrogates... While a state could regulate [surrogate motherhood]...it could not ban or refuse to enforce such transactions... It might even be argued that refusal to enforce these contracts...would constitute an unconstitutional interference with procreative liberty... [58]

So far has the "right" to artificially conceive a child advanced that an inmate of a Federal prison recently filed suit against the government over its refusal to permit him to father a child through artificial insemination. [59]

When, in early 1987, the Roman Catholic Church issued its statement on reproductive technology, [60] calling for a genuine respect for human persons, procreation and parenthood, there was widespread opposition to the statement.

The document itself sensitively affirms the dignity of persons from the moment of fertilization to the last moment of life and cautions that "the connection between *in vitro* fertilization and the voluntary destruction of human embryos occurs too often", thus subjecting life and death to the decision of man, who sets himself up as the giver of life and death by decree. [61]

Voluntary destruction of human embryos was noted by a Glasgow, Scotland physician who recently wrote that, "out of every four embryos conceived *in vitro*, three are subjected to selective reduction". [62]

The Vatican statement opposed surrogate motherhood because, among other reasons, "it sets up, to the detriment of families, a division between the physical, psychological, and moral elements which constitute those families". [63]

Confusion in identity is exemplified in the case of a South African woman who recently gave birth to her own triplet grandchildren. The woman, 48-year-old Pat Anthony, had been implanted with her daughter's ova, which had been fertilized with her son-in-law's sperm.

58. "Excerpts from the ruling on Baby M," *The New York Times*, April 7, 1987.
59. "Prisoner and wife sue for right to artificially conceive a child," *The New York Times*, September 20, 1987, p. 17.
60. "Instruction on Respect for Human Life in Its Origin and on the Dignity of Procreation," issued by the Congregation for the Doctrine of the Faith, February 22, 1987. Hereafter cited as Vatican Statement.
61. Ibid., Part II, para. 3.
62. Letter by Colum O'Reilly, "Selective Reduction in Assisted Pregnancies," *The Lancet*, September 5, 1987, p. 575.
63. Vatican Statement, Part II, A, Question 3.

According to the news reports, the "grandmother" who gave birth to the triplets is considered their legal guardian. [64]

The Vatican document called for public policy to protect the rights of all human beings, stating, "When the state does not place its power at the service of the rights of each citizen, and in particular of the more vulnerable, the very foundations of a state based on law are undermined". [65]

There are those who say that neither the Vatican nor anyone else has a right to call for limitation of reproductive technology. Any concern about the harmful use of reproductive technology is, according to those wishing wide open availability, merely alarmist hysteria.

However, Dr. Robyn Rowland, who was, until her 1984 resignation, the head of the research coordination committee for the Monash University Queen Victoria-Epworth Hospital In Vitro Fertilization Program in Melbourne, Australia (the program which made history by successfully impregnating women with embryos which had been frozen, thawed, and implanted in uterii) sees grave social implications of reproductive technology.

According to Rowland, "test-tube" children are considered brighter and more socially skilled due to genetic factors; therefore some people have requested *in vitro* fertilization to achieve such characteristics in children. A belief is growing, warns Rowland, that people will *want* to produce children of special personality types. The logical conclusion is, therefore, that *all* couples should be allowed to produce children in this way, since the children will be superior offspring. "The seeds of genetic breeding and manipulation are hence sown," says Rowland. [66]

This, she explains, could have great impact on the child born to order, particularly during the child's adolescence. Pressure because of their so-called perfection has already placed an "unjustified expectation of perfect performance" on children born of the new technologies. [67]

Further concerns noted by Rowland include the question of ownership of frozen embryos. In 1984, 250 frozen embryos were residing at Queen Victoria Hospital. Emphasis related to the status of the embryos was placed on who owned them, "reflecting the obsession our society has with the ownership of, as opposed to the caring for, children". [68]

---

64. John D. Battersby, "Woman in South Africa has daughter's triplets," *The New York Times*, October 2, 1987, p. 6.
65. Vatican Statement, Part III, para. 5.
66. Rowland, p. 191.
67. Ibid., p. 195.
68. Ibid., p. 196.

Quoting Edward Grossman, Rowland predicted that if the current progression continues, the artificial womb and placenta will become a reality and "natural pregnancy may become an anachronism...the uterus will become appendix-like". [69]

"Will we," asks Rowland, "soon be fighting for the *right* [of fertile couples] to have babies, and to have them naturally?" [70]

THE END OF THE ROAD, OR A CHANGE IN THE PATHWAY

Changes in biomedical ethics engendered by reproductive technology and the euthanasia movement threaten the heart of civilization. If unchecked, the prospect looms of a society where children may be produced only under quality controlled conditions and, if they do not live up to expectations, be disposed of much as any other flawed piece of merchandise. The euthanasia movement, with its emphasis on death for the vulnerable and unproductive, may eventually require, as has been suggested, "that the normal ordinary expected thing to do is to do your dying relatively early, relatively easily, in a way in which you won't impose a burden on others". [71]

A challenge faces all who recognize the nightmare world that will result if the current pathway is followed. A change can take place. But this change will require patient, firm, untiring work to shift attitudes.

On November 22, 1981, Pope John Paul II issued *Familiaris Consortio*, An Apostolic Exhortation on the Family. In it he wrote:

> Families should be the first to take steps to see that the laws and institutions of the state not only do not offend, but support and positively defend the rights and duties of the family. Along these lines families should grow in awareness of being "protagonists" of what is known as "family politics" and assume responsibility for transforming society; otherwise families will be the first victims of the evils that they have done no more than note with indifference. [72]

---

69. Ibid., p. 197.
70. Ibid., p. 198.
71. Rita L. Marker, "Euthanasia: The New Family Planning, Part II," *International Review of Natural Family Planning*, vol XI, no. 2, (Summer, 1987), p. 123. Quoting Margaret Pabst Battin, associate professor of Philosophy at the University of Utah and member of the advisory committee of Concern for Dying.
72. Pope John Paul II, *Familiaris Consortio*, November 22, 1981, (The Human Life Center, University of Steubenville, Ohio, 1984), p. 24, no. 44.

It is crucial that all families recognize both their ability to transform society and their responsibility to do so.

Steps that must be taken in changing the pathway are:

...Acknowledgment that the pathway *can* be changed.
...Awareness of the current activities and goals of those who are setting the biomedical ethics agenda.
...Involvement in policy making processes on all levels.
...Recognition that productive change takes patience, time, energy and financial commitment.
...Refusal to be intimidated by self-proclaimed "experts".
...Support for those who recognize the value of personhood and parenthood.
...Maintenance of a sense of humor.

And, above all, prayer that soon a respect for life and family, personhood and parenthood will be restored.

5

THE HUMAN UNBORN: RESEARCH SUBJECT, ORGAN DONOR, OR ONE OF US?

Joseph R. Stanton, A.B., M.D., F.A.C.P.
Clinical Associate Professor, Tufts University School of Medicine

Clearly visible in the media are a spate of recent stories and items justifying euthanasia. They move under the banner of a "right to die", "aid in dying" and "death with dignity". With this increasing emphasis against life at its other extremity, less well noticed is the fact that *pari passu* justification of non-therapeutic research on the human embryo and fetus has been escalating. By "non-therapeutic research" we mean research not for the benefit of the one on whom the research is conducted. While the Federal Government presently does not fund non-therapeutic fetal research, there is much evidence to suggest that this resistance is being significantly eroded. While seventeen states carry on their books laws forbidding or restricting non-therapeutic research on the living embryo and fetus, the landmark Massachusetts statute has been repeatedly subject to criticism and editorial denigration. Within two weeks, one major Boston TV station carried as news a discussion of the use of human fetal tissues and organs taken from abortions for transplantation experiments. Within the month, a New York Times article raised the question of deliberately bringing into existence a human fetus for the purpose of sacrificing its life to supply organs for transplantation. Similarly, pressure is being exerted for removal of the hearts of human newborns at or near death for transplantation into other infants with fatal heart lesions.

A review of the present state of fetal research with an analysis of the idealization behind advocated changes may be instructive. The pressure for embryonic and fetal research today exists both at the beginning of embryonic life, on the early embryo, and on the fetus as organogenesis develops or is completed, i.e., the laying down of the organs (heart, liver, pancreas, brain, etc.). Let us discuss both categories.

The Early Human Conceptus

Since the birth of Louise Joy Brown on July 25, 1978 (the first baby whose conception occurred in a petri dish), the superovulation of women by drugs with the harvesting of human ova by laparoscopy has provided an unprecedented supply of human ova, one of the two essential gametes (sex cells) necessary for generation of a new member of the human species. Sperm banks have long existed from which the other vital gametes may be drawn. As a result of the spread of *in vitro* fertilization in hundreds of laboratories in England, Australia, America and South America today, sperm and ova are brought together daily, perhaps hourly, in laboratories; fertilization occurs, and new human lives are begun. From the published evidence it is clear that not all of these newly created embryos are being implanted. We know, for instance, that much research on the freezing and reconstituting of embryos has occurred. We know also that human embryos not transplanted in embryo transfer have been subject to laboratory experimentation and study. Scientists talk of the necessity for research on the human conceptus to understand problems in fertilization, implantation, genetic abnormalities, etc.

An unsigned editorial, "When Life Begins", in *The Economist*, which appeared November 15, 1986, as well as a paper by the Animal Rights advocate Peter Singer, delivered at a meeting of the Society of Law and Medicine, August 1986, suggests that human status be conferred on the embryo and fetus *only* when the brain has organically developed enough to perceive pain, an event which they place at nine weeks after conception. Others have suggested that human status be denied until full brain development has occurred. Unrestricted research would be allowed before this time, but forbidden after this date. How successful this line of dehumanization can be is seen in a subsequent statement in the editorial. "Examining small clusters of cells to save life and fight disease would continue." I would point out that the terms "a clump of cells", "a mass of protoplasm", and "fetal tissue" have long been used by abortion counselors to describe what they call the "product of conception" so as to desensitize pregnant women for whom abortion is a consideration. An extension of this kind of dehumanization can be seen in the adult person in a "chronic vegetative state." In the spring of

1986, the A.M.A. Judicial Council approved the withdrawal of nutrition and hydration from non-dying patients "in a vegetative state". Dehumanization of that which is clearly human must be successfully accomplished before unrestricted research and the use of the human unborn as research objects can occur.

A similar application has recently arisen in the discussion of organs used for donation from the anencephalic child born with little or no cerebral cortex but with intact brain stem and the ability to breathe for hours or days. "Kidney Transplantation From Anencephalic Donors" (Holzgreve, W., Beller, F.K., Buchholz, B., Hansmann, M., and Kohler, K., *N. Engl. J. Med.*, 1987; 316: 1069-70) reports the use of newborn anencephalics as a source for organ transplants. They consider as brain dead one whose brain stem is alive and functioning. This has raised the slippery slope argument and produced ethical concern and discomfort. In the recent paper in the *New England Journal of Medicine*, the doctors in Muenster, Germany knew before delivery that one twin had anencephaly. Immediately upon delivery, the anencephalic baby was incubated and supported until its organs could be harvested. It would be fatuous at this time to point out that ideas have consequences; that is obvious. But the rationalization that "they are going to die anyhow and we might as well make use of them" was the guiding philosophy in the experimentation on those piteous subjects marked for death in the concentration camps of the Third Reich. At Nuremburg, these experiments were condemned as crimes against humanity. This latest sally by science merits critical examination.

Non-Therapeutic Experimentation on the Fetus

In the files of the Value of Life Committee, there are 25 or 30 papers from the literature of the 60's and 70's dealing with non-therapeutic human fetal research carried out for scientific purposes. In many of these, for pregnant women planning abortions, the abortion is delayed. Drugs or vaccines are given to the mother and 24-48 hours later the pregnancy is aborted by hysterotomy, and the organs harvested for research purposes. In other instances, fetal organs are taken for transplantation. Human fetal liver cells were used at Chernobel in radiation cases after the explosion and fire.

Fetal research usually depends upon the fetus being delivered intact; in most instances, the fetus is delivered by hysterotomy, often called miniature caesarean section. The fetus is always alive at delivery, while it is still connected to the placenta. A paper in the Hastings Center Reports, "Ethical Options in Transplanting Fetal Tissue," (Mahowald,

M.B., Silver, J., and Ratcheson, R.A., Feb. 83, pages 9-15), is of interest. It points out that "clearly, electively-aborted healthy fetuses are the primary source for transplantation of fetal tissue". In another section it is noted that "the process is straightforward, abortion is induced and performed through a method intended to preserve the fetal tissue — a specific segment of brain tissue is then removed from the fetus". Brain tissue is the most sensitive tissue to the lack of oxygen in the human body. Brain tissue, especially the cells of the cerebral cortex, dies promptly when oxygen is interrupted, and there are papers that suggest ordinary standards of brain death used in the adult should not be applied in dealing with newborns. Is the human fetus alive when portions of or entire organs are removed? If not, how long are they dead? If alive, we are talking about human vivisection of those destined to die. I suggest that if this were being proposed with puppies, cats, or monkeys, public outrage would be enormous and instantaneous.

The current successful auto-transplantation of human adrenal medulary cells into the brain to improve the state of individuals having Parkinson's disease has led to using the human embryonic brain in transplantation experiments. These are presently being carried out in Sweden. If these experiments show success in treating Parkinson's disease, the pressures will increase exponentially to allow such programs in the United States. Additionally, there is speculation about the use of fetal brain tissue transplantation in cases of brain damage such as extensive stroke injury, or in specific brain deterioration such as Alzheimer's type dementia. It is elemental that the brain tissue transplanted *not* be dead. The hard question our society must ask and answer is "Should our society, for the benefit of others, condone human vivisection or something very close to human vivisection?" It is crucially important that these hard questions be asked now and policy be established. For if federal constraints on funding non-therapeutic research on the human fetus are swept away, federal funding will absolutely guarantee that more and more non-therapeutic experimental research will occur on the human fetus.

It is crucial that one appreciate the fact that federal moneys are the most important driving force in the funding of the research laboratories of America. Significant, too, is the false assumption that what is legal is *de facto* ethical, a presumption often made. Thus, in addressing the question of non-therapeutic embryonic and fetal research and its funding, this nation faces a policy question of profound moral significance. The way we answer that question will determine the kind of society we are to be. For how a society regards and protects the most defenseless among itself determines the kind of society it is.

On January 22, 1973, the Supreme Court abortion decisions *Roe v. Wade* and *Doe v. Bolton* came down. In *Roe v. Wade*, we now know, the original plaintiff's allegation that she was pregnant as a result of gang rape was admitted to have been a lie. ("A Wink from the Bench," Uddo, B.J., *Tulane Law Review*, vol. 53 No. 2398, 1978 and *AMA News*, Pg. 5, September 18, 1987, "Roe Plaintiff Recants Rape Story.") In 1968, well before *Roe v. Wade* became the law, the recently retired Chief Justice of the Supreme Court, Warren Berger, wrote, "No adult has the legal power to consent to experiment on an infant unless it is for the benefit of the infant...." ("Reflections of Law and Medicine," Berger, W., *15 UCLA Law Review*, 436-38, 1968.)

In 1974, the State of Massachusetts passed legislation (Ch. 112 12V) widely called the "fetal research law". It includes the following proscription: "No person shall use any live human fetus whether before or after expulsion from its mother's womb for scientific, laboratory research or other kind of experimentation." The law further states, "No experimentation may knowingly be performed upon a dead fetus unless the consent of the mother has first been obtained." Additionally, the law forbids the selling, transfer, distribution or giving away of any fetus which is in violation of provisions of the law. It does allow such research procedures as are therapeutic, i.e., specifically for the benefit of that particular child, and it does allow routine autopsy in the instance of a dead fetus.

Author of the law was the late Professor James Smith of the faculty of Boston College Law School. Massachusetts Citizens for Life invited Professor Smith to write the law. Research background for the law was contributed from the books and files of The Value of Life Committee.

At legislative hearings before passage, key historic documents were cited, including the World Medical Association's declaration of Geneva, 1949. "I will maintain the utmost respect for human life from the time of conception." Cited as well was the United Nations Declaration on the Rights of the Child, affirmed by this nation in 1969: "Whereas the child, by reason of his physical and mental immaturity, needs special safeguards and care including appropriate legal protection *before* as well as after birth."

The World Medical Association Declaration of Geneva and its subsequent Helsinki Declaration of 1964 were strongly influenced and, indeed, constituted a response to the violation of medical ethics that in

Nazi Germany led to the Nuremburg trials and to the imposition of death sentences on participating doctors for "crimes against humanity".

The Massachusetts law, as well as a subsequent Federal decision not to fund non-therapeutic research on the human fetus, were a direct response to research carried out on the human fetus scheduled for abortion and on the fetus produced as a result of a planned induced abortion.

As long ago as February 24, 1972, Professor Arthur Dyck of Harvard had testified before the Massachusetts legislature on then current research on human fetuses. He cited a paper in *Science Magazine* (August 27, 1971), where in Rochester, New York, explants of (human) fetal cerebral cortex had been kept alive and growing up to a total of nine months. This was done by transplanting them into animals.

Professor Dyck was but one of an increasing number of perceptive citizens across the land concerned by the fact that the early liberalization of abortion laws in Colorado, New York, and several other states had produced an opportunism with regard to the availability of the human fetus for use in non-therapeutic experimentation. Increasingly, the medical literature presented articles where soon-to-be-aborted fetuses were used as the subjects of experimentation. Indeed, it was implied that abortion provided an unparalleled opportunity to test all manner of drugs and procedures on an ideal experimental subject, the human fetus to be aborted.

In the spring of 1973, the American Society for Pediatric Research met in San Francisco. There, Dr. Peter A.J. Adam, of Case Western Reserve Medical School, described a fetal research project carried out in Sweden and supported by U.S. National Institute of Health funds. *Medical World News* (June 8, 1973) reported that presentation as follows:

> No one even raised an eyebrow when Dr. Peter A.J. Adam, associate professor of pediatrics at Case Western Reserve University in Cleveland, reported on a study of 'cerebral oxidation of glucose and D-beta hydroxy butyrate in the *isolated perfused human fetal head*'. The research was carried out in Helsinki, summer of 1972 and supported in part by NIH funds.
>
> ... the investigators severed the heads of twelve previable fetuses obtained by abdominal hysterotomy at 12 and 20 weeks gestation.
>
> ... once society has declared the fetus dead and abrogated its rights — I don't see an ethical problem," said Dr. Adam.

Dr. Adam's presentation did not "raise an eyebrow" at the doctors' meeting where it was presented. But, as knowledge that human fetuses were being delivered alive, the circulation to their brains maintained by a pump, and then the heads severed from the bodies while the experiment on the brain continued, a wave of revulsion reached the halls of Congress. Although carried out in Sweden, the fetal research Dr. Adam reported had been supported by a federal NIH grant. A ban on the use of any federal funds for non-therapeutic live fetal research was quickly followed by action of the U.S. Congress. State legislatures in 17 states passed legislation specifically forbidding or restricting non-therapeutic research on the human conceptus. Several states exactly copied the pioneering work of Professor Smith in the Massachusetts fetal research law. Non-therapeutic fetal research in the U.S. has not been funded since that moratorium went into effect.

However, at present, new pressure is arising in the area of fetal research and organ transplant. Primarily, it is a call for tissue and organs from fetuses aborted or to be aborted to be made available for transplantation. Further, papers in publications dealing with ethics have raised the question of whether a woman could deliberately become pregnant by her husband whose own kidneys were failing. In the *New York Times* (March 14, July 1, and August 16, 1987), there are articles reporting on human fetal research. In Sweden, human brains from fetuses of six to nineteen weeks gestation have already been transplanted into rats. The call is now to repeat the experiments in humans with Parkinson's disease. The Sunday, August 16, 1987, *New York Times* ran an article about a woman who called an ethician to ask "whether she could be artificially inseminated with sperm from her father who suffers from Alzheimer's disease. The resulting fetus would have been aborted for brain tissue to transplant into her father's brain."

It is interesting to speculate whether Dante, in his conception of hell, could have dreamed up a scenario such as society faces today. Presently, we are being taken up to the mountain top. The promised possible amelioration of Parkinson's disease, Alzheimer's, and brain and spinal cord damage is dangled before us. But let us understand that there is a price. That price is to place upon the altar of science the living bodies of the to-be-aborted, or those aborted alive for sacrifice. From the aborted brain and kidney and heart of the least members of the human family comes the promise of the fountain of youth and restored health.

Such utilitarianism has temporarily held sway before, and the Pandora's box which was opened produced the darkest chapter in medical history. The earlier publications of Frederick Wertham, Dr. Leo Alexander, and others fully detail the horrors of that chapter in human history. Dr. Robert Jay Lifton's recent book, *The Nazi Doctors*, has focused renewed attention on the problem. At the Nuremburg War Crimes Trial of doctors, non-therapeutic experiments on non-consenting humans were condemned as "crimes against humanity". It is also a matter of the historic record that many of those scientific experiments, which required the death of the participants, were later judged to be sloppy, poorly done, and of little lasting value. And yet even if the ends achieved were scientifically impeccable and of great value to the human race, a larger question remains: at what price?

Two quotations from the literature stimulate reflection. In Freund's "Experimentation with Human Subjects", philosopher Hans Jonas writes:

> Let us not forget that progress is an optional goal not an unconditional commitment, and that its tempo in particular, compulsive as it may become, has nothing sacred about it. Let us also remember that a slower progress in the conquest of disease would not threaten society, grievous as it is, to those who have to deplore that their disease is not yet conquered, but that society would indeed be threatened by the erosion of those moral values whose loss, possibly caused by too ruthless a pursuit of scientific progress would make its most dazzling triumphs not worth having.

Professor Paul Ramsey of Princeton in his book *The Ethics of Fetal Research*, comments:

> So here we have an entity too alive to be dead, not mature enough to be a viable baby, yet human enough to be specially protectable.

This nation has celebrated the 200th Anniversary of the ratification of the U.S. Constitution. As the pealing of the Liberty Bell reverberates into history, how will this nation respond to present agitation for human fetal sacrifice in the name of science? I believe that the way our American society answers this question may well determine whether this nation will survive yet another 200 years. A prestigious National Bioethics Board has recently been appointed by the U.S. Congress (AMA News, p. 11, August 14, 1987). It is to study and make recommendations about fetal research, genetic engineering, and other ethical problems. 2.5 million dollars was appropriated for this committee in 1987 and 3 million dollars for fiscal year 1988. It will be powerful and have great influence. From the scientific community will come great pressure to allow federal funding of non-therapeutic research on the human fetus. I will confess, regrettably, that I would rather trust the fate of the human unborn to a committee of simple citizens than to judges or experts. But it is most crucial that this committee be instructed to seek out and find citizens and organizations willing to stand up and speak out against non-therapeutic fetal research.

Finally, for the Christian in American society, there is a haunting reminder that echoes down the ages into our own time. It was uttered long ago by One Who throughout His public ministry loved the little ones. He made this remarkable statement; "Whatsoever you have done unto the least of these my brethren, you have done it unto me." The human embryo and fetus, whose moral status is before us, is today what each one of us once was, a tiny island of humanity surrounded by the body of a woman called mother. Like that tiny atom of humanity, each of us was also totally vulnerable, totally dependent on the value judgement of a woman and a society and its laws. The question before us today and for the future is, "Does the humanity we share in common with the unborn child place particular demands upon us as citizens at this moment in history?"

6

RESEARCH ON THE PSYCHOSOCIAL IMPACT OF ABORTION: A SYSTEMATIC REVIEW OF THE LITERATURE 1966 TO 1985

John S. Lyons, Ph.D.
Assistant Professor
Northwestern University Medical School

David B. Larson, M.D., M.S.P.H.
Wendy M. Huckeba, B.A.
James L. Rogers, Ph.D.
Candace P. Mueller, M.S.W.

Editor's note: This research was performed by the Family Research Council of America under contract (#86A029390501D) with the Office of Population Affairs, Department of Health and Human Services. It was presented at the Values & Public Policy Conference by John S. Lyons, Ph.D.

INTRODUCTION

The legalization of abortion in 1973 set the stage for a raft of opinions from legal, religious, and media scholars. It also set the stage for research literature on its effects. Legalized abortion has been and remains a controversial subject. The annual rate of abortions has risen from 744,600 in 1973 to 1,573,900 in 1982. (1) This latter number represents 28.8 abortions per 1,000 women aged 15 through 44. Reportedly, 26% of all pregnancies in 1982 ended in abortion.

The complex legal issues of abortion correspond to the growing involvement of courts in the area of medical treatment. (2) These issues concern the rights of patients both to receive treatments they desire and to not receive treatment not desired. In the area of obstetrics in general, court involvement in medical decisions is a growing controversy.

(3) Legal concerns specifically regarding abortion involve protection of the rights of the patient. (4,5) As Chervenak, et al. (6) point out, the decision to terminate pregnancy represents a moral conflict. These authors provide data from scientific study to establish guidelines for the moral justification of abortion in the third trimester. Their work documents the complex relationship among legal, moral and scientific enterprises.

Scientific study of the abortion issue with its defined, objective standards offers one means of attempting to moderate this often intense debate. By operationalizing constructs to allow for reliable and replicable measurement and study, science can avoid the polemics that have made resolution of this issue difficult. (7)

Although a critical question in the abortion issue remains the definition of the genesis of life, science is not well-suited for providing answers to such definitional questions. (8) Other questions, more empirical in nature, can be usefully addressed by the scientific method. However, in the application of science to controversial issues regarding the human condition, one must always remain cognizant of the warnings of Hutchinson (9) of the need to proceed with science in a cautious manner in order to avoid harmful, unintended effects.

A most important question regarding the use of abortion which can be studied scientifically is the later impact of an abortion on the female who decided to abort her pregnancy. The impact of the abortion on the fetus is clear. The impact on the man who impregnated the woman has received less study. (4,10) Finally, the impact of abortion on society is too broad a question to be addressed with any clarity. The specification of dependent variables at a societal level constitutes many values choices as to the priorities of that society. Thus, the psychosocial consequences of abortion for the woman represents the most easily researchable issue. The following is, therefore, a systematic review of the scientific literature on the psychosocial sequelae of abortion. That is, what is the status of research efforts designed to determine the nature and extent of the psychosocial outcome following abortion?

Systematic review represents a specific strategy for identifying the "state-of-the-art" in a particular substantive area. (11) Fashioned with a careful eye toward the sampling of studies, this review strategy identifies all articles that cover a topic within a given time frame and/or published in particular journals. (12) Each article is then classified according to its characteristics, such as qualitative (e.g., case series, reviews, opinions) versus quantitative (i.e., including at least descriptive statistics), issues of internal and external validity, and so forth. The aggregation of these characteristics then documents the status of the literature over the sampled time period for that topic. Systematic reviews avoid many of the sampling biases associated with traditional syntheses of the literature. (11) This level of objectiveness is particularly important when controversial topics such as abortion are reviewed. Systematic review also avoids some of the restrictive assumptions of meta-analysis, which is a statistical strategy for combining the results from a literature. (13)

Systematic review of the literature on the psychosocial sequelae of abortion, therefore, represents an important strategy for identifying the quantity and quality of this literature using a stated, replicable method. By specifying this "state-of-the-art", we can then understand that which can now be said with some scientific confidence regarding the psychosocial consequences of abortion.

METHODS

Sampling Procedure: English language, quantitative post-abortion research articles were reviewed using systematic analysis in order to evaluate the adequacy of their empirical methods. A comprehensive search was completed for all abortion studies published in referred journals over the past two decades (1966-1985). Specifically, a computer search of six scientific databases was done using the keyword "abortion". The search strategy varied somewhat based on the database source. The following databases were used: *Family Resources, Medline, Mental Health Abstracts, Population Bibliography, PsycALERT, and PsycINFO*. Multiple searches using varying keywords were used to provide maximum identification of relevant articles for inclusion in the review. Multiple searches on overlapping databases allowed for greater confidence in the identification of articles. Sacks, et al. (13) report this strategy results in a reliable (0.66) way of identifying all articles in a substantive area. Quantitative studies were analyzed, including cross-sectional, retrospective or prospective designs, while qualitative studies, such as reviews, case series, editorials, and letters to the editor were not analyzed. The present review did not study research reported in books, dissertation abstracts, supplements, newsletters, or magazines. A total of sixty-one quantitative research articles on the psychosocial effects of abortion were identified during the two decades under review.

Review Procedure: For each of the 61 identified studies, the following aspects of research methods were determined: 1) sampling frame, 2) number of subjects (N), 3) response rate, 4) age of those in the sample, 5) presence or absence of controls, 6) times of measurement, 7) type and reliability of measures used, and 8) level of statistical significance.

Many studies involved multiple measurement events; therefore, both the N and the response rate were assessed as of the final measurement event. Measures were defined simply as any quantified assessment reported in the results of the study, and thus included a range of physical, social, and psychological scales. A broad-based approach was used to clarify reliability of the measure; that is, even if the reliability coefficients were unstated in the study, any reference to previous publication was accepted as evidence for the reliability of that measure.

Additionally, each study's outcome was categorized based upon the author's (s') opinion, as stated in the discussion of the article, of whether the results indicated that abortion: 1) had no negative effects; 2) did have negative effects; or 3) had mixed effects and/or remained neutral.

A random sample of 5 articles was taken from the 61 in the present review and a second reviewer categorized these articles to determine the reliability of the classification scheme. For this sample of articles the reliability was .92 for the present categories of analysis.

RESULTS

Of the 61 quantitative studies published between 1966 and 1985 (14-74), thirty-three were published in the first decade (1966-1975), whereas twenty-eight were published in the second decade (1976-1985).

Sample Characteristics

Thirty-six (59%) of these 61 articles had no sampling frame. Of those articles that used a sampling frame, fifteen used all of the given population, nine used consecutive subjects, and only one article used a random sample.

Turning to sample size, forty-one (67%) of the articles had less than 100 subjects. This large proportion of studies with relatively small sample sizes suggests the potential for problems with the power of any statistical comparison. (74) Excluding two relatively large studies (N's of 4018 and 1391), the range was 10 to 326, with a mean of 86.7.

No response rate was reported in seventeen (29%) of the articles. For those that did report, the mean response rate was 62.6%, with nineteen having a response rate of 75% or greater; fourteen with a rate between 50% and 74%; and eleven with a rate less than 50%. Three studies had response rates below 25%.

Age of subjects was not specified in fourteen (23%) of the articles. Twenty-six (43%) only specified the average age of the full sample but did not subcategorize subjects by age nor provide any indices of dispersion such as the standard deviation or the range. The remaining twenty-one (34%) of the articles stratified the subjects into multiple age groups.

Design Characteristics

More than two-thirds of the studies (70.5%) failed to use any type of control group.

Twenty-six (43%) of the studies measured only at a single time post-abortion. Twenty-seven (44%) measured two times. Eight (13%) measured three or more times. Of the studies that used at least two measurement events, fifteen did not specify when the first measure was taken. Fourteen administered the first measure within twenty-four hours before the abortion; two administered the first measure sometime after the abortion; and one study administered the first measure one week before the abortion.

The time at which the final measure was administered ranged from five hours to more than a year after the abortion. Two studies took the final post-abortion measure at five hours; four studies at 2-3 weeks; twenty-five (41%) at 1-6 months; six at 7 months to 1 year; and ten (16%) at more than one year. For six studies, the time of the final post-abortion measure was not specified, varying greatly among subjects; the time of final measure was described as a range, e.g., 2 days to 37 months, 2 months to 10 years. Eight studies (13%) did not specify the timing of the measurements relative to the abortion.

Measurement Characteristics

The number of measures used per study to assess either the dependent or independent variables ranged from one to eight. Twenty-four (39%) of the studies used only one measure; twenty-three (38%) used two measures; and fourteen (23%) used three or more measures. Thirty-four (56%) of the studies used no reliable measures, while the remaining twenty-seven used one or more.

Twenty-seven (44%) studies used descriptive statistics only (mean, standard deviation, percentage). The remaining majority of studies used inferential statistics.

Outcome Characteristics

The authors of thirty-eight (62%) of the articles concluded that abortion had no negative psychosocial sequelae. Ten (17%) other articles found that abortion did have negative effects. The authors of the final thirteen (21%) articles were neutral or cited mixed effects.

DISCUSSION

The results of the present systematic review on the psychosocial sequelae of abortion presents the picture of literature without sufficient methodological standards to assure the reader of the conclusions. Few studies had adequate control groups or used reliable assessments. No standards existed for studying the impact of abortion over time as most studies utilized only one or two measurement points. Poor methods can have a substantial impact on the results found. (75)

The present results are consistent with those reported by Rogers, et al. (76), that controlled studies of abortion lack sufficient statistical power to detect significant effects. Most studies had power less then .30. Thus, the potential for failing to identify actual negative psychosocial outcomes remains large. Therefore, it is not surprising that the majority of studies did not detect any psychosocial effects of abortion.

A substantial amount of the reported research failed to study the age of the patient in any systematic manner. It would seem, given the reports regarding teenage pregnancy and abortion, (22,60,73) that it would be important to, at minimum, separate teenage from adult women in all analyses to determine if these two populations are comparable.

Two studies with large samples examined only severe psychopathology post-abortion and have reported contradictory results. On one hand, a Swedish study (23) reported an incidence of post-abortion psychosis at 19.2 per 1000 with an incidence of puerperal psychosis of 6.8 per 1000. An English study, (20) on the other hand, found a lower rate in their post-abortion sample (0.3 versus 1.7). In fact, the differences may be accounted for by methodological artifact. The Swedish study utilized a large, computerized national database, whereas the English study surveyed physicians, thus relying on the memory and/or records of their participants. In addition, the British study did not match on prior psychiatric history, whereas the Swedish study did. Although the Swedish study is clearly superior in terms of methods, both studies suffer from a lack of specificity of the outcome criteria (inpatient psychiatric hospitalization was used as a proxy for psychosis). Such research, in the absence of great vigilance on the part of the investigators, is subject to false negatives.

SUMMARY AND RECOMMENDATIONS

In summarizing the "state-of-the-art" in research on post-abortion psychosocial sequelae, what recommendations can be made to advance scientific investigation of this controversial issue?

1. Multiple carefully selected control groups that are comparable in terms of age, supports, and socioeconomic status should be used within the same study. The following groups may represent important control groups for a post-abortion sample:
   a. Post-delivery women who had considered an abortion.
   b. Post-spontaneous aborting women.
   c. Post-delivery women who did not wish an abortion.
   d. Post-delivery women who were refused an abortion.
2. Utilization of a random sampling frame.
3. Measurement at multiple time points. Prospective follow-up of the identified sample should involve measurement well past the actual event.
4. Measures should be used which vary in sensitivity from the least sensitive (e.g., psychiatric hospitalization) to more sensitive self-report and observational measures of psychiatric symptoms and psychological well-being. Multiple outcome measurement should be the standard. Reliability of measures should be assessed specifically for the study sample.
5. Identification of risk factors which predict both the choice of abortion and the psychiatric response to abortion. Gibbons (77) reports that attempts to specify risk factors indicates that women with previous psychiatric vulnerability are particularly at risk for post-abortion psychiatric complications. Other factors related to increased risk were ambivalence, coercion, medical indications, concomitant psychiatric illness and the woman's feeling that the decision was not her own.
6. Conceptual and theoretical models of response to abortion are necessary to guide research initiatives. For example, Payne, et al. (58) have proposed a social-psychological model of abortion as a crisis and crisis resolution experience. Adler (15) reports that often women feel both relief and happiness and guilt, regret, or anger in the aftermath of an abortion. This author goes on to discuss aspects of the individual, the environment, and the surgical team that may impact on the patients' adjustment to the procedure.
7. Finally, and perhaps most importantly, if one is to scientifically address the impact of abortion on the woman, it would seem that documentation of no negative impact is not sufficient. Thus, instead of one-tailed tests of whether or not abortion leads to increased negative psychosocial sequelae, two-tailed tests of the impact using both positive and negative outcomes must be done. This recommendation would be of primary importance in situations

where the decision to abort is not based on concerns for the physical well-being of the pregnant woman.

It is apparent that the scientific study of the impact of abortion on the psychosocial status of the pregnant woman has suffered from significant methodological shortcomings. The importance of careful science is magnified in the study of controversial issues. Only through well-designed and controlled studies with reliable and appropriately timed measurement which follow prior hypotheses can one hope to even begin to deal with the polemics of this controversy. (7) Without this rigor, science has little to offer to the understanding of the role of abortion in our society. Without the time, effort and thoughtfulness needed to employ this rigor, emotions, not reason, will continue to mediate this debate.

REFERENCES
CHAPTER 6

1. Morbidity and Mortality Weekly Report, Centers for Disease Control, July 6, 1984, 374.
2. Glans, L: The role of personhood in treatment decisions made by courts. *Milbank Mem Fund Quarterly*, 1983, *61*: 76-100.
3. Kolder, VEB, Gallagher, J, Parsons, MT: Court-ordered obstetrical interventions. *NEJM*, 1987, *316*: 1192-1196.
4. Annas, GJ: Protecting the liberty of pregnant patients. *NEJM*, 1987, *316*: 1213-1213.
5. Melton, GB: Legal regulation of adolescent abortion. *American Psychologist*, 1987, *42*: 79-83.
6. Chervenak, FA, Farley, MA, Walters, L, Hobbins, JC, Mahoney, MJ: When is termination of pregnancy during the third trimester morally justifiable? *NEJM*, 1984, *310*: 501-504.
7. Yankauer, A: Abortion: The divisive issue. *Am J Pub Health*, 1985, *75*: 714-715.
8. Zack, BG: Abortion and the limitations of science. *Science*, 1981, *213*:
9. Hutchinson, GE: What is science for? *American Scientist*, 1983, *71*: 639-644.
10. Shostak, A, McLouth, G, Seng, L: *Men and abortion: lessons, losses, and love*. New York: Prager, 1984.
11. Larson, DB, Pattison, M, Blazer, DG, Omran, AR, Kaplan, BH: Systematic analysis of research on religious variables in four major psychiatric journals, 1978-1982. *Am J Psychiatry*, 1986, *143*: 329-334.
12. Mulrow, CD: The medical review article: State of the science. *Annals of Int Med*, 1987, *106*: 485-488.
13. Sacks, HS, Berrier, J, Reitman, D, Ancona-Berk, VA, Chalmers, TC: Meta-analyses of randomized controlled trials. *New Eng J Med*, 1987, *316*: 450-455.

14. Abrams, M, DiBiase, V, Sturgis, S: Post-abortion attitudes and patterns of birth control. *J Fam Prac*, 1979, *9*: 593-599.
15. Adler, NE: Emotional responses of women following therapeutic abortion. *Am J Orthopsyhiat*, 1975, *45*: 446-454.
16. Ashton, JR: The psychosocial outcome of induced abortion. *Brit J Ob Gyn*, 1980, *87*: 1115-1122.
17. Belsey, EM, Greer, HS, Lal, S, Lewis, SC, Beard, RW: Predictive factors in emotional response to abortion: King's termination study — IV. *Soc Sci & Med*, 1977, *11*: 71-82.
18. Blumberg, BD, Golbus, BD, Hanson, KH: The psychological sequelae of abortion performed for a genetic indication. *Am J Ob Gyn*, 1975, *122*: 799-808.
19. Borins, EFM, Forsythe, PJ: Past trauma and present functioning of patients attending a women's psychiatric clinic. *Am J Psychiatry*, 1985, *142*: 460-463.
20. Brewer, C: Induced abortion after feeling fetal movements: Its causes and emotional consequences. *J Biosoc Sci*, 1978, *10*: 203-208.
21. Cohen, L, Roth, S: Coping with abortion. *J Human Stress*, 1984, 140-145.
22. Cvejic, H, Lipper, I, Kinch, RA, Benjamin, P: Follow-up of 50 adolescent girls 2 years after abortion. *CMA Journal*, 1977, *116*: 44-46.
23. David, HP, Rasmussen, KK, Holst, E: Postpartum and post-abortion psychotic reactions. *Family Planning Perspectives*, 1981, *13*: 88-92.
24. Devore, NE: The relationship between previous elective abortions and postpartum depressive reactions. *JOGN Nursing*, 1979, 237-240.
25. Evans, DA, Gusdon, JP: Postabortion attitudes. *NCMJ*, 1973, *34*: 271-273.
26. Ewing, JA, Liptzin, MB, Rouse, BA, Spencer, RF, Werman, DS: Therapeutic abortion on psychiatric grounds. A follow-up study. *NCMJ*, 1973, *34*: 265-273.
27. Ewing, JA, Rouse, BA: Therapeutic abortion and a prior psychiatric history. *Am J Psychiatry*, 1973, *130*: 37-40.
28. Ford, CV, Castelnuovo-Tedesco, P, Long, KD: Abortion. Is it a therapeutic procedure in psychiatry? *JAMA*, 1971, *218*: 1173-1178.
29. Freeman, EW: Abortion: Subjective attitudes and feelings. *Family Planning Perspectives*, 1978, *10*: 150-155.
30. Freeman, EW: Influence of personality attributes on abortion experiences. *Amer. J. Orthopsychiat.*, 1977, *47*: 503-513.

31. Freeman, EW, Rickels, K. Huggins, GR, Garcia, CR, Polin, J: Emotional distress patterns among women having first or repeat abortions. *Obstetrics and Gynecology*, 1980, *55*: 630-636.

32. Greenglass, ER: Therapeutic abortion, fertility plans, and psychological sequelae. *Amer. J. Orthopsychiat.*, 1977, *47*: 119-126.

33. Greenglass, ER: Therapeutic abortion and its psychological implications: the Canadian experience. *CMA Journal*, 1975, 754-757.

34. Greenglass, ER: Therapeutic abortion and psychiatric disturbance in Canadian women. *Can. Psychiatr. Assoc. J.*, 1976, *21*: 453-460.

35. Greer, HS, Lal, S, Lewis, SC, Belsey, EM, Beard, RW: Psychosocial consequences of therapeutic abortion: King's termination study III. *Brit. J. Psychiat.*, 1976, *128*: 74-79.

36. Horowitz, NH: Adolescent mourning reactions to infant and fetal loss. *Social Casework*, 1978,: 551-559.

37. Kretzschmar, RM, Norris, AS: Psychiatric implications of therapeutic abortion. *Am. J. Obst. & Gynec.*, 1967, *98*: 368-373.

38. Kumar, R, Robson, K: Previous induced abortion and ante-natal depression in primiparae: preliminary report of a survey of mental health in pregnancy. *Psychological Medicine*, 1978, *8*: 711-715.

39. Jacobs, D, Garcia, CR, Rickels, K, Preucel, RW: A prospective study on the psychological effects of therapeutic abortion. *Comprehensive Psychiatry*, 1974, *15*: 423-434.

40. Jacobsson, L, Solheim, F: Women's experience of the abortion procedure. *Social Psychiatry*, 1975, *10*: 155-160.

41. Jansson, B: Mental disorders after abortion. *ACTA Psychiatrica Scandinavia* 2, 1965, *41*: 87-110.

42. Jorgensen, C, Uddenberg, N, Ursing, I: Ultrasound diagnosis of fetal malformation in the second trimester. The psychological reactions of the women. *J. of Psychosomatic Obstetrics and Gynecology*, 1985, *4*: 31-40.

43. Lask, B: Short-term psychological sequelae to therapeutic termination of pregnancy. *Brit. J. of Psychiatry*, 1975, *126*: 173-177.

44. Lazarus, A: Psychiatric sequelae of legalized elective first trimester abortion. *Journal of Psychosomatic Obstetrics and Gynecology*, 1985, *4*: 141-150.

45. Levene, HI, Rigney, FJ: Law, preventive psychiatry, and therapeutic abortion. *The Journal of Nervous and Mental Disease*, 1970, *151*: 51-59.

46. Lloyd, J, Laurence, KM: Sequelae and support after termination of pregnancy for fetal malformation. *British Medical Journal*, 1985, *290*: 907-909.

47. Mackenzie, P: Before and after therapeutic abortion. *CMA Journal*, 1974, *111*: 667-671.

48. Major, B, Mueller, P, Hildebrnadt, K: Attributions, expectations, and coping with abortion. *Journal of Personality and Social Psychology*, 1985, *48*: 585-599.

49. Margolis, AJ, Davison, LA, Hanson, KH, Loos, SA, Mikkelsen, CA: Therapeutic abortion follow-up study. *Amer J. Obstetr. Gynec.*, 1970, *110*: 243-249.

50. Meikle, S, Gerritse, R: A comparison of husband-wife responses to pregnancy. *The Journal of Psychology*, 1973, *83*: 17-23.

51. Meyerowitz, S, Satloff, A, Romano, J: Induced abortion for psychiatric indication. *Amer. J. Psychiatr.*, 1971, *127*: 1153-1160.

52. Moseley, DT, Follingstad, DR, Harley, H: Psychological factors that predict reaction to abortion. *Journal of Clinical Psychology*, 1981, *37*: 276-279.

53. McCoy, DR: The emotional reactions of women to therapeutic abortion and sterilization. *J. Obstet. Gyneac. Brit. Cwlth.*, 1968, *75*: 1054-1057.

54. Niswander, KR, Patterson, RJ: Psychological reaction to therapeutic abortion: I. Subjective Patient Response. *Obstetrics and Gynecology*, 1967, *29*: 702-706.

55. Niswander, KR, Singer, J, Singer, M: Psychological reaction to therapeutic abortion: II. Objective response. *Am. J. of Obstet. Gynecol.*, 1972, *114*: 29-33.

56. Osofsky, JD, Osofsky, HJ, Rajan, R, Fox, MR: Psychological effects of legal abortion. *Clinical Obstetrics and Gynecology*, 1971, *19*: 215-234.

57. Patt, SL, Rappaport, RG, Barglow, P: Follow-up of therapeutic abortion. *Arch. Gen. Psychiat.*, 1969, *20*: 408-414.

58. Payne, EC, Kravitz, AR, Notman, MT, Anderson, JV: Outcome following therapeutic abortion. *Arch. Gen. Psychiatry*, 1976, *33*: 725-733.

59. Peck, A, Marcus, H: Psychiatric sequelae of therapeutic interruption of pregnancy. *The Journal of Nervous and Mental Disorders*, 1966, *143*: 417-415.

60. Perez-Reyes, MG, Falk, R: Follow-up after therapeutic abortion in early adolescence. *Arch. Gen. Psychiatry*, 1973, *28*: 120-126.

61. Pion, RJ, Wagner, NN, Butler, JC, Fujita, B: Abortion request and post-operative response: A Washington community survey. *Northwest Medicine*, 1970, 693-698.

62. Robbins, JM: Objective versus subjective responses to abortion. *Journal of Consulting and Clinical Psychology*, 1979, *47*: 994-995.

63. Robbins, JM, DeLamater, JD: Support from significant others and loneliness following induced abortion. *Soc. Psychology*, 1985, *20*: 92-99.

64. Schmidt, R, Priest, RG: The effects of termination of pregnancy: A follow-up study of psychiatric referrals. *Brit. J. of Med. Psychology*, 1981, *54*: 267-276.

65. Sclare, AB, Geraghty, BP: Therapeutic abortion: A follow-up study. *Scot. Med. J.*, 1971, *16*: 438-442.

66. Shusterman, LR: Predicting the psychological consequences of abortion. *Soc. Sci. & Med.*, 1979, *13A*: 683-689.

67. Simon, NM, Rothman, D, Goff, JT, Senturia, AG: Psychological factors related to spontaneous and therapeutic abortion. *Am. J. Obstst. & Gynec.*, 1968, *104*: 799-808.

68. Simon, NM, Senturia, AG, Rothman, D: Psychiatric illness following therapeutic abortion. *Amer. J. Psychiat.*, 1967, *124*: 59-65.

69. Smith, EM: A follow-up study of women who request abortion. *Amer. J. Orthopsychiat.*, 1973, *43*: 574-585.

70. Smith, EM: Counseling for women who seek abortion. *Social Work*, 1972, *March*: 62-68.

71. Todd, NA: Follow-up of patients recommended for therapeutic abortion. *Brit. J. Psychiat.*, 1972, *120*: 645-646.

72. Tsoi, WF, Cheng, CE, Vengdasalam, D, Seng, KM: Psychological effects of abortion: A study of 1739 cases. *Singapore Medical Journal*, 1976, *17*: 68-73.

73. Wallerstein, JS, Kurtz, P, Bar-Din, M: Psychosocial sequelae of therapeutic abortion in young unmarried women. *Arch. Gen. Psychiat.*, 1972, *27*, 828-832.

74. Weston, F: Psychiatric sequelae to legal abortion in South Australia. *The Medical Journal of Australia*, 1973, *1*: 350-.

75. Lipsey, MW: A scheme for assessing measurement sensitivity in program evaluation and other applied research. *Psychological Bulletin*, 1983, *94*: 152-165.

76. Rogers, JL, Phifer, J, Lyons, JS, Larson, DB: Estimating the psychosocial impact of abortion using meta-analytic techniques. Unpublished manuscript.

77. Gibbons, M: Psychiatric sequelae of induced abortion. *Journal of the Royal College of General Practitioners*, 1984, *34*: 146-150.

PART III

AGING AND FAMILY

RELATIONSHIPS

7

HOW OLD IS "OLD AGE"?

Peter Uhlenberg, Ph.D.
Associate Professor of Sociology,
University of North Carolina Chapel Hill

The recently completed Carnegie Corporation-sponsored report on America's aging society begins by asserting that "the inexorable aging of our population" is a demographic revolution that "will affect every individual and every institution in the society". The remarkable transformation in age distribution is clearly borne out by the data: The proportion of the American population over age 65 tripled between 1900 and the present (from 4 to 12 percent), and it is projected to nearly double again between now and the year 2050 (from 12 to 22 percent). The effects of this pattern lead us to ask the crucial question of whether the arrangements for supporting the older population that have evolved over the past fifty years can or should be maintained.

During these past five decades a variety of social policies were enacted (most of them since 1960) that enable the elderly both to disengage from economically productive activities and to experience an improved standard of living relative to the younger population: Social Security benefits were significantly increased and protected against the threat of future inflation; Medicare provided the old with national health insurance, while Supplemental Security Income provided them with a guaranteed minimum income; special tax benefits for the elderly protected their assets during the later years of life; and the Older American's Act supported an array of services specifically intended for older persons. As a consequence of these policies, poverty among the elderly declined, the need to work past age 62 or 65 declined, and opportunities to enjoy leisure activities proliferated. To achieve these benefits for the old it was necessary, of course, to increase greatly the amount of federal money spent on the elderly. Currently (1987), expenditures on the population over age 65 capture 30 percent of the annual federal budget. If these arrangements are maintained, projections show about 60 percent of the federal budget going to support the old by the year 2030.

Yet this possible outcome is not due simply to population aging. Rather, the potential crisis results from a combination of assumptions regarding (1) future population aging, (2) removal of the old from economically productive roles, and (3) entitlement of the old to the variety of cash and noncash benefits now existing. While each of these three factors contributes to the projected cost of supporting the older population, discussions of options for the future usually focus only on the issue of economic transfer policies. Implicitly it is assumed that the population aging and retirement rates are fixed for the future. Thus, the possible options include moving the responsibility for support back to individuals and families, limiting the cost of transfer programs by imposing means tests, and increasing the tax burden on the working population to meet the growing costs of these programs. There is, however, an alternative option for dealing with the aging of the population that raises a more important issue: Should the proportion of old people in the population be reduced by changing the standard criteria age of "old age"?

How to Define Age

A perspective for considering the contemporary and future definitions of old age is provided by research on aging conducted by anthropologists and historians. Three useful generalizations can be extracted from the cross-cultural and historical literature on aging. First, old age is a socially recognized phase of life in virtually every society. That is, certain individuals are recognized as "old," and having achieved the status of being "old" has consequences concerning how individuals are expected to behave. Second, societies differ greatly in the criteria they use to distinguish the old from the non-old, and rites of passage into old age range from clear rituals to ambiguous transitions. Third, the meaning of "old age" is highly variable across cultures and across time. Using these generalizations as guides to the future, we anticipate that "old" will continue to be a meaningful status, but that when it begins and what it means may change.

While no one denies the social reality of old age in contemporary America, many would insist that the choice of age 65 as its beginning seems to be too arbitrary. Given the biological, social, psychological, and economic heterogeneity of individuals at any particular age, how can one chronological age be used to classify people as "old"?

Nevertheless, most individuals in the United States do cross some threshold into old age by the time they celebrate their sixty-fifth birthday. Identification of old age with the age of 65 should be seen in the context of the increasing "chronologization" of the entire life course. Chronological age is widely used to define distinctive life stages from infancy through old age. Today there are two distinct changes in a person's life, both correlated with chronological age, that are the best markers of the transition into the last stage of life. One is taking retirement, and the other is beginning to receive old age benefits. Both of these changes are nearly universal among those aged 65 and over. Regardless of other characteristics or attitudes, it is meaningful to say that a person has entered old age when he receives old age entitlements and is no longer significantly engaged in the labor force.

The obvious query, of course, is why does one's relationship to an employer and to the welfare state tend to change around age 65? This age, it seems, has figured prominently in social legislation enacted over the past fifty years. As the numbers of people attaining old age and needing extra benefits was recognized as a social problem, policy makers were challenged to design social policies to alleviate the problem. Designing programs to aid a segment of the population (the old) that cannot be precisely defined might appear difficult. This was not the case with legislatures, however. They simply selected a chronological age as the standard criterion for defining who would be eligible for old age benefits. Starting with old age insurance in 1935, a gamut of special benefits has since been created for those individuals who can prove that they have been alive for more than a fixed number of years. And these benefits are essential for making retirement a viable option for most older people.

Although several different ages (55, 60, 62, 65) are used in various federal programs designed to benefit the elderly, the most significant age is clearly 65 — the age at which full social security benefits, Medicare, and special tax advantages are available. Reflecting the semi-official status of age 65 as the marker of old age, statistics reporting on the older population routinely use a category of "65 plus". Researchers use this same category. Thus, despite the diversity of opinions regarding who "really" is old, chronological age is an accurate indicator. Many Americans have achieved the status of being "old" by age 62 (they are substantially retired and receive old age benefits), and most are in the category of "old" by age 65.

In recent years, several experts on aging have urged that the increased use of age to structure the life course be reversed. Bernice Neugarten, past president of the Gerontological Society, for example, sees chronological age as an irrelevant basis for defining groups in contemporary society. She advocates removing irrelevant age constraints that operate in such areas as employment, housing, education, and community participation. Others (for example, Matilda White Riley, president of the American Sociological Association) protest the chronological division of life into three boxes — education, work, leisure —and support a reorganization of the social structure that will encourage interspersing of each of these activities throughout the life course. The case for beginning to deinstitutionalize the life course is not persuasive, given the heterogeneity of the population within each age category. It is not likely, however, that old age will be eliminated as a distinctive stage of life.

Aging is a multifaceted process, involving biological and psychological change as well as social change. Attempts to socially eliminate old age as a distinctive last phase of life, without breaking the association of biological decline with aging, are probably futile and counterproductive. The absence of a specific age to mark the transition into old age would leave old age to be defined by negative biological changes, such as physical and mental deterioration. Under this condition, old age could be viewed only as an unmitigated disaster — that phase of life characterized by undesirable and irreversible losses. Despite its arbitrariness, then, the use of chronological age to determine when old age begins has certain advantages.

Establishing an age for entitlement to old age benefits aids individuals and governments in long-range planning. Further, this approach leaves open the definition of old age, since it simply says that, after a set age, the social expectation of being engaged in the labor force is lifted and the person qualifies for special benefits. Having a clear marker of old age does not limit the flexibility of what the elderly do, nor does it necessarily encourage an unproductive old age. On the other hand, it does provide added protection during a stage of life when physical limitations are increasingly likely to restrict activities.

The Trouble With 65

If establishing a chronological age to mark the beginning of old age is reasonable, continuing to use age 65 for that purpose is not. Ongoing changes since 1935, when the Social Security Act was established, have made 65 an obsolete standard. For as successive cohorts bear fewer children and live longer, the age at which they enter the privileged status "old" needs to be increasing. Several of the more salient reasons for increasing the age of old age can be briefly stated.

Old age dependency burden. The economic impact of an aging population is sure to receive increasing attention as the baby-boom generation ages. No society in the history of the world has experienced a situation in which over 20 percent of its population was over age 65. The options available for supporting a future older population of this size are quite limited: taxes could be increased substantially or the level of per-capita benefits could be reduced substantially. Faced with these alternatives, the possibility of reducing the size of the older population by increasing the age of eligibility for old age benefits becomes relatively attractive.

Potential of the old to contribute. The potential productive contributions by cohorts after reaching age 60 or 65 has been increasing, while actual productivity has declined. There is a growing gulf between what older people could contribute to societal welfare and what they actually do contribute in the areas of work, family and leadership in organizations. The members of cohorts reaching age 65 now and in the future, compared to those in earlier cohorts, are better educated and more skilled in their roles in a complex bureaucratic society. But as retirement has become pervasive and has begun earlier in life, the productive contributions of the old to society have diminished. Advancing the age of old age will encourage continued independence and productivity among individuals who are capable of making significant contributions to the larger society.

Social roles for old people. It is frequently noted that role expectations for old people in our society are vague and ambiguous. They are not expected to work or support others economically, but it is unclear what their social responsibilities ought to be. The challenge of creating meaningful social roles for the older person is exacerbated by the expanding average length of time spent in old age. But the added years of life after age 60 resulting from declining mortality need not extend the old age stage of life. Rather, these added years can extend the middle-adult phase of the life course, when individuals are expected to be economically productive. At the same time, a distinctive, and hopefully more positive, last phase of the life course can be developed.

High relative expectations. Social and economic changes occurring over most of the twentieth century have produced a situation in which each successive birth group has been better educated, more urban, and wealthier than any preceding group. Consequently, the older population has consistently had, on average, less education and lower income than the middle-aged population. This gap in socioeconomic states between age groups is maximized during periods of rapid transition, such as the first half of the twentieth century. However, as a result of stability (or stagnation) since 1970, it appears that these differences in education and earnings will decline or disappear in coming decades. More recent cohorts of young people are not receiving more education than those preceding them, and their earnings trajectories are not exceeding those of earlier cohorts. The potential leveling of education and earnings across cohorts has two interesting implications for the elderly in the future. First, if the old no longer suffer an educational disadvantage, their ability to compete with younger workers for desirable occupational positions may be enhanced; this would be especially true if there is an increase in lifelong education, which could keep skills from declining as workers age. Second, the ability, or the willingness, of the young to support the old at levels considered adequate by the old may become problematic. Up to the present, the income expectations of the old (based on their past earnings) have been modest compared to the actual incomes of the middle aged. This may not be true in the future, as the middle aged no longer are advantaged vis-a-vis the old. Will middle-aged workers be willing to support retired persons who, on average, have a higher standard of living than they themselves?

Future productivity of today's youth. The experience of adolescents in recent years raises further doubts regarding the ability of the future middle-aged to support the old at relatively high income levels. If the early years of life are a time of accumulating "human capital," such as education, that determines future productivity, there is reason for concern. The academic performance of successive cohorts of young people, as measured on standardized exams, has deteriorated in recent years. Furthermore, there have been increasing rates of adolescent criminal behavior, drug and alcohol use, and out-of-wedlock births. And an increasing number of children are living in poverty and being raised in single-parent families. These children and adolescents of the 1970's and 1980's will be the middle-aged adults of the 2020's to whom, if current arrangements persist, the old must look for support. Perhaps renewed concern for the well-being of children will produce changes that will reverse these pernicious trends. But the recent experiences of children at least adds another note of uncertainty regarding the future security of the old.

Racial-ethnic age stratification. The rapid growth of minority populations, compared to the majority, suggests another dimension of the future population composition. It is expected that the Hispanic,

Black, and Asian populations will contribute over 56 percent of the total growth of the U.S. population between 1980 and 2000. Since more rapid growth implies a younger age distribution, the minority populations will have quite a different age structure than the non-Hispanic white population. Projections for 2030 indicate that 41 percent of the children, but only 24 percent of the old, will be minorities. Thus, various racial-ethnic groups in the population will differ in the stake they have in programs that support different age groups. Might the growing number of middle-aged minorities, who are parents of a disproportionate number of children, resist increasing federal expenditures for the old, who are predominately nonminority whites?

Generational equity. As government expenditures on the elderly increased in recent years, the proportion of old people below the poverty line fell from 25 percent in 1970 to 12 percent in 1984. During this same time period, the proportion of children in poverty increased from 14 to 20 percent. Will the growing costs of supporting a much larger older population in the future prevent adequate investment in children? Increasing the economically productive years of adulthood and decreasing the size of the dependent older population would not automatically solve the problem of underinvestment in children. These changes could, however, alleviate tensions between age groups by increasing the resources available for redistribution.

Marking Up Age

Thus far I have argued that the state largely controls access to old age by establishing a chronological age at which individuals are entitled to major old age benefits. Establishing such an age is reasonable: It allows long-term planning, it recognizes the reality of increasing risks in later life, and it avoids causing old age to be defined as a state of physical or mental disability toward the end of life. Yet if chronological age is to be a component of an aging policy, it is crucial that increased attention be given to the question of where to mark the beginning of old age. Congress, in 1983, indicated some willingness to change the age when it passed an important amendment to the Social Security Act. The age for full social security benefits is now scheduled to increase gradually until it reaches 67 in 2027. Although this change is a significant step toward removing 65 as an untouchable symbol, it is only a first small step.

The problem with replacing one fixed age (65) with another (67) is that this approach does not appreciate the uncertainty of the future age distribution. To be sure, demographers can, and do, provide precise projections of the future population, broken down by age and sex. Before accepting these projections as reliable predictors of what is to come, however, it is well to remember the heading of a *Wall Street Journal* article appearing a few years back: "Demographers Are Wrong Almost as Often as Economists".

To make a population projection, one must begin with assumptions regarding the future course of mortality, fertility, and migration. The difficulty of accurately anticipating these trends can be seen by reviewing the recent history of population projections made by the Census Bureau. A number of projections were made between 1960 and 1975, each providing a range of estimates for the population aged 65 and over in 1980. These projections turned out to be wide of the mark. Not only was each middle estimate too low, but the range of projections never even included the figure of 11.3, the actual percentage over age 65 in 1980. These projections were technically correct, but they could not accurately forecast what would really happen over the succeeding five to twenty years.

The most recent population projections were made by the Census Bureau in 1983. In this report, the median projection of the percent of the population over age 65 in 2030 is 21.2, up from a "best guess" projection of 18.3 percent in 1975. The low projection in 1983 shows 17.5 percent of the population to be old in 2030, while the high projection shows 25.4. Three observations on future population aging are in order. First, each projection indicates a substantial future increase over the 12 percent of the population now aged 65 and over. Second, with the high figure being about 50 percent greater than the low figure, the economic and social implications of plausible outcomes are surely quite different. Third, we cannot be confident that the actual proportion who are old will in fact fall within this wide range. This last observation needs further elaboration.

What happens if the "low" mortality assumption of the 1983 projections is replaced with an even lower level of future mortality? This type of calculation was made with the assumption that age-specific death rates would decline at the same rate in the future as they did over the past decade and a half — not a wholly plausible situation. [1] Should this occur, in conjunction with low fertility and low immigration, 36 percent of the population would be over 65 in the year 2050. At the other extreme, the proportion of old people in 2030 could be as low as 13 percent, should there be a combination of slow mortality improvements, medium immigration, and an increase in fertility to the level

---

1. Jacob S. Siegel and Cynthia M. Taeuber, "Demographic Perspectives on the Long-Lived Society," *Daedalus* (Winter 1986), Vol. 115, No. 1, pp. 77-117.

existing in the mid-1960's. Admittedly, the extremes of 13 percent and 36 percent are unlikely outcomes. But substantial uncertainty regarding what the age distribution will be in the year 2030 does exist. Given this uncertainty, there is an advantage to incorporating flexibility in the age criteria used in social policy that will affect the future older population.

Any method of determining a chronological age to mark the transition into old age will, admittedly, involve some arbitrary choices. Nevertheless, it is possible to view the beginning of old age as a variable that can change over time and can be defined by a formula responsive to demographic changes. In addition, the formula should be simple to calculate and easy to explain to the general public. Details regarding its implementation would need to be specified, perhaps along the following line: (1) every ten years, using current information, a revised marker of old age would be calculated; (2) the new marker would be gradually phased in, beginning twenty years later (for example, old age could be advanced two months per year until the new level was obtained). Such an approach avoids any abrupt change and provides enough lead time for future retirement planning.

Four formulas for establishing a variable marker of old age are described below. Modifications on these proposals could be suggested, as well as altogether different approaches. The essential point, however, is that a feasible formula could be established and implemented to guide planning for the future older population.

Proposal 1. Establish a fixed limit to the span of old age. Rather than defining the beginning of old age by a fixed number of years after birth (e.g., 65), this approach suggests counting back a fixed number of years from expected age at death. Using a current life table, it is simple to calculate the age at which the average number of remaining years of life is, for example, 15 (or whatever number is preferred). As life expectancy increases, the onset of old age also increases. Thus, any added years of life would expand the length of the middle years of life rather than old age. Nevertheless, with this definition most members of each cohort could anticipate a substantial period of life in the privileged status of old age.

Proposal 2. Establish an old age limited to one-fourth of the adult life. Barbara Torrey, a demographer at the Census Bureau, suggests a formula for calculating a normal retirement age, which is also determined by using life-table values. By selecting the age at which life expectancy is equal to 25 percent of the life expectancy at age 20, individuals would spend an average of one-fourth of their adult lives in old age. Compared with Proposal 1, this alternative allows the length of both old age and middle age to grow in response to longer life expectancy.

Proposal 3. Establish a fixed ratio of old to middle-aged populations. Rather than starting with life tables, this approach keeps constant the ratio of old to middle-aged adults in the population. The age distribution of the population, as provided by the Census Bureau, would be used to determine an age X such that the population over age X was equal to 17 percent of the population aged 20 to X. Thus, the old age dependency ratio would not increase as the population aged chronologically.

Proposal 4. Establish a fixed proportion of old people in the population. A variation on the previous proposal would keep the proportion of old people in the population constant at 10 percent. Again, this involves a simple calculation using the age distribution of the population. Under this proposal, there would be no future growth in the relative size of the older population, regardless of what demographic changes might occur.

Calculating with Variables

Using any of the above proposals, old age would become a variable determined by future demographic trends. The "new" age of old age in the year 2030 under each proposal can be calculated by assuming that the most recent middle-range projections are accurate. The results of these calculations are shown in Table 1. For comparison, 1985 is used as a baseline with age 67 used as the starting marker of old age in that year (reflecting the change in future age eligibility for full social security benefits). Proposal 1 (old age begins when average years of life remaining equals 15) and Proposal 2 (ratio of older years to middle years of life equals .25) produce the same result — the transition to old age would occur at age 72. By so advancing old age 5 years (from 67 to 72) over the next 45 years, there would be about a 24 percent increase in the ratio of old to middle-aged adults. Proposal 3, which keeps this ratio of old to middle aged constant, would start old age at 74 years. Under this proposal, average length of the last stage of life would decline to 13.7 years. Finally, Proposal 4, which keeps the proportion of old people in the population constant at 10 percent, requires the biggest change — old age would begin at 75. This alternative, which still provides an average of thirteen years of life remaining for those who reach old age, would reduce the proportion of all adults who were old.

Table I. Implications of Alternative Definitions of Old Age [a]

Year and definition of old	Old age threshold	Average length of old age	Years old as proportion of adult life	Old pop. Adult pop.	Old pop. Adult pop.
1985 (baseline)					
Age 67	67	15.4	.275	.17	.10
2030 (projection)					
Proposal 1	72	15.0	.250	.21	.13
Proposal 2	72	15.0	.250	.21	.13
Proposal 3	74	13.7	.229	.17	.11
Proposal 4	75	13.0	.219	.15	.10

[a] *Source:* Population data are from U.S. Bureau of the Census, 1984; life table values are from *Life Tables for the United States: 1900-2050* (Actuarial Study No. 89, Social Security Administration, 1983).

Once the implications of maintaining our current old age policy under new demographic conditions are understood, the idea of changing the age criteria of old age may not appear preposterous. Indeed, raising the age for entrance into old age to 72 through 74 over the next forty or forty-five years becomes a modest proposal. Unfortunately, such ideas have not yet received much attention, and the mechanisms to accomplish such a goal are still sketchy and tentative. Nevertheless, the number of options for dealing with the potential problems of future population aging is not very large, and there are risks involved in postponing the selection of one. To avoid serious social disruption, substantial lead time is needed to implement any significant change in the arrangement for supporting older persons. At the same time, the unknowns about future conditions suggest the need for a policy that is sufficiently flexible to adapt to a range of possiblities. A plan for periodically adjusting the age of old age for cohorts who will be entering old age twenty years later is a reasonable and not terribly painful way to meet these requirements.

Objections to enacting legislation that gradually increases the age for entitlement to old age benefits are sure to be raised by those currently approaching old age. Yet no change is proposed for individuals who will be reaching 65 over the next twenty years. Further, cohorts approaching old age in the future differ from the current older population in a number of significant ways. There are, however, legitimate objections to increasing the age of old age without making concomitant changes in other aspects of the social system. If changing the threshold of old age is to have a positive consequence for individuals during their later years of life, some profound changes in the organization of society are needed.

First, changes must be made in the organization of work. The growth of early retirement has occurred because it makes economic sense within the existing structure of work. It will be necessary to introduce greater flexibility in work careers. For example, possibilities for horizontal job mobility and opportunities for moving to jobs with less responsibility and lower incomes need to be expanded. A variety of work options (part-time, flexible hours, contract work, etc.), if expanded, would permit an individual to choose an option that meets his or her particular work needs and ability in later life.

Second, changes are needed in the organization of education. If older workers are to have skills needed to be productive or to make job changes, opportunities for education and learning throughout adulthood must be expanded. New forms of lifelong education could not only increase possibilities for extending the work life, but also promote greater opportunities for continuing productivity in non-economic areas of life.

Third, extending the middle years of life into the seventies requires that more attention be given to problems of disability before old age begins. Despite some contrary views, most studies of morbidity trends in recent years suggest that declining mortality has not been accompanied by improved health status. If disability in later adulthood does not decline (or increases), then advancing the normal retirement age would increase the number of persons unable to work because of physical disabilities. Increased efforts to prevent disability should be encouraged along with ways to provide more adequately for those with disabilities.

Finally, attention to delaying entrance into old age does not address the equally important question of what happens during old age. Shortening the duration of old age and reducing the proportion of the population that is old should facilitate efforts to improve the quality of the last years of life. But how to make old age a more productive and meaningful stage of life also needs direct attention.

8

AGING AND LIFELONG LEARNING

Robert Strom, Ph.D.
Director, Office of Parent Development Int'l, and
Professor of Education, Arizona State University

Until recently, the need for education was seen as limited primarily to children and adolescents. Schools were expected to provide them with the knowledge and skills they would require for the rest of their lives. Few people today would agree with this formula for success. Instead, there is a growing emphasis on self-improvement at every age level. The emerging view is to regard personal growth as a never-ending obligation. This fundamental revision in the public attitude toward learning presents families with new opportunities and greater responsibility. Each of us can benefit by considering how we are involved in educational change.

INCREASING THE SOURCES OF LEARNING
Learning in a Past-Oriented Society

When the older people of today were children, the world was changing less rapidly. Because there was a slower rate of progress, the past dominated the present. Consequently, the young learned mostly from adults. In those days a father might reasonably say to his son "Let me tell you about life and what to expect. I will give you the benefit of my experience. Now, when I was your age ..." In this type of society, the father's advice would be relevant because he had already confronted most of the situations his son would one day have to face. Because of the slow rate of change, children could see their future as they observed the day-to-day activities of parents and grandparents.

There are still some past-oriented societies in the world, places where adults remain the only important source of a child's education.

This continues to be so among aboriginal tribes in Australia as well as among religious groups like the Amish in America. In each of these settings the future is essentially a repetition of the past. When life is so predictable it seems justified to teach the young that they should adopt the lifestyle of their elders. For this reason, in every slow-changing culture, grandparents are viewed as experts, as authorities, as models by all age groups. The role expected of the children is to be listeners and observers, to be seen but not heard (Mead, 1978).

Learning in a Present-Oriented Society

Something happens to a society when technology is introduced and begins to accelerate. There is a corresponding increase in the rate of social change. Longstanding lifestyles are permanently modified. Successive generations of grandparents, parents and children have less in common. In effect, the children of today are having experiences that were not part of their parents' upbringing. This means there are some things adults are too old to know simply because they are not growing up now. It is a reversal of the traditional comment to children that "You're too young to understand". Certain situations children currently encounter are unique in history to their age group. Access to drugs, life in a single-parent family, computer involvement and global awareness are common among children. Adults cannot remember most of these situations because they never experienced them.

The memory of one's own childhood as a basis for offering advice ("When I was your age...") becomes less credible as the pace of change quickens and young people's experiences begin to diverge significantly from those of their parents and other adults. As the generation gap widens, a peer culture develops. We live in a time when both adults and children prefer to learn from people whose experiences are similar to their own. In America's age-segregated environment, peers are turning more and more to one another for advice. Peer influence is strong within every age group. We are just beginning to understand something about the pressures that older adults impose on one another, particularly when they leave their home towns and move to retirement communities.

Obviously a peer orientation undermines cultural continuity as it divides the population into special interest groups. Furthermore, because a technological society assigns greater importance to the present than the past, older people cease to be seen as models for everyone. Instead, each generation chooses to identify with well-known individuals of their own or next higher age group. So, in a technological nation, respect for the elderly declines. Older people are no longer regarded as experts about much of anything except aging (Strom, Bernard & Strom, 1987).

Learning in a Future-Oriented Society

The phase of civilization we are entering now is commonly referred to as the Information Age (Hofmeister, 1984; Naisbitt, 1985). In this context school for children begins at an earlier age, continues longer, and includes a vast amount of knowledge which was unavailable to previous generations of students. Given these conditions, young people are bound to view the world from a different perspective than their elders. As a result, the gap in experience between age groups keeps growing wider, so much so that intergenerational misunderstanding becomes common.

Another fundamental change that accompanies high technology is increasing public concern about the future, especially preventing nuclear war, preserving the environment and preparing for retirement. Certainly it is wise for each of us to look ahead, set goals and make plans — as long as we also attend to current affairs. For those who become preoccupied with the future, there is no longer any spontaneity; everything must be planned. These people are forever looking forward to the time when they graduate, get a job, have children, receive a promotion, save enough money to travel. It appears that they avoid living in the present. Instead they wait, they save, they are going to do so many things, have such good times someday — and life goes by.

All of us know people who live for tomorrow. They look forward to the freedom and economic security that will come after their children grow up. But, in their anticipation of the future, they fail to enjoy their children now, their jobs now, their lives together now — and then, when the days of retirement arrive, they regret that the children are gone, they resent the loss of their vocational role and they painfully face their failure to have established intimacy. It is just as possible to become fixed in the future as in the past or the present.

EXPANDING THE SCOPE OF THINKING
Schooling in the Past

The kind of education students encounter is influential in shaping their attitudes. For example, when persons who are middle aged or older attended school, the main emphasis was on analytic thinking. Students spent most of the time memorizing events that had already happened. They tried to figure out what could have been done differently and, in hindsight, judge how certain situations might have been avoided. Every class heard the warning: "Those who do not understand the mistakes of the past are destined to repeat them."

Therefore, knowing about the past was considered the best preparation for the future. By studying people and happenings of bygone days, Americans could learn who they were, understand their national identity and know the principles for which their country stood. Subjects like history and literature were given priority and expected to instill a common attitude of patriotism.

Schooling in the Present

More recently, in our present-oriented society, schools have tried to prepare students for a technological society. Alvin Toffler (1970; 1980) told us that we would soon live in a time of overchoice. Cable television is perhaps the most familiar example of overchoice. There are more kinds of cereals, automobiles, movies, books, clothing, and leisure pursuits than ever before. Since our children will experience overchoice more often than we do, they need preparation to cope with it. Although most parents would agree that growing up and decision making go together, it does not always turn out that way. Instead, adults often justify their takeover of children's decisions by insisting that wrong choices could bring serious consequences. This presents a dilemma. Boys and girls need preparation in making choices so they can establish a sense of self-direction and not be misled by others; yet the chance to make decisions is often denied them for their own protection. Because children are expected to remain students longer than their parents, the initial chance to decide for themselves may not come until the stakes are high (Chance, 1986).

The importance of making one's own decisions has been reinforced by the self-concept movement. Although this movement has sometimes been used to support selfish motives, it has also enabled our country in a short time to enlarge the population that experiences respect from only older people and whites to include men and women of every age and ethnicity, the handicapped and children. Of course, we still believe that elders deserve respect, but now they are obliged to respect young people as well. A guiding premise of the self-concept movement is that every person is special, important, one of a kind. It follows that everyone should be encouraged to make their own choices. When this view became popular in the late 1970's, schools added critical thinking to the list of goals for learning (Strom & Bernard, 1982)

Schooling in the Future

Schools have also been obliged to accept more responsibility for helping students cope with the future. Students can read about problems of the past, but they cannot do anything about them. They cannot stop the assassins of Presidents Lincoln and Kennedy, nor can they can buy Hitler's paintings so he will become an artist instead of a dictator. Students cannot affect events that have already taken place, but they can influence the future by thinking about it and learning to plan cooperatively. That is, the physical and social technology are available to make the future what we wish it to become. But first there is a need to conceptualize alternative futures and then decide which of these to pursue. On both the individual and societal level, planning for the future requires creative thinking (Torrance, 1986)

Futurists agree that if children are encouraged to be creative, they can more readily avoid boredom, resolve personal conflict, cope with increasing consumer choice, accept complexity and ambiguity, make independent judgments, use leisure time constructively, and adjust to the rapid development of new knowledge. In an era of overchoice there is also good reason for education to include moral development and commitment to others. It is not just that a multitude of options can overwhelm people if their learning lacks a coherent set of values; but as technology makes a greater range of goals possible, decisions need to be made about what goals ought to be achieved and the priority of their importance (DeBono, 1984; Naisbitt, 1985).

It appears that in a changing society successive generations will differ in the kinds of thinking they need to acquire at school. This makes it unreasonable to judge children by how well they perform tasks that were emphasized several decades ago. For example, handwriting and spelling receive less attention now as students rely on computers with word processing that includes a choice of print styles and spelling correction. Everyone could benefit by recognizing that the knowledge base of children is up-to-date. Indeed, information is growing at such a rapid rate that each generation is necessarily better informed. When adults fail to acknowledge this important and continuing change, children are denied the respect they deserve.

PROMOTING INTERGENERATIONAL UNDERSTANDING

In order to properly shape the future in a democratic society, intergenerational dialogue has to become more common. Unless such contacts are sustained and mutually beneficial, the future could bring conflict as low birth rates provide fewer working-age taxpayers to meet the needs of a growing elderly population. Some social scientists expect the relationship between young and old to replace the relationship between classes and races as the dominant source of domestic conflict during the next half century. The National Council on the Aging and the Child Welfare League of America are trying to prevent this forecast from coming true. Recently they formed a coalition of organizations called Generations United. The affiliates agree they are mutually "troubled by a divisive and growing movement promoting the claim that the elderly receive too large a share of public benefits and entitlements at the expense of younger age groups, particularly the nation's children" (Angelis, 1987). Plans are underway to increase public awareness of the need for intergenerational cooperation and harmony.

The potential for better relationships is being recognized in other ways as well. During the past several years intergenerational programs have been established throughout the country (Stamstead, 1985; Struntz & Revelle, 1985; Thorp, 1985). These initiatives contend that it is not enough to just extend life for older people — the quality of their lives must be enriched as well. They need younger people to spend time with them. This is because at every age we define our importance in terms of the amount of attention others give us and the impact we have on human affairs. Conversely, senior citizens should accept their reciprocal obligation to share time with youngsters. Instead, some men and women choose to isolate themselves by accepting the proposition that retirement ends their responsibility to society. The reality is that however long one lives it is the commitment to others that generates their respect.

Intergenerational programs are often identified by family terminology, but their purpose is to promote relationships between nonrelatives of differing age groups. For example, the nationwide Foster Grandparent program pays low income elderly people to ease the caretaking burden for one-parent families, parents of retarded children, and school-attending teenage mothers (Butler & Gleason, 1985). The University of Florida has an Adopted Grandparent program in which primary grade children rotate as daily visitors to a nearby nursing home. This prototype has served as a model for public schools and long-term care partnerships throughout the country (Hegeman, 1986). The Grandpersons program in Michigan matches retired mentors who share self-defined competencies with interested elementary children (Tice, 1985). In all these programs, older participants experience a sense of purpose and satisfaction. For children the benefits include receiving help, establishing friendships, and recognizing older people as a population who cares about the welfare of other age groups.

It would be pleasing to report that corresponding gains have accompanied studies of the grandparent-grandchild relationship. But the absence of family-oriented educational programs for grandparents would not support such a conclusion. The lack of curriculum for them obtains in part because researchers have limited their concern to the symbolic meaning of grandparenthood. For more than 20 years, descriptive studies have tried to place grandparents into categories based on their behavior styles. During the 1960's, grandparents were identified as *formal* (occasionally helping out, but expecting parents to raise their own children), *fun-seeking* (maintaining a playful and informal relationship with grandchildren), *surrogate* (grandmothers who assume regular caretaking responsibilities), and *distant* (the benevolent figure who emerges on holidays and special occasions) (Neugarten & Weinstein, 1964).

More recent research informs us that grandparents now qualify for new categories such as *companionette* (affectionate but somewhat passive), *remote* (geographically distant but not necessarily emotionally so), and *involved* (ready to enforce discipline and family rules) (Cherlin & Furstenberg, 1986). Other investigators emphasize the relationship of grandparent styles to such variables as age, gender, ethnicity, divorce, or family separation (Bengston & Robertson, 1985; Hagestad & Burton, 1986; McCready, 1985; Mitchell & Register, 1984). These studies commonly conclude that there is a need for more help to build mutually satisfying relationships between older and younger family members.

Considering that education has proven to be an effective way for parents to improve their family relationships, a similar orientation that acknowledges and treats grandparents as individuals ought to be available. Although nearly fifty million Americans are grandparents, they currently lack educational support. No reported investigations of the extended family have resulted in a programmatic attempt to apply what is known about the changing role of grandparents. Instead of continuing the nearly exclusive emphasis on non-relative intergenerational programs, some attention should be placed on resolving cross-age problems within families, developing ways to facilitate communication and counteract alienation.

Assumptions for Grandparent Education

The program at Arizona State University to help grandparents become more influential and experience greater respect began by scheduling a free course for them at senior centers in metropolitan Phoenix. Persons who enrolled in the "Becoming a Better Grandparent" class were promised a better understanding of child and adolescent developement. In return, they were expected to make known certain aspects of their grandparent experience. The emphasis was placed upon sharing, because our earlier search of the literature had revealed a patronizing attitude toward grandparents and no programmatic response to their educational needs. A similar observation about the need to replace sentimentality with involvement was recently expressed by the National Council on the Aging (Manheimer, 1987).

It seemed a contradiction to affirm the importance of grandparents while failing to offer them guidance in a time of change, to applaud their ability to learn without proposing anything in particular that they should be expected to know. So, accompanied by graduate students in gerontology, the author met with small groups of grandparents to hear and record their comments about specific issues. These meetings, conducted over a period of two years and attended by more than 400 grandmothers and grandfathers, provided useful data on which to base a tentative curriculum for grandparents. In additon, several assumptions emerged from the preliminary work that guide the continuing project.

Assumption 1: The grandparent role can be made less ambiguous.

There is general agreement that the grandparent role is no longer clearly defined (Bengston & Robertson, 1985). Parents can take courses to remain competent in their changing role, but such opportunities do not exist for the approximately 75 percent of older people who are grandparents. Instead they are left alone to wonder: "What are my rights and responsibilities as a grandparent?" "In what ways can this role be more influential and satisfying?" "How can I know how well I am doing as a grandparent?" These kinds of questions will persist until norms of behavior are established for grandparents to use in goalsetting and self-evaluation.

Assumption 2: Grandparents can learn to improve their influence.

There is evidence that parent education has enabled many mothers and fathers to increase their effectiveness (Bronfenbrenner, 1984; Strom, 1984). Similarly, family life specialists assert that grandparents can enhance the lives of grandchildren when they are prepared to fulfill their guidance function (Peterson & Quadagno, 1985). However, even though studies of learning potential during middle and later life indicate that people remain capable of acquiring new knowledge, an educational curriculum focusing on the changing role of grandparents is unavailable (Pifer & Bronte, 1986). This missing element in adult education lessens the possibility of a meaningful life for many grandmothers and grandfathers.

Assumption 3: Grandparenting curriculum ought to be developed.

Senior adults have been led to believe that learning in later life should consist of whatever topics a person finds interesting, without any consideration of societal expectations (Euster, 1982; Peterson, 1983). But, as people continue to age, they should also continue to grow — and not just in terms of leisure-oriented skills. Some of one's education should emphasize obligations and roles, just as a work-related curriculum does for younger age groups. By balancing what they want to learn with what they need to know, grandparents can remain a valued resource to their families and society. As things now stand, senior citizens are the least educated subpopulation and, ironically, the only one without any defined educational expectations. Given that the size of this age group is expected to grow faster than any other age segment, it would be a mistake to perpetuate the current situation (Dienhart, 1987).

Assumption 4: The benefit of grandparent education can be assessed.

Popular support seems likely for educational programs that would help grandparents to enlarge their scope of influence, improve their ability to communicate and understand loved ones, become more self-confident, and experience greater satisfaction in their family role. These benefits would be even more credible if the sources confirming them included other persons than just the participating grandparents. By combining results from three generational versions of the author's "Grandparent Strengths and Needs Inventory", the merits of this approach to family development can be determined.

ELEMENTS OF A GRANDPARENT PROGRAM

Building a relevant curriculum for grandparents and presenting it in an effective way requires some trial and error. A convenience sample of volunteers has provided regular feedback about the suitability of our evolving program. The components we have developed thus far include the following: sharing feelings and ideas with peers; listening to younger people; studying lifespan personal development; improving family communication skills; and focusing self-evaluation on relevant behavior. Each of these elements will be described.

Sharing feelings and ideas with peers. Sharing feelings is the basis of intimacy, and self-disclosure permits us to unload emotions for the sake of mental health. Grandmothers and grandfathers have much to gain by sharing anxieties, hopes, satisfactions, and observations with other grandparents. They need to inform, challenge, and reassure one another in their common quest to attain a respected role. For these reasons every session begins with discussion in small groups. To help grandparents prepare for each topic, the discussion questions are provided a week in advance. This practice allows time for reflection and promotes a more stimulating exchange of views.

Most of the topics apply to everyone. For example, a unit on "Parents and Grandparents as Teaching Partners" calls for discussing these issues:

Now that your children have grown up, what do you find most satisfying about your relationship with them?

Compare your problems as a parent with those your children seem to be having in raising their children.

How are your views on childrearing similar and different from those of your children?

What do you think parents should teach children to expect of their grandparents?

Listening to younger people. After sharing with their peers, the participants become listeners to a younger source of feelings and ideas. Grandparents seldom have a chance to be observers when grandchildren carry on discussions with their friends. Our age-segregated lifestyle prevents it. Once in a while parts of a conversation among youngsters may be overheard, but in isolation this occurrence does not significantly increase adult understanding. There should be a better way to acquaint older people with the perceptions of children and teenagers.

The approach we use is to show grandparents videotaped interviews with junior and senior high school students. These observations reveal what it is like to be growing up today. Teenagers are asked to express their views on topics that correlate with the agenda for grandparent discussions. Some of the subjects include peer pressure, self-esteem, gender roles, classroom learning, personal stress, and family communication. The participating students, identified only by first name and age, are not related to the grandparents who watch them. It follows that the grownups are less likely to be offended or suffer a loss of self-esteem. The video conversations offer insights for understanding how one's grandchildren resemble and differ from peers.

Grandparent development also calls for learning what it is like to be raising school age children today. The satisfactions and difficulties of people in the middle generation are often misunderstood by their aging parents and dependent children. Again, a videotape format is used; none of the taped men and women who discuss their experience as parents and as adult children are related to the viewing grandparents. This nontraditional method for educating older people about younger people has great potential.

Studying lifespan personal development. Grandparents need to know the views of peers who have a similar family role. They should be familiar with the perceptions of teenagers and parents of school age children. A third important source of guidance in our program comes from short lectures focusing on research studies with implications for family relationships. Each minilecture corresponds to the weekly grandparent discussion topic and is accompanied by an easy-to-follow outline in large print. All of the themes involve learning to grow as a grandparent (e.g. parents and grandparents as partners, the learning potential of grandparents), learning to respect grandchildren (e.g., the student experience in today's schools, building self esteem and achievement), and learning to overcome obstacles (e.g., being grandparents from a distance, family separation and divorce).

Improving family communication skills. Most of the grandparents we work with admit they sometimes have difficulty in getting a conversation started with grandchildren. It is also recognized that unless grandchildren are encouraged to share information about their experience, older family members increase the risk of being ignored as a source of guidance. One of the communication strategies for the grandparent program involves televiewing, the most common activity in which family members spend time together. Three out of four parents regularly see television with their children; the proportion of grandparents who watch with grandchildren is approximately the same (Gallup, 1985; Cherlin & Furstenberg, 1986). When full advantage is taken of this opportunity for interaction, a better relationship can be expected.

During televiewing grandparents and grandchildren look at the same pictures and hear the same words. But previous experience causes them to sometimes reach dissimilar conclusions (Bryant & Anderson, 1983). It is these differences in perception that ensure each party can benefit from the other. Watching television together can be an excellent way to learn about the impressions, understandings, and values of grandchildren. When adults ask questions, it shows they care about what children think and are interested in understanding them. To illustrate, these questions can be used occasionally while watching almost any television program.

"What has happened in the story so far?" A fundamental goal in learning to read is comprehension. Memorizing the alphabet and being able to identify words is not enough. Understanding the sequence of events is also important. In the books from which children learn to read, the words are necessarily short and the story line is uneventful. On the other hand, television programs usually have a beginning, middle and end. Indeed, most of them are better suited for the assessment of understanding sequence than are beginning children's books.

"What do you suppose will happen next?" Everyone needs to anticipate events. By asking hypothesis-type questions we motivate children to explore beyond what can be observed directly, to imagine what is unseen, to express a futuristic perspective. This procedure encourages boys and girls to talk more, because there is no single correct answer. It also permits children to express opinions that differ from adults.

"What do you think she/he learned from this experience?" Moral learning should occur throughout life. Long ago the Greeks effectively used the theater to teach morality because they realized this type of learning is best acquired through observation. When members of an audience focus attention on the behavior of others, they are less defensive and more able to consider changes in their own conduct. Some of the moral dilemmas portrayed on television can be personalized when grandparents describe related events and struggles in their own lives.

"What do you suppose _____ means?" Learning the definition of words is a lifelong task. Many of the words children hear on television can be the focus of this question, e.g. "witness", "victim", "emergency". An emphasis on vocabulary building calls for the more informed of the viewing parties to define the word. It is also helpful to provide corrective feedback when statements reveal misunderstanding. To confirm the need for this approach, ask a child in your family to repeat aloud any words she/he does not understand during one segment of a mutually-viewed program.

Focusing self-evaluation on relevant behavior. Grandparents want to think well of themselves. But the respect they desire is difficult to attain because it depends on fulfilling a relatively undefined role. They aspire to success, but lack a common set of reasonable criteria for self-evaluation. Grandparents need norms of constructive behavior so they can become more influential and satisfied. The method for focusing self-evaluation begins with grandparent groups brainstorming a list of rights they feel are appropriate for persons in their role. The important outcome is to help individual grandparents define aspirations based on their family situation.

They do so by selecting from a list of rights developed by peers:

Right to visitation with grandchildren where there is a divorce.
Right to hear from grandchildren when separated by distance.
Right to express personal feelings, including childrearing advice.

The same procedure of group brainstorming followed by individual goal-setting is used to help grandparents define their responsibilities.

Naturally grandparents are not alone in determining what their relationships will be with grandchildren. The parents are involved, too, and hopefully will encourage grandparents to assume a significant family role with:

> Responsibility to model the constructive use of leisure time.
> Responsibility to help grandchildren know how their parents behaved as children.
> Responsibility to understand contemporary childrearing practices.

At the end of each session grandparents are given a self-evaluative homework assignment. For example, the following questions are given for the unit on "Parents and Grandparents as Teaching Partners":

> How do you suppose your family views you as a source of guidance?
> How do you feel about offering childrearing advice to your children?
> How do you let your children know they are doing a good job as parents?
> How does your performance as a grandparent compare with how well you did as a parent?

Finally, responses of family members on the Grandparent Strengths and Needs Inventory are used to focus growth for individuals. All three generations are asked to express their feelings about the merits and limitations of a particular grandparent's behavior. The rationale for using this approach is that better decisions about self-improvement can be made when the viewpoints of other people are taken into account. Certainly grandmothers and grandfathers are the best persons to identify the demands placed upon them. However, if they serve as the only source of perception about their competence, some pivotal concerns might be overlooked. More specifically, a grandchild's perception is worth knowing and can motivate a change in behavior. Then too, grandparents who understand how their adult children see them can continue some response patterns and reconsider others.

There is benefit in becoming aware of how grandparents are assessed in other families. This common view or norm deserves attention by older persons who wish to grow. Grandparents have a peer reference group too. By comparing experiences with others who have adult children and grandchildren, it is possible to determine the merit of likenesses and differences. An individual profile, drawn from the combined grandparent, adult child and grandchild responses, can give a comparative overview of personal success and progressive change.

CONCLUSION

The developmental phase of this project will continue until all curriculum elements are considered suitable for dissemination. Our field test population will soon enlarge to include grandparents who live in long-term care facilities. Many of them experience frustration and disappointment in their attempts to communicate with children and grandchildren. While members of this dependent group often function in a mentally normative way, physical impairment causes them to be isolated from family and friends. Loneliness, coupled with the lack of mental stimulation, poses a situation equally as detrimental to health as their physical disabilities.

Most people are surprised to learn this is the first educational program for grandparents in our country. It is common to suppose the government agencies and private organizations which assert that lifelong learning is essential must be supporting curriculum development for older people. This is seldom the case. Our efforts to date have reinforced the belief that grandparents need more than competent health care and a decent pension. They need a well-defined, constructive role in our society. Before this transition takes place, however, they need education to identify the relevant and obsolete aspects of their traditional role. They need to accept new functions as well as the task of revising others. It seems clear that the emerging role will be a more difficult one, but the personal growth it requires can also mean the grandparent experience becomes more worthwhile than ever before.

BIBLIOGRAPHY
CHAPTER 8

Angelis, J. (1987). Generations united. *Continuance/Interface*, 2 (1), 1.
Bengston V., & Robertson, J. (1985). *Grandparenthood.* Beverly Hills, CA: Saga Publications.
Bronfenbrenner, U. (1984). The changing family in a changing world. *Peabody Journal of Education*, 61(3),52-70.
Bryant, J. & Anderson, D. (1983). *Children's understanding of television. Research on attention and comprehension.* New York: Academic Press.
Butler, R., & Gleason, H. (1985). *Productive aging.* New York: Springer Publishing Company.
Chance, P. (1986). *Thinking in the classroom.* New York: Teachers College Press.
Cherlin, A., & Furstenberg, F. (1986). *The new American grandparent.* New York: Basic Books.
DeBono, E. (1984). *Tactics: The art and science of success.* Boston: Little Brown & Co.
Dienhart, P. (1987). Anna's Future. *University of Minnesota Update.* 14(4), 6-8.
Euster, G. (1982, Fall). Serving older adults through institutions of higher education. *Gerontology and Geriatrics*, 3(1),69-75.
Gallup, G. (1985). Forecast for America. *Television and Families.* 8(1),11-17.
Hagestad, G., & Burton, L. (1986). Grandparenthood, life context and family development. *American Behavioral Scientist*, 29(4),471-484.
Hegeman,C. (1986). *Grandparents and childcare.* Albany, NY: Foundation for Longterm Care.
Hofmeister, A.M. (1984). The special educator in the information age. *Peabody Journal of Education*, 62(1),5-21.

Kornhaber, A. (1986). *Between parents and grandparents.* New York: St. Martin's Press.

Manheimer, R. (1987). Older adults enriching their communities. Cultural Enrichment of Older Adults, 5(2),1.

McCready, W. (1985). Styles of grandparenting among white ethnics. *Granparenthood,* edited by V. Bengston & J. Roberston. Beverly Hills, CA: Sage Publications, 49-60.

Mead, M. (1978). *Culture and commitment.* New York: Columbia University Press.

Mitchell, J., & Register, J. (1984). An exploration of family interaction with the elderly by race, socioeconomic status and residence. *The Gerontologist,* 24(1),48-54.

Naisbitt, J. (1985, August). Megachoices: Options for tomorrow's world. *The Futurist,* 19(4),13-16.

Neugarten, B., & Weinstein, K. (1964). The changing American grandparent. *Journal of Marriage and the Family,* 26(2),199-204.

Peterson, D. (1983). *Facilitating education for older learners.* San Francisco, CA: Jossey-Bass.

Peterson, W., & Quandago, J. (1985). *Social bonds in later life.* Beverly Hills, CA: Sage Publications.

Pifer, A., & Bronte, L. (1986). *Our aging society.* New York: Norton.

Stamstead, M. (1985, Summer). The Intergenerational Educational Volunteer Network Act of 1985. *Intergenerational Clearinghouse,* 3(1),2.

Strom, R. (1984). *The parent as a teacher inventory.* Chicago: Scholastic Testing Service.

Strom, R., & Bernard, H. (1982). *Educational psychology.* Belmont, CA: Wadworth.

Strom, R., Bernard, H., & Strom, S. (1987). *Human development and learning.* New York: Human Sciences Press.

Struntz, K., & Revelle, S. (1985). *Growing together: An intergenerational sourcebook.* Washington, D.C.: American Association of Retired Persons and the Elvirita Lewis Foundation.

Thorp, K. (1985). *Intergenerational programs.* Madison: Wisconsin Positive Youth Development Initiative, Inc.

Tice, C. (1985). *The states speak: A report on intergenerational initiatives.* Ann Arbor, MI: New Age, Inc.

Toffler, A. (1970). *Future shock.* New York: Random House.

Toffler, A. (1980). *The third wave.* New York: William Morrow & Co.

Torrance, P. (1986). Glimpses of the promised land. *Roeper Review.* 8 (4), 246-251.

PART IV

TEEN SEXUALITY: RESEARCH, PUBLIC POLICY & PROGRAMS

9

DECISION MAKING IN ADOLESCENT PREGNANCY: A REVIEW OF INTRAPERSONAL AND INTERPERSONAL FACTORS

Everett L. Worthington, Jr., Ph.D.
Associate Professor of Psychology,
Virginia Commonwealth University

Teenage pregnancy has become a national concern. In 1981 approximately 1.3 million pregnancies occurred among teenagers. In adolescents aged 15 to 19, the pregnancy rate was 134 per 1,000 (Henshaw et al., 1985). Most teen pregnancies are unintended. Adolescent pregnancy is characterized by numerous instances of emotion-laden decision making (Rosen, 1982). Generally, these decisions affect the girl, the baby, the girl's family, and often the putative father.

Adolescent pregnancy often involves uncertainty, turmoil and crisis. Pregnant adolescents can be faced with four major decisions: (a) to end the pregnancy or bear to term; (b) assuming bearing the baby to term is chosen, to rear the child or place it for adoption; (c) assuming rearing is chosen, to rear the child within the adolescent's family of origin or outside of it; and (d) to determine the future of her relationship with the putative father. Of course, each major decision may necessitate numerous other decisions, leading to almost continual feelings of uncertainty, bewilderment, and upheaval in families of pregnant adolescents — especially those eschewing abortion.

This paper consists of three sections. In the first, models of decision making are briefly reviewed. In the second, research concerning the decision to abort or bear to term are reviewed. In the third, the decision to relinquish the baby for adoption or to rear the child is examined, with emphasis on the mothers and their families once the girls have decided to bear to term.

Theories and Models of Decision Making

There are several approaches to making good decisions, stemming from a variety of theoretical perspectives. Generally, decision making models can be classified as based on social exchange theory, humanistic theory, psychodynamic theory, cognitive theory, or social psychological theory.

Models of decision making based on social exchange theory emphasize the analysis of the costs and benefits of the various alternatives among which the person must decide. Krumboltz and Hamel (1977) have proposed a social exchange model of career decision making. Ainslie (1975) has proposed a social exchange model of self-control decision making. Janis and Mann (1977), although they also trace their roots to social psychology, advocate vigilant information processing as optimal decision making. Vigilant information processing involves careful consideration of the pros and cons of the various alternatives and is thus derived from social exchange theory.

Models of decision making based on humanistic psychology emphasize the effect in decision making. For humanistic theoreticians, a good decision feels correct and is congruent with one's self-concept. Such models of decision making have been proposed almost *en passant* by May (1953), Rogers (1961) and Maslow (1971).

Models of decision making based on psychoanalytic theory have emphasized that decisions be congruent with the person's ideal of "good". Unconscious factors might motivate decisions. Intrapsychic conflict can lead especially to guilt and post-decisional regret. Psychodynamic models have been expounded by Adler (1939), Frankl (1967), Fromm (1950), and Jung (1933).

Models of decision making based on cognitive theory have generally emphasized problem solving skills and psychological processes that short-circuit effective decision making. For example, Tversky and Kahneman (1974) identified several uses and misuses of heuristics — problem-solving strategies — in the process of decision making. Hunt (1982) and others have investigated the ways in which people think, make decisions, and support their decisions after the fact. Herbert Simon (Simon & Barenfeld, 1969) and other researchers in artificial intelligence have implemented decision making strategies in computer programs that simulate human decision making (Kahneman, 1973; Neisser, 1976).

Models of decision making that are based on social psychology draw from theories of interpersonal influence (Ajzen & Fishbein, 1980), cognitive dissonance theory (Festinger, 1957), or attribution theory (Nisbett & Borgida, 1975).

Janis and Mann's (1977) theory of decisional conflict is generally accepted as the most complete overview of the entire decision making period. It draws from social exchange approaches, cognitive approaches, and social psychological approaches. Essentially, it suggests that vigilant information processing leads to optimization strategies of decision making or at least to strategies that approach optimization strategies. Optimization strategies are systematic examinations of the pros and cons of all major alternatives and decisions that weigh the relative merits of the alternatives (e.g., consanguineous with information processing models). Often, though, in emotionally "hot" decisions (ego-involving decisions with real risks of harm or loss), people use suboptimization decision making strategies, such as *satisficing* (considering whether one alternative meets minimum acceptable criteria and is satisfactory and ignoring other alternatives) or *muddling through* (making small incremental changes to deal with a specific problem without considering the effects of the decisions on the entire system).

Janis and Mann propose a decision tree that predicts whether people will terminate their decision making at nonoptimal levels or will persevere to vigilant information processing. Decision making that is terminated prematurely may lead to (a) *unconflicted inertia* (if the person decides that continuing without change is not risky enough to merit more time spent in decision making), (b) *unconflicted change* (if the person decides that the first option considered satisfices), (c) *defensive avoidance* (if there is no perceived hope of a better alternative), or (d) hypervigilance (or panic, if time is too brief to consider other alternatives).

According to Janis and Mann, when hope is lost for a good solution and the person engages in defensive avoidance, the person may choose one of three alternatives: (a) if risks are not perceived to be great when the decision is postponed, the person will *procrastinate* and may lose interest in the decision until it has become irrevocable; (b) if the decision cannot be postponed, the person might allow others to make the decision, thus *shifting responsibility* away from himself or herself; (c) if the decision cannot be postponed and responsibility cannot be conveniently shifted, the person might *defensively avoid* vigilant information processing through "bolstering" an easy alternative with biased search, appraisal and contingency-planning strategies (e.g., similar to cognitive dissonance theory).

Janis and Mann specify conditions under which vigilant and less than vigilant strategies of decision making are employed. For example, the person is more likely to employ vigilant decision making if:

1. moderate stress is felt (high perceived stress leads to defensive avoidance, unconflicted change, or hypervigilance; low perceived stress leads to unconflicted inertia);

2. significant others are involved in the decision making but not over-involved to the extent of coercing compliance or assuming decision making for the adolescent (e.g., similar to social psychological theories, such as Ajzen & Fishbein, 1980).

If the adolescent eschews premature decision making and uses optimization decision making strategies, Janis and Mann hypothesize that decision making will proceed in five stages: (1) appraising the challenge, (2) surveying the alternatives, (3) weighing the alternatives, (4) deliberating about commitment, and (5) adhering to the commitment despite negative feedback. The weighing of alternatives requires consideration of gains and losses for self and others and of approval and disapproval of self and others.

Despite the thoroughness and realism of Janis and Mann's (1977) model of decision making, some elements of their theory receive short shrift. For example, Janis and Mann are relatively nonspecific about how decision makers weigh the pros and cons of their alternatives. Ainslie (1975) has proposed a model of optimization of decision making that may be adapted to predict the reward potential (RP) of a potential consequence as

$$RP = p v e^{-kt}$$

where p = the expected probability of a reward or punishment, v = the value of the reward or punishment (which may be either positive or negative), t = the time in the future that the reward or punishment is anticipated, and k = an empirically-derived constant. The overall consequence potential (CP) of an alternative is the sum of the separate RP's for the various rewards and punishments associated with the alternative. The alternative with the highest CP is selected. Ainslie's theory of behavioral self-control is applicable to decision making only when the person uses an optimization strategy.

Another area of weakness in Janis and Mann's theory concerns the social influence of significant others in the girl's life. Although the importance of others is acknowledged — especially if their influence attempts are clumsy or coercive — Janis and Mann do not describe how the influence occurs or how the various significant others' opinions are considered. Ajzen and Fishbein (1980) describe how a girl's attitude or decision might be influenced by the significant others in her life. They describe the girl's behavior (B) or behavioral intention (BI) by:

$$B \text{ or } BI = Att + {}_i^N(OA_i \times MC_i)$$

where Att = the girl's attitude, OA_i = other's opinion, MC_i = the motivation to comply with the other's opinions, and N = the number of significant others considered important *for that opinion* by the girl.

A third area of weakness for Janis and Mann's theory is the recognition that decisions often occur within families and that others are involved in the decision making because the decision is part of a *family* crisis. Family crisis theories consider many variables that influence decision making that are not recognized when a decision is considered to be an individual enterprise.

McCubbin and Patterson (1983) have proposed the Double ABCX model of family crises, which expanded the earlier ABCX model by Hill (1949). In the ABCX model, factor A is the stressor, factor B is the family and other physical and psychological resources, and factor C is the family's perception of the stressor and the resources available to deal with the stressor. Factor X represents the product of the three factors and it stands for the subjective experience of crisis (or not). The Double ABCX model acknowledges that crises, once experienced, take time to be resolved. Resolution is affected by factor aA, pile-up of other stressors; factor bB, use of existing and new resources, and factor cC, ongoing perception of the crisis. The family ultimately experiences resolution (factor xX) ranging from bon-adaptation (good adaptation) to mal-adaptation (bad adaptation).

Adolescent pregnancy can be conceptualized as a family crisis using the Double ABCX model. Resolution of the crisis should be expected to involve more than vigilant decision making, but effective decision making should mediate the crisis. On a more microscopic level, each of the decisions required during the adolescent's pregnancy might be considered a separate family crisis — especially the decision between parenting the child within the family of origin and relinquishing the child for adoption. That decision might take place over a protracted time period, being very applicable to family crisis theory (McCubbin &

Patterson, 1983). Previous decisions contribute to pile-up of stressors (factor aA). Decision making strategies contribute to family resources (factor B) and contributions of the opinions of others outside of the family of origin, (e.g., the putative father, friends, peers, church members, counselors, school teachers) contribute to new resources (factor bB).

The Decision to Abort or Bear to Term

Teen pregnancy is generally a long-lasting, unanticipated, non-normative and untimely stressor that may result in family stress, crisis and transitional disruption because of the way the events affect almost all family members.

Between 1972 and 1976, the abortion rate (the number of abortions per 1,000 women aged 15-44) among teenagers rose by more than three-fifths; this rate nearly doubled for girls under the age of fifteen (Baldwin, 1976). Teenagers obtained 28 percent of all abortions in 1981. About 13 per cent of 15- to 19-year-olds and about three per cent of girls aged 14 became pregnant in 1981 (Henshaw et al., 1985). Women between 18 and 19 years old had the highest rate of abortion for any age group (Chilman, 1980).

In earlier studies, abortion seemed more acceptable to white than to black women. This trend has changed, however. National data from 1973 through 1977 showed that abortion rates were higher for black than for white women (Forrest et al., 1979). In 1981 the nonwhite abortion rate was more than two times the rate for whites. Although nonwhites have a relatively high abortion rate, their fertility rate (births per 1,000 women aged 15-44 years) is 35 percent higher than that of whites. Therefore the higher abortion rate in nonwhites is a result of higher birth rate in nonwhites (Henshaw et al., 1985). Nonwhites are less likely than whites to terminate pregnancies that occur outside of marriage but are more likely than whites to terminate marital pregnancies through abortion.

Although most of the teenage pregnancies are unwanted, the majority of these pregnancies are nevertheless carried to term. In 1981, 56 percent of the pregnancies (excluding those ending in miscarriages or stillbirths) occurring before age 15 resulted in live births, while 44 percent were terminated by abortion (Henderson et al., 1985).

Methodological Considerations

Much research has been conducted during the past ten years in regard to teenage sexuality and pregnancy. Some of this research investigated contraceptive use and nonuse, retrospectively comparing effective contraceptors to those who experience unwanted pregnancy (DeAmicis et al., 1981). Other studies examined pregnancy resolution in groups of teens who abort and in those who bear the baby to term (Fishman, 1975; Klerman et al., 1982). Still other studies compare all three groups — aborters, childbearers and contraceptors (Gispert & Falk, 1976; Landry et al., 1986; Nadelson et al., 1980). Comparative studies of the above groups have been criticized, however, because in most cases, samples are drawn from different agencies. Such studies may be confounded due to the effect of different influences or presentations of options by different agency workers. In addition, different agencies may attract differing populations of teens. Michaels and Fanelli (1986) maintain that it is usually not possible to find these groups (including those who relinquish their children for adoption) in the same institution.

Research that investigates teenage pregnancy has generally fallen into one of three categories. Such studies have looked at (a) factors that discriminate between two or more of the groups mentioned above, (b) factors involved in the decision-making process, or (c) consequences or sequelae of the pregnancy resolution decision (i.e., to abort or to carry the pregnancy to term).

A major criticism of many of the studies has been their bivariate nature, which does not take into account relationships among several of the variables associated with abortion or pregnancy continuation decisions. For instance, Bracken et al. (1974) perceived degree of support as being only one aspect of the decision to abort or deliver. They pointed out the need to look at the interaction of personality variables within a sociocultural milieu. Other objections raised by Chilman (1980) have been the failure of the research to adequately consider the probable confounding effect of subject differences (i.e., developmental level, socioeconomic status, ethnicity, race, religion, etc.) with respect to the causation and outcome of early childbearing. She maintains that variables found to be associated with early childbearing are mistakenly presumed to be caused by early childbearing. Chilman (1980) further points out the tendency to design research and interpret its results in a framework that views the causes and consequences of adolescent childbearing in personalistic terms; the problems are seen as residing almost exclusively within individuals, rather than at least partly in the society in which they live.

One of the first studies using multivariate analysis (Eisen et al., 1984) compared the decisions of those teens who aborted and those who kept their babies. This study explored sociodemographic, financial, educational, attitudinal and social interaction variables.

Data collection of pregnancy resolution studies is typically done through structured interviews (including telephone interviews) or (more commonly) self-administered questionnaires. Some studies have combined these two techniques. The use of questionnaires alone has been debated because of the complexity and ambivalence of human attitudes and because answers to the survey are often sensitive to the wording of questions (Granberg & Granberg, 1980).

In much of the research, assessment has been conducted at only one point in time, i.e., preabortion, predelivery, post-abortion, or postpartum (Rosen, 1980; Eisen & Zellman, 1984). A few studies include multiple assessment points (Bracken et al., 1974; Eisen et al., 1983; Swigar et al., 1976), but these are exceptions. Resnick (1984a) proposed that more research using longitudinal design be conducted. This would allow assessment at a number of decision-making points. These points would include decisions to contracept, to abort, and to relinquish the child for adoption.

Eisen et al., (1983) found that the pregnancy-resolution decision was made in stages for some adolescents. During the first stage, the girl made a decision to deliver her baby or to abort it. If the pregnancy continued, during the second stage of decision making the girl decided to keep her baby and marry or to keep her baby and remain single. Adoption decision making was not investigated due to the small sample size. Other women in Eisen et al.'s study seemed to make all three decisions simultaneously, weighing the costs and benefits of each.

A Conceptual Framework for Understanding Abortion — Bearing to Term Decision Making

Despite the plethora of models and theories of decision making, few studies have actually investigated a theoretical model. Chilman (1980) reviewed research on adolescent pregnancy and concluded that much of the research on adolescent sexuality and pregnancy conducted in the 1970's was funded by the federal government and was pragmatic and atheoretical in nature. The few times theoretical models have been investigated they have identified some factors that influence decision making in adolescent pregnancy resolution.

Because research has been primarily atheoretical, it is helpful to use some conceptual framework to organize the research concerning decision making during adolescent pregnancy. In general, three categories of factors are thought to influence decision making by pregnant adolescents: societal, intrapersonal, and interpersonal factors. These factors are shown graphically in Figures 1 and 2.

ABORTION VS BEAR TO TERM

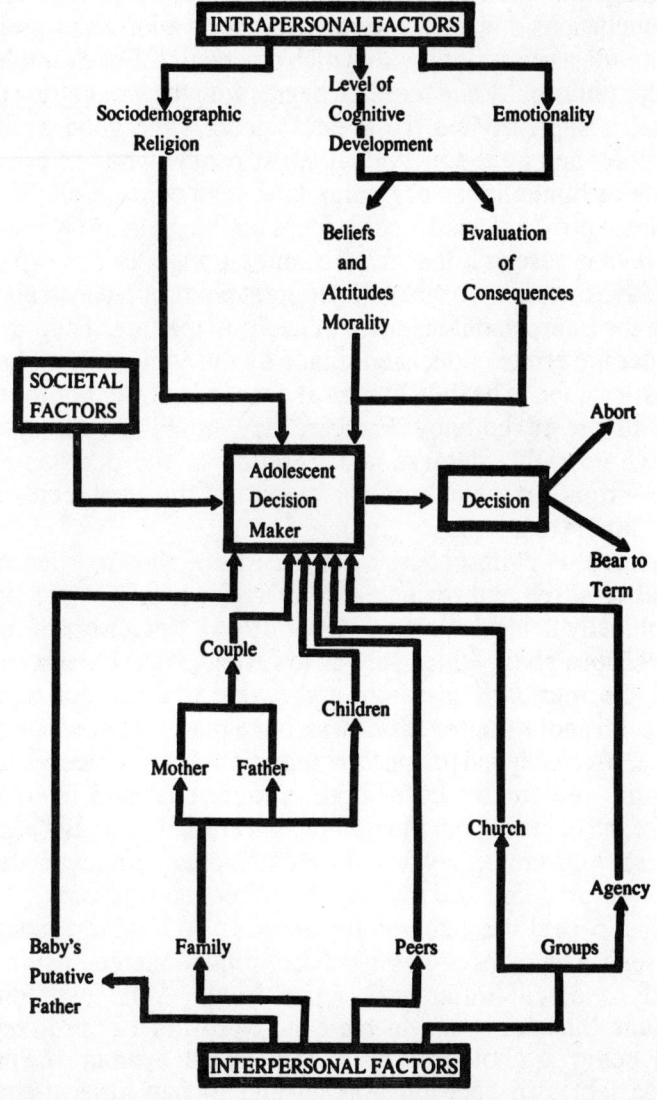

In Figure 1, we summarize factors affecting the decision to abort or to bear to term. We concentrate on the psychologically-oriented intrapersonal and interpersonal factors rather than the more sociologically-oriented societal factors. In Figure 2 (to be discussed later), we summarize factors affecting the decision to relinquish for adoption or to parent the child.

Using such a conceptual scheme to understand decision making in pregnant adolescents is not philosophically or politically neutral. Many of the conclusions one draws from research on adolescent pregnancy depend on the assumptions with which one begins. For example, most pro-choice philosophy and research begins with the assumption that the individual is supreme and the greatest good is the good as idiosyncratically defined by the individual. Most people who are pro-choice define life or humanity as beginning later than conception (Williams, 1982). Since pro-choice advocates focus on the pregnant woman, they tend to review research that reveals and emphasizes *her* experience. Pro-life advocates often begin with different philosophical assumptions, stressing the interpersonal context of decision making. They are likely to consider the effect of decisions made by the adolescent on her baby (which is assumed to be fully human at conception), her family, and the putative father of the baby. Further, they emphasize the system of people whose rights deserve consideration in the decision-making process — rights of the unborn, the parents of the adolescent, and the putative father (to a lesser degree).

As numerous philosophers of science have shown, science (both empirical research and reviews of research) cannot (in principle) be philosophically neutral (Polanyi, 1958, 1964). Reviewers of research make decisions about which studies to review, what criteria to use to evaluate the merits of research, and which findings are worthy of reporting. It is not a matter of fairness, but a matter of how one defines relevance, which depends on one's assumptions. Pro-choice researchers and pro-life researchers cover both intrapersonal and interpersonal aspects of the decision, but their emphases are different. Because their emphases are different, they treat different findings as relevant data that demand interpretation and thus draw different conclusions.

In this paper, we attempt to consider both intrapersonal and interpersonal aspects of adolescents' decisions about their pregnancies. Obviously, we will differ in balance from people with different assumptions than our own, which are more pro-life than pro-choice. In addition, being psychologists, we have chosen to examine the psychological variables in decision making and to pay little attention to societal variables, which might be of more interest to sociologists and which require consideration for a full understanding of the problem.

Societal Factors

Societal Acceptance. Pregnant adolescents look for support from their families and from their sexual partners in their decisions to abort or to bear the baby to term. They also look for acceptance and support from the larger society. The growing acceptance in the last two decades of single parenthood has further contributed to the girl's decision to bear her baby to term and raise her child. Research has found that teens who chose to bring a pregnancy to term were more likely to have a friend that had been pregnant or to know an unwed teenage mother (Eisen & Zellman, 1984; Landry et al., 1986).

Adolescents who reported knowing an unmarried teenage mother were less likely to abort and more likely to deliver and remain single than those adolescents who did not know an unwed mother (Evans et al., 1976). These findings would seem to indicate that one factor in the pregnancy resolution decision is societal acceptance of illegitimacy and the possibility of social support from other women in a similar situation.

Intrapersonal Factors

Sociodemographic Variables. Sociodemographic variables have been most often studied in determining differences between adolescents who choose abortion over those who choose to carry their pregnancies to term. One association that has been found is between the adolescent's family's financial situation and the pregnancy resolution decision. Evans et al. (1976) looked at unmarried white and Mexican-American pregnant adolescents. They found that white adolescents were most likely to abort when they were less dependent on parental or family financial aid, were not receiving financial aid from the government (e.g., AFDC), or were not enrolled in Medicaid at the time of pregnancy. Fischman (1977) investigated social and psychological factors that influence black pregnant teenagers' decisions to abort or deliver their babies. Black adolescents whose families received AFDC and who reported lower scores on measures of socioeconomic status were more likely to carry their pregnancies to term than those adolescents from a higher socioeconomic status (SES).

Landry et al. (1986) studied three groups of black teenage girls aged 12 to 18. One group carried their pregnancies to term, the second group aborted, and the third group was composed of never-pregnant contraceptors. In contrast to previous findings regarding the adolescent's family's financial situation, Landry et al. found that teens who carried a pregnancy to term were less likely to be living with their parents than nonpregnant teens. Teens who aborted were likely to be living with at least one parent. These conflicting results indicate that for adolescents who are dependent upon their families for financial support, the decision to abort or keep the baby is largely dependent upon the family's financial situation, and in particular, upon whether or not that family receives state financial aid or is enrolled in Medicaid. Teens less dependent upon their families for financial aid fall into one of two subgroups. They either choose to abort or they carry their baby to term while not living with their parents. It might be hypothesized that these two groups of adolescents decide to deliver or abort for different reasons. Adolescents who abort may do so on the basis of their own educational or career goals, whereas teens who deliver their babies do so despite their family's inability or unwillingness to support the teenage mother and her baby. The groups may also differ on the basis of socioeconomic status. For example, Rosen et al. (1976) examined five groups of pregnant teens: (a) whites who kept their babies, (b) whites who aborted their babies, (c) whites who gave their babies up for adoption, (d) blacks who aborted their babies, and (e) blacks who kept their babies (The number of blacks who gave their babies up for adoption was so small that this group was dropped from the study). Rosen et al. found that pregnant adolescents who chose abortion, compared to those who carried to term, were more apt to come from skilled working class or white collar families. Another study (Landry et al., 1986) shows that adolescents who did not reside with their parents but delivered the baby lived with a relatively large number of people. This might indicate an alternative source of financial support. Further research is needed to determine if the pregnancy resolution decision of teens not living with their parents is influenced by SES.

Regardless of whether the pregnant teen is financially independent of her parents, educational attainment has been repeatedly associated with the decision to abort or to bear the baby to term. Adolescents who had completed high school or who had some post-secondary education and those who reported better school grades were found to be more likely to abort than less educated adolescents and those with low grades (Eisen & Zellman, 1984; Evans et al., 1976). Fischman (1977) found that black adolescents who were at the appropriate grade level for their age were more likely to have an abortion than black adolescents who were at grade levels below their peers. Girls who were behind grade level for their age were overrepresented in country live-birth statistics (see also Hansen et al., 1978).

Teens who aborted were more likely to aspire to college (Landry et al., 1986). The girls who aborted, compared to pregnant adolescents who carried to term, had higher educational goals (Rosen et al., 1976). Further, the girls who chose abortion were likely to come from skilled working class or white collar families (Fischman, 1977; Hansen et al., 1978). Family values stressing the importance of educational and career attainment became part of the adolescent's values as well. This is also supported by the finding that teens whose mothers had more education were more likely to abort than deliver (Zelnik et al., 1981).

Religion. Many studies that examine the association between religious beliefs and attitudes about abortion have been conducted. Harris and Mills (1985) examined data that came from the National Opinion Research Center's General Social Survey for 1974 and 1982. They found that religious *participation* better explained the impact of religion on attitudes toward abortion than did religious *preference*. Their belief was based on social learning theory, which maintains that influence of religion on attitudes and behaviors is due primarily to reinforcement of group-specific norms and values through social interaction. Harris and Mill's study was consistent with other research that found an inverse relationship between religiosity and support for abortion (Balakrishnan et al., 1972; Clayton & Tolone, 1973; Ebaugh & Haney, 1980; Finner & Gamachem, 1969; Hedderson et al., 1974; Hedderson & Hodgson, 1976; Hertel et al., 1974). Support for this relationship has been found on a variety of populations using different control variables and measures of religiosity. Three studies using National Opinion Research Center data found religiosity, as measured by frequency of church attendance, to be positively and significantly related to opposition to abortion (Ebaugh & Haney, 1980; Hedderson et al., 1974; Hedderson & Hodgson, 1976). Researchers using multi-dimensional measures of religiosity (Finner & Gamachem, 1969) and religious ideology (Clayton & Tolone, 1973) have also found relationships between religiosity and opposition to abortion. Religious affiliation has been consistently associated with abortion attitudes, with Jews and nonaffiliates of religion generally supporting abortion and Catholics and Protestants generally opposing abortion (Ebaugh & Haney, 1980). Comparisons between Catholics and non-Catholics show significant differences in abortion attitudes as well (Bouvier & Rao, 1975; Hedderson et al., 1974). The above studies reflect attitudes toward abortion, not the decision to abort. Few studies have addressed religious beliefs, participation, or affiliation in regard to the actual decision to abort.

Williams (1982) examined religious beliefs and beliefs about the beginning of life in actual abortion/bearing decisions of women with unwanted pregnancies. In contrast to findings concerning attitudes toward abortion, neither conservative religious affiliation nor high religiosity were related to actual rejection of abortion. Catholics and non-Catholics did not differ. Groups also did not differ significantly in their perceptions of religious teaching concerning abortion. However, beliefs about the beginning of life and attitudes towards abortion were highly related to the decision to abort or to bear the baby to term. Williams argued that the discrepancy between religiosity and attitudes toward abortion on the one hand and religiosity and the decision to abort on the other hand may reflect a respondent's post-decisional attempt to make her attitudes and beliefs consistent with her behavior, as cognitive dissonance theory would suggest (Festinger, 1957). In earlier research, though, Bracken et al. (1978) maintained that data did not support a cognitive dissonance theory explanation. Women who have had repeated abortions generally have a more negative attitude toward abortion than those aborting for the first time.

Williams (1982) concluded that personally held convictions regarding the beginning of human life cannot be assumed to always derive from religious doctrine. In a somewhat related study, Worthington and Danser (1987) found that late adolescents' willingness to engage in unmarried cohabitation was more related to their definition of cohabitation as a lifestyle or moral issue than to religious beliefs or intensity. Both lines of research suggest that religion contributes to some adolescents' decisions of whether to abort (or cohabit), but many adolescents who are not religious arrive at the same decision on moral, and not religiously motivated, reasoning.

One possible reason that even religious adolescents might not use their religion to arrive at pregnancy-related decisions is that teens lack knowledge of religious doctrine. This may be because of their failure to use formal operational thought or their failure to learn or be taught doctrine. More research is needed to assess the impact of religious affiliation and commitment upon abortion attitudes and also the relationship of religious doctrine to personal beliefs and decisions concerning abortion.

Levels of Cognitive Development. A controversy exists about the degree to which the level of cognitive development in adolescents affects their decision making in pregnancy resolution decisions. Piaget and Inhelder (1969) have described ways in which the mental capabilities of children change as they develop. Most preteens are supposed to be capable of thought involving concrete operations, which are mental manipulations concerning specific objects and situations. Thinking is presumed to be governed primarily by what is in the child's physical environment. When a pregnant adolescent uses concrete operations, she will have difficulty in anticipating the future and in examining the logical consequences of her decisions. Her thinking will generally be egocentric, meaning that she will usually fail to consider options from the perspectives of others while making her decisions (Elkind, 1967). About the age of 11 or 12, the early adolescent becomes capable of formal operational thought, which involves symbolic and abstract thinking. Logic can characterize decision making.

Fully mature adults often engage in both concrete and formal operational thinking throughout their adult life span (Keating, 1980). Although they are able to foresee some of the logical consequences of their actions, fully mature adults sometimes do not exercise their capabilities (Janis & Mann, 1977). This suggests that as adolescents move from early to middle to late adolescence and then into the various states of adulthood, two tasks must be learned: (a) to develop their capabilities to use formal operational thought during decision making, and (b) to apply formal operational thinking with increasing frequency to emotionally-charged decisions.

In a number of decisions within the judicial system, justices have repeatedly voiced the common assumption that adolescents are generally not as competent as adults at making mature decisions. This is thought to be especially true for early adolescents and to become less true as the adolescent nears early adulthood. Despite this common wisdom, the American Psychological Association and various psychologists have recently concluded that adolescents and adults do not differ in their decision making *competence* (Interdivisional Committee on Adolescent Abortion, 1987; Lewis, 1987; Melton, 1983, 1987; Melton & Russo, 1987). For instance, in the APA's recently submitted *Amicus curiae* brief in *Thornburgh v. American College of Obstetricians and Gynecologists*, the APA claims "that there is no empirical basis for concluding that minors fourteen and older are less capable of making informed decisions than adults" (quoted in *Interdivisional Committee on Adolescent Abortion*, 1987, p.77). This conclusion is based largely on the *absence* of detected differences in decision making in selected laboratory tests. Besides the obvious weakness of proving the null hypotheses, the argument — even if it were proved conclusively to be true — is weak. Lewis's (1987) review, upon which the conclusions rest, suggests that actual decision making differs substantially across adolescence. She attributes differences in decision making performance to different social situations of adolescents relative to adults. The social fact is, however, that unemancipated minors will always differ in their social circumstances from emancipated adults.

Thus, the main controversy at present boils down to the meaning of "competence" in adolescent decision making. Is an adolescent competent if he or she is *capable* of employing formal operational thinking? Or is an adolescent competent only if he or she is likely to *use* formal operational thinking in real-life, emotionally-charged decisions with a frequency approximately equal to adults?

The conclusion that adolescents and adults are equally capable of reasoning logically in a decision making task is based on the following evidence.

1. Wiethorn and Campbell (1982) have tested volunteers aged nine, fourteen, eighteen and twenty-one on their choice of treatment options in four hypothetical vignettes concerning health care. Participants were given detailed information about the purpose, risks, and benefits of treatments. Generally, there were no differences between participants aged 14, 18, and 21, but all of those differed from participants aged 9. Scales measured inferential understanding, reasoning, reasonable outcome, and evidence used to support one's choice.

2. Reviews of research on health care decision making have generally found similar results (Grisso & Vierling, 1978; Melton, 1981, 1984; Melton, Koocher, & Saks, 1983; Wiethorn, 1982).

3. A study by Lewis (1980) failed to find differences between minors at three California pregnancy clinics. Minors at different ages did not differ in knowledge of laws concerning abortion and adoption. They did not differ from adults in the number of people consulted, the tendency to consult parents, boyfriends or peers, and expectations about advice they were likely to receive.

To the contrary, there is substantial evidence that adolescents do differ across the adolescent years and differ from adults in ways in which they actually make decisions.

1. Younger adolescents consult different people for advice than older adolescents and adults (Ashton, 1979; Clary, 1982; Lewis, 1980; Rosen, 1980; Torres, Forrest, & Eisman, 1980). The relative influence of parents and peers changes with age and topic area (Larsen, 1972).

2. Adolescents between age 15 and adulthood consider different factors in pregnancy decisions (Hatcher, 1976) and in potential

childrearing decisions (Leibowitz, Eisen, & Chow, 1984; Lewis, 1980; Musick, Handler, & Waddill, 1984).
3. Adolescents consider future solutions and goals less than adults (Rowe, 1984; Verstraeten, 1980).
4. Adolescents delay their decision more than adults (Bracken & Kasl, 1975; Russo, 1986).
5. Adolescents differ from adults in consideration of future consequences in hypothetical dilemmas (Eisen et al. 1983; Lewis, 1981; Rowe, 1984).
6. Adolescents have been found to differ from adults in their ability to understand aspects of moral decisions from the viewpoint of others (Whitbeck & Mullis, 1987).

Two studies have investigated decision making in pregnant adolescents. Cobliner (1974) interviewed 211 single adolescent girls, free of known psychiatric disturbances, who had each undergone an elective abortion. Data relating to birth control measures used was obtained and compared to data for the control group (girls who had effectively practiced contraceptive measures for at least six months). About three-fourths of the pregnancies were unintended. Three cognitive mechanisms were uncovered that virtually blocked the conversion of birth control knowledge into successful practice: (a) erroneous belief without concrete knowledge (beliefs without knowledge), (b) concrete knowledge that was subsequently dismissed (knowledge without beliefs) and, (c) probabilistic appraisal or risk taking. Probabilistic thinking is characterized by the absence of planning. Girls using this cognitive mechanism were sexually active and were aware of the risks involved, but did not bother or plan to protect themselves from unwanted pregnancy. When they became pregnant, however, they were galvanized into action.

Cobliner looked at adolescents' decision making for resolution of their pregnancies in terms of Piaget's model of cognitive development. Cobliner maintained that the inability to contracept effectively was indicative of a lack of formal operational thinking. The teen was unable to imagine the negative consequences and therefore did not use contraception. The decision to abort was viewed as an example of figurative thinking — thinking that is essentially set into motion by sensory input. It mobilizes resources in order to overcome present pressing situations and obstacles. Figurative thinking apprehends states and situations. Pregnancy allows for sensory feedback, with abortion being the immediate reaction to the situation.

Eisen et al. (1983) maintained that previous studies of adolescent pregnancy resolution lacked explicit models of decision sequence and a relatively large group of psychosocial variables for exploratory analysis. Eisen et al. studied the decision to abort or bear the baby to term in white and Mexican-American unmarried teens. They found that the pregnancy resolution decision constituted a two-stage model for many adolescents. During the first stage, the girl made a decision to bring her baby to term or to abort. If the pregnancy was allowed to continue, during the second stage the girl decided to keep her baby and marry or keep her baby and remain single. Adoption was not included in this study due to the small sample size. Other women looked at these three decisions simultaneously, weighing the costs and benefits of each.

In Eisen et al.'s (1983) study, the explicit model of decision making used was based on the assumption that pregnancy resolution decisions incorporate some form of expected utility analysis by adolescents. In making a decision, the adolescent (a) identifies options, (b) weighs the perceived benefits and costs in economic, social and psychological terms, and (c) chooses the option that appears to be preferable. This decision making process may not be logical or rational in a Piagetian formal operational sense (see Cobliner, 1974); however, it is perceived by the teen to further some important goal. In this sense, the decision making is "rational" or reasonable (i.e., has reasons) to the adolescent, although it is egocentric (in Piaget & Inhelder's theoretical terms). Egocentrism is thought to be characteristic of early formal operational thinking (Hudson & Gray, 1986). Eisen et al.'s findings supported Cobliner's theory by concluding that many teens do not have the ability to reason abstractly or to foresee consequences in the future.

Emotionality. The propensity for most people to make reasonable decisions likely depends on their ability to handle emotion during emotion-laden decisions. Lazarus and Folkman (1984) describe two styles of dealing with stress: emotion-focused coping and problem-focused coping. Emotion-focused coping is aimed at managing one's reactions to the stressful situation and is found most often in situations that afford little perceived control to the decision maker. Problem-focused coping is more likely when the person perceives that he or she has a measure of control. Little effort has been made to employ Lazarus' cognitive theory of stress (or any other theory of stress, such as McCubbin and Patterson's, 1983, family stress theory) to adolescent decision making about how pregnancy is to be resolved. Presumably, various buffers such as social support and perceived control should be expected to influence perceptions of stress and thus affect the decision making styles of adolescents (Cohen & Wills, 1985). As yet, research has not investigated adolescent decision making within such theoretical frameworks.

Some research has investigated the emotional reactions to various decisions of pregnant adolescents. Janis and Mann's (1977) model was used in one theoretical study of pregnancy resolution decision making. Bracken et al. (1978) studied unmarried pregnant women who chose either to abort or to bear their babies to term. They were compared on four variables: (a) happiness about being pregnant, (b) initial acceptance or rejection of their eventual decision, (c) ease or difficulty of the decision making process, and (d) gladness or sadness about their ultimate choice. Results indicated that women who delivered, in comparison to those who aborted, were relatively happier, had a closer relationship with their sex partners and received greater support for their decision to deliver from their partners, mothers, and friends. Women who aborted were less happy about their pregnancies. The closeness of their relationship with their sex partners, the length of their involvement, and the support for their decision were not associated with levels of sadness in these women. Women with low ego resilience were happier about their pregnancies than women with high ego resilience, but some went on to abort due to an inability to resist their mothers' pressure to abort.

The decision to deliver was significantly more likely to be initially accepted than the decision to abort. The decision to deliver was also more likely to be supported by significant others. Women who initially rejected abortion and those who did not have adequate coping skills to deal with conflict or to make their own decisions appeared unable to prevail when persuaded by others to abort.

The decision to deliver was reported to be easier to make than the decision to abort. For women delivering, this decision was easier to make if they had support from significant others and if other women's decisions to abort were perceived to receive little support from significant others. Women choosing delivery who had been persuaded by a significant other to abort found the delivery decision to be more difficult.

Likewise, the abortion decision was easier to make when supported by significant others and when the decision was discussed with the partner. The decision to abort was also easier if the women knew other single women raising children. The decision to abort, as with delivery, was easier for women of higher ego resilience and internal loci of control.

Women who chose delivery were happier about their choice than those who had abortions. Support from significant others for the decision to deliver increased satisfaction. Among those choosing abortion, women who had not completed high school, who reported no income or were on welfare and who were not living at home were sadder then other women about their decision. Women who were high on ego resilience and who had internal loci of control were more satisfied with their decisions to abort.

Evaluation of the Consequences or Sequelae of the Decision to Abort or Bear to Term. There are two aspects of the evaluation of the consequences or sequelae of the two primary ways that pregnancy can be resolved. First, there is the scientific evaluation of the options. This involves evaluating the weight of studies that assess consequences of each decision or that compare the two options. Numerous review papers have attempted to make such evaluations (for a few examples, see Adler, 1976; Huckeba & Mueller, 1987; Illsley & Hall, 1976; Rogers, Phifer, & Nelson, 1987; Rue, 1985; Shusterman, 1976, for reviews). Second, there is the manner in which the adolescent evaluates the evidence that she believes applies to each alternative.

Many studies have scientifically investigated the consequences of an adolescent's decision, often the negative consequences of both abortion and adolescent parenthood. At the most general level, research shows there to be no psychologically painless way to deal with an unwanted pregnancy (David, 1972).

A number of studies have examined the consequences of abortion. Although the predominant response following abortion is experienced as relief (Adler, 1975), women often experience feelings of guilt, depression, regret and anxiety after an abortion (Adler, 1981; Brody, Meikle, & Gerristse, 1971; Osofsky & Osofsky, 1972; Smith, 1973). These generally diminish over time; however, longitudinal studies to determine the effects of abortion later in life on the women and their relationships with others have not been conducted. Kent (1977) noted that only in-depth post-abortion interviews with a trusted person truly reveals the personal agony and relational trauma that abortion induces. It cannot be denied that abortion is a stressful experience. Adler (1975), who studied the emotional responses of women following an abortion, found two sources of stress associated with abortion. One source is derived from external social conflict associated with disapproval and stigmatization of abortion. The second source of stress is derived from internal conflict regarding loss of both the pregnancy and the potential child. Adler (1979) maintains that responses to the abortion will be a function of the meaning of the pregnancy to the individual, her defensive and coping style and her social environment. Payne et al. (1976) studied the psychological outcome of abortion in 102 patients requesting abortion in a hospital setting. Self-administered questionnaires, the Minnesota Multiphasic Personality Inventory, Profile of Mood States, and Symptom Rating Scale were given along with post-abortion interviews that were conducted during the first 24 hours in the hospital, 6 weeks and again 6 months following the abortion. Payne et al. concluded that a complex multivariate model based on conflict and conflict resolution was appropriate to conceptualize the unwanted pregnancy and abortion experience. Results from Payne et al.'s study support Adler's (1979) findings by identifying seven factors that predicted difficulties for working through conflicts associated with abortion. The factors were: (a) prior history of mental illness, (b) immature interpersonal relationships, (c) unstable, conflicted relationships with one's parents, (d) history of a negative relationship with one's mother, (e) ambivalence regarding abortion, (f) a religious or cultural background hostile to abortion, and (g) single status, especially if the woman has not borne other children. A variety of intrapsychic, interpersonal and socio-environmental factors interact to determine a woman's response. The response itself is multidimensional and may manifest itself in different spheres of the woman's life.

Proponents of abortion argue that the choice of abortion brings greater personal freedom to the woman. Freeman (1977) researched women requesting a legal abortion during their first trimester. These women responded to questionnaires one hour after the abortion and again four months later. Freeman hypothesized that women who chose abortion would see themselves as an "agent" (i.e. one who denies passive acceptance of unwanted pregnancy) rather than a "patient". The findings did not support this hypothesis. Rather, it was found that the need for abortion resulted from *not* perceiving oneself as an agent. The majority of women chose abortion from necessity. For women who fell into a cluster of a negative self-image or an avoidance of feelings, less than half changed their contraceptive patterns in favor of greater or more consistent use. These women were unable to contend with their emotions about abortion and denied their sexual behavior. Many of these women found it difficult to accept themselves as persons who had made a significant decision that affected themselves and others. Freedom of choice for such women was out of context and experienced in a negative, rather than positive, way.

Abortion affects not only the pregnant adolescent, but also her relationships with family and others. Cotroneo and Krasher (1977) have noted that it is impossible to lift a pregnant woman out of her primary loyalty system for the purpose of decision making without manifesting a complementary therapeutic concern for the relationship fallout of her decision on her mate, parents, children (born and unborn), siblings, grandparents and other significant relationships. If this is the case for mature women, it is all the more true for the pregnant adolescent who is most often dependent upon her family for emotional, as well as financial, support. It has been found that, in relationships, abortion provides "pseudo-homostasis", that is, a stability through non-adjustment rather than through readjustment, which promotes even more serious relational disequilibrium; induced abortion promotes mystification and masking within the family, which is dysfunctional for the individual in every context (Lennard & Bernstein, 1970).

Other research has studied the consequences of adolescent childbearing. There has also been much research conducted that investigates the consequences of the pregnant adolescent bearing her baby to term. Most of these consequences relate to the girl's decision to keep and raise her child herself. It has been found through various studies that the adolescent girl runs a higher risk of pregnancy complications than do women who deliver in their 20's (Hutchins, 1978; Ventura & Hendershot, 1984). Some of these complications are prenatal bleeding, premature delivery, low birth weight, preeclampsia, perinatal death and toxemia. It has been noted, however, that this risk becomes greater if the teenager does not get adequate prenatal care (Spellacy et al., 1978). Such adverse effects of early childbearing on the health of the mother tend to disappear when free or low cost, high quality medical care is made available to these girls. The earlier observed negative health consequences seem to have been a confounding variable associated with the poverty situation of many of these adolescents. This poverty results in an inability to obtain adequate obstetrical care and does not directly result from the age of the girl (Baldwin & Cain, 1980).

Despite the high volume of research that has compared the consequences of abortion with those of bearing to term and research that has investigated the consequences of each alternative individually, it is not the research evidence per se that will persuade an adolescent to abort or bear to term. Rather, it is her personal evaluation of the evidence (in addition to the multitude of other factors considered in this paper). Further, her evaluation of the evidence is often influenced by (a) the beliefs of those who provide her with evidence, (b) which evidence she is aware of, (c) how much evidence she is aware of, (d) the credibility she affords to the evidence, (f) her cognitive ability and willingness to evaluate the evidence, and (g) her emotional state. Given that she decides to accrue and investigate evidence about the consequences of abortion and bearing to term, she must use some criteria for evaluation. Janis and Mann (1977) suggest that people evaluate evidence in terms of four categories: (a) utilitarian costs versus benefits for the self, (b) utilitarian costs versus benefits for others, (c) self-approval versus self-disapproval, and (d) approval or disapproval of others. Almost no research has investigated *how* adolescents who are pregnant evaluate the evidence bearing on their perceived alternatives.

Adolescents judge alternatives in light of the impact each has on the adolescent. Apparently, financial considerations are part of their evaluation of costs and benefits to the self (Evans et al., 1976). Further, occupational aspirations are also apparently considered (Eisen & Zellman, 1984; Evans et al., 1976; Fischman, 1977; Hanson, 1978, Landry, et al., 1986; Rosen et al., 1976).

On the other hand, there is little evidence that adolescents consider the costs and benefits to others as part of their evaluation of the alternatives. Generally, adolescents have been found to seek support from their parents and others (Eisen et al., 1983; Rosen, 1980), but there is no evidence that the adolescents considered the impact of their decisions on their parents or others.

Evaluations of the adolescent's consideration of the impact of a decision on her self-image, self-concept, or self-esteem are infrequent. Klerman et al. (1978) found that never-married women who were persuaded against their initial wishes often were vulnerable to decreases in self-esteem. There is evidence that the morality of the adolescent plays a part in her decision making (see Williams, 1982). Presumably, the adolescent acting either in concordance with or in opposition to her morality would have an impact on her self-esteem; however, no empirical investigations have substantiated this common sense hypothesis.

Contrary to the other aspects of the adolescent's evaluation, she is highly likely to consider the possibility of approval or disapproval of others as part of her decision making. There are several important findings from this vast amount of research. First, adolescents who are supported in their decisions by their parents — whether to abort or bear to term — are likely to cope better with the consequences of the decision than are adolescents who are not supported (see Melton, 1987). Second, most pregnant teens are initially afraid to consult their parents, but when they do, their parents are often more supportive than the adolescents had anticipated (Adler, 1981; Barglow, 1967; Bernstein, 1971; Bolton, 1980; Bowerman, Irish, & Pope, 1966; Furstenberg, 1976b; Swigar et al., 1976). Third, girls can have negative reactions to their decisions whenever they are coerced into a decision with which they strongly disagree (Friedman et al., 1974; Klerman et al., 1978; Simon et al., 1967; Swigar et al., 1976). Fourth, some girls use the decision about resolution of their pregnancy as a power tactic with their parents (Friedman, 1971; Group for the Advancement of Psychiatry, 1985; Klein, 1978; Paulker, 1969).

Overall, the weight of the evidence is that most adolescents' primary consideration in how they decide to resolve the pregnancy are the consideration of the social approval or disapproval of others, especially their parents, and the effects of the consideration of each decision on herself. Generally, research has not investigated the role of self-esteem and of the adolescent's consideration of the effects of her decision on others.

Beliefs and Attitudes About the Morality of Abortion. Bracken et al. (1978) studied never-married adolescents who either chose abortion or kept their babies. One of the strongest factors that differentiated those who abort from those who bear their babies to term was a difference in beliefs and attitudes regarding the moral aspect of abortion. In other studies it was discovered that teenagers who held a more favorable opinion about abortion were also more likely to choose abortion (Evans et al., 1976; Fischman, 1977). Williams (1982) examined the relationship of religion and beliefs about the beginning of life to the decision for or against abortion among 58 women with unwanted pregnancies. He found that those opting for abortion tended to believe that human life begins subsequent to conception or that the beginning of life cannot be determined. These women were highly favorable to abortion. Women expressing the belief that life begins at conception were more likely to reject abortion. In a study of women initially seeking abortion who later changed their minds and delivered their babies, the most important factor in their change of decision was the belief that abortion is morally wrong (Swigar et al., 1976).

Intrapersonal Factors

Social Support in the Family of Origin. Another factor affecting pregnancy resolution decision making has been the pressure and opinions from the adolescent girl's family of origin. Social influence or pressure from others has been shown to be related to the outcome of this decision. Social support by family members during the crisis is even more important for the pregnant adolescent than for pregnant adult women, since adolescents are generally financially, physically and emotionally dependent on their parents (Adams, 1964; Lee, 1980; Litwak & Szeleniyi, 1969). Rosen (1980) examined the extent to which black and white pregnant adolescents involved their parents in the decision regarding the resolution of their pregnancies. She found the pregnant adolescent's mother to be the most significant influence on the girl's decision in all cases except for those white teens who kept their babies. One half of the pregnant teens between 12 and 17 in Rosen's study consulted their own mother about their decision.

Black mothers also had a relatively great influence on their daughters who chose abortion. In Fischman's (1977) study of black and white pregnant teenagers, it was found that black teens who reported more emotionally supportive relationships with their mothers were more likely to deliver their babies. Those adolescents who reported making their decisions alone rather than with family or friends were more likely to choose abortion.

Mosely et al. (1981) investigated demographic and psychological factors relating to positive or negative reactions to legal abortions performed during the first trimester in 62 females in an urban southern community. They found that social (i.e., familial and relational) context for those seeking an abortion proved more important to predicting reaction to abortion than any demographic variable. In Bracken et al.'s (1978) study of decision making and satisfaction with the decision of pregnant women choosing to either abort or deliver, the girl's reaction to abortion, one hour before the procedure, was found to be significantly more favorable when her partner's perceived support and her anticipated parental support was greatest. A further analysis indicated that the partner's support was more important in predicting favorable abortion reaction among older women, whereas parental support was a more powerful predictor among younger women. Eisen et al. (1983) found that if the adolescent's boyfriend and mother both thought she should have an abortion, she was more likely to abort than bear to term. The girl's best girlfriend's opinion related only to the girl's attitude toward abortion for others.

Women tend to discuss their pregnancy resolution decision with people whom they perceive to support it; this is particularly true for women who decide to continue their pregnancy (Bracken et al., 1978). Not only are pregnant teenagers influenced by others, but they also choose to discuss their pregnancy with others who will support their decisions.

Rosen (1980), in her study of pregnancy resolution in black and white adolescents, noted that some teens who rejected their parents as a resource seemed to be doing so less out of fear and weakness than out of desire for independence and autonomy. In Rosen's study, independence of decision making was positively associated with the perception of competence. For all five groups (white aborters, white keepers, white relinquishers, black aborters, and black keepers), the mother's influence was positively and significantly associated with conflict. From this data, the important conclusion is drawn that when pressure is exerted upon the pregnant teen to resolve her pregnancy as others see fit, conflict results. Simon et al. (1967) found that women who felt coerced into terminating their pregnancies, either because of pressure from parents or partners or because of a medical problem, were at a greater risk on developing post-abortion problems. This is supported by Klerman et al. (1978) in their study of pregnancy resolution among never-married women. Women most vulnerable to loss of self-esteem were those who were persuaded to deliver or abort against their initial wishes. In teenagers, coercion from significant others in regard to the pregnancy resolution can backfire and be expressed in resistance or rebellion on the part of the teen. In Swigar et al.'s (1976) study of abortion seekers who changed their minds and delivered their babies, the one reason given for this change in decision was resistance on the part of the adolescent to her family's wish that she abort. This reason was more commonly given by adolescents than adults.

One common finding in the literature on adolescent sexuality is that a substantial number of adolescents use sexual acting out (often resulting in pregnancy) as a power tactic against their parents (Friedman, 1971; Group for Advancement of Psychiatry, 1985; Klein, 1978; Paulker, 1969). When adolescents do accede to their parents' wishes for an abortion, some may have a subsequent pregnancy that they carry to term (Hatcher, 1976).

Although social support is a necessary component of the teen's satisfaction with her pregnancy resolution decision, a coercive approach that leaves her out of the decision making process can be detrimental to her, especially post-abortion.

Social Support of the Putative Father. Whereas the adolescent's parents control her physical well-being and largely influence her psychological well-being, the putative father (when the pregnancy is not due to incest or rape) can most strongly affect the adolescent's emotional well-being. The effects of parents and the putative father are, consequently, different. Generally, the putative father only has influence to the extent that the adolescent is willing to empower him. Several studies illustrate this.

Rosen (1980) investigated 432 pregnant adolescents younger than 18 to determine who affected their decisions about the resolution of their pregnancies. She found the mothers generally were influential. In cases in which the adolescent was white and decided to keep her baby, the father of the baby gained influence. Bracken et al. (1978) studied decision making and subsequent satisfaction with the decision in pregnant women who chose to abort or deliver. For aborters, the adolescent's satisfaction at one hour post-abortion was enhanced if both the partner and the mother were perceived as supporting the abortion. In a further analysis, it was found that the partner was relatively more influential for women who were older and that parents were more important for younger adolescents. Eisen et al. (1983) also found that concurrence in support between the girl's mother and partner was more predictive that the girl would abort than bear to term.

In sum, the role of the putative father appears to be one of support for the adolescent. There is no suggestion in the empirical literature that a partner who disagrees with the adolescent has any substantial impact on her decision. Obviously, this needs investigation.

Professional Counseling. Still another source of social support available to adolescents is that of professional counselors and social agencies. Research indicates, however, that in general, pregnant adolescents rarely avail themselves of this support. Bracken et al. (1978) found that information about pregnancy options for pregnant adolescents came from friends and not from professionals. Lewis (1980) found minors to be less likely than adults to anticipate consultation with a professional regarding their pregnancy. Minors did not differ from adults, however, in their knowledge of the legality and confidentiality of abortion, nor did they make pregnancy decisions on the basis of legal misinformation. In a subsequent study, Lewis (1981) evaluated changes in adolescents' approaches to decision making in grades seven to twelve. She found that grade level groups differed with regard to the advice to another for outside consultation with a specialist.

Whereas 62 per cent of twelfth-grade responses suggested outside consultation, 46 per cent of tenth graders and 21 per cent of the seventh-eighth graders suggested obtaining an outside opinion.

The Decision to Relinquish or Rear the Child

Methodological Considerations

The decision of white adolescents to relinquish their children for adoption has become statistically infrequent in recent years for a number of reasons (National Committee for Adoption, 1985). Black adolescents almost never relinquish their children for formal adoption. Much more common in families of Blacks is to relinquish the child to a relative or friend for rearing while retaining legal custody of the child. This informal adoption is particularly difficult to study because it is *sub rosa* (Sandven & Egeland, 1985).

The main result of the small number of adolescents who make decisions to relinquish their children is that samples to date have been largely geographically restricted and small. In a typical study, a local agency supplies a list of girls who are contacted after the birth (at varying times). Over the course of the study, usually 20-50 girls are either surveyed or interviewed about their remembrances of the births. Or girls are surveyed about their demographic characteristics and groups are compared to distinguish relinquishers and parenters.

This mythological typical study illuminates a number of criticisms of the methodology of extant research.

1. Samples are small. Only one study (McLaughlin et al., 1987) has used over 100 girls as participants. They used 269 girls.

2. Samples are geographically restricted. Most samples are local, or data have been drawn from only two agencies. The exception to this generalization is that national surveys have been used to examine gross demographic variables (Bachrach, 1986), or uncontrolled (and biased) samples have been used (e.g., Deykin et al., 1984; Panner et al., 1978; Rynearson, 1982; Winkler & Van Keppel, 1984).

3. Groups for comparison have not been carefully delineated. Small sample sizes have prevented sufficient experimental or statistical control to learn more than general truths about the decision making process. For example, extant research has shown a variety of controls to be needed: (a) age, (b) race or ethnic background, (c) SES, (d) girl's living arrangement pre-conception and post-birth (e.g., with both parents, with one parent only, with

one parent and a step-parent, cohabiting with a minor or adult male, emancipated, at a boarding school, in a foster home), (e) relationship to the putative father post conception, and (f) educational aspirations of the girl. At a minimum, in future research, it is necessary to account for age, post-delivery marital status, post-delivery living status, and race via design considerations. For example, in the largest and best controlled study to date, McLaughlin et al. (1987) compared relinquishers and parenters selected from a local adoption-promotion program. Both parenters and relinquishers included girls who remained at home after the birth and girls who established their own households (or lived in foster care). Clearly, the decision making and the impact of decisions differ greatly depending on whether girls live with their parents after delivery.

4. There have been few examinations of *how* decisions about relinquishment or parenting have been made. Studies of decision making have been limited by being:
   a. Retrospective rather than longitudinal;
   b. Limited to the adolescent's perspective, even though others (e.g., putative father or family members) will be affected by the decision and will likely influence the decision;
   c. Unrelated to *theories* of decision making (most examinations being atheoretical or testing empirically-derived differences among groups);
   d. Unrelated to theories of family interaction.

5. Instrumentation has generally been developed solely for the purpose of each individual study. Instruments with psychometric data available to support them have rarely been used. Even instruments that measure demographic characteristics are not used repeatedly across studies; thus, there is little potential for accurate comparison from study to study.

A Conceptual Framework for Understanding Relinquishment/ Parenting Decision Making

Objectively, the net advantages of relinquishing the child generally appear to outweigh those of rearing the child. Nonetheless, the rate of adoption has decreased within the most recent 15 years. Further, the increase in sheer numbers of pregnant teenagers (Alan Guttmacher, 1973; Mech, 1973; National Research Council, 1987) has created a problem of giant proportions.

Pregnant adolescents are placed under intense psychological stress (in addition to the physical stress of pregnancy, childbirth, and postpartum recuperation) because of the consequences of the decisions they must make. Families are stressed and strained because of the impact the decisions could have on each family member. The girl faces enormous change in her peer relationships as a consequence of her decision. Social agencies and counselors become involved in the decision making. Waves from the adolescent's decision rock numerous boats.

With the social and psychological costs of both parenting and relinquishing the child, it becomes imperative to understand factors affecting girls' decisions, how they make decisions, the ways their families become involved in the decisions, and the family stress that is experienced during periods of decision making.

A framework for understanding parenting-relinquishing decision making involves three types of factors: societal, intrapersonal, and interpersonal (see Figure 2).

At least seven *societal trends* are thought to have caused the dramatic reduction in adoptions within the United States over the last two decades (National Committee for Adoption, 1985).

1. The legalization of abortion.
2. The impact of the "sexual revolution" and the "pill generation".
3. Title IX, which requires school districts to offer schooling to pregnant girls.
4. The rights of putative fathers increasing due to recent Supreme Court decisions (*Caban v. Mohammed*, 1979; *Stanley v. Illinois*, 1972).
5. The stigma of out-of-wedlock childbearing and welfare being reduced (see Chilman, 1980).
6. The increase in numbers of households headed by females.
7. The closing of many comprehensive maternity homes.

Intrapersonal determinants of decisions between relinquishment and parenting involve two broad classes of variables: girls' assessments of their abilities and desires to assume the roles of mothers, and girls' attitudes toward the babies. Girls' abilities and desires to assume the roles of mothers involve their maturity, financial status, attitudes toward motherhood, future plans, knowledge of the sacrifices associated with motherhood, their preexisting mothering skills, their psychological involvement in pregnancy and with the fetus, and the month of discovery of the pregnancy. Girls' attitudes toward the baby include their expectations about the baby, the reward value of the babies for the adolescents, the costs to the adolescents of rearing a child, considerations for the welfare of the baby, moral beliefs about family, abortion, and adoption, and consideration of the needs of non-family members.

RELINQUISH VS PARENT

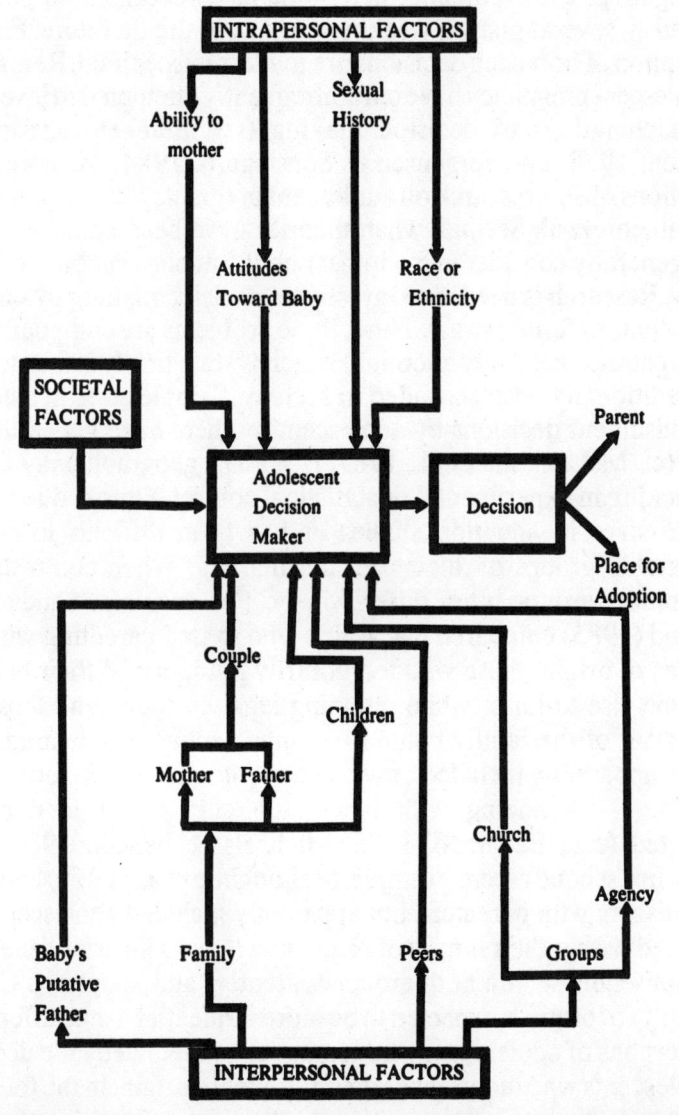

Interpersonal determinants of decisions between relinquishment and parenting involve relationships (and perceptions of relationships)

between the adolescent and (a) the putative father, (b) the parents —especially the mother (Clapp & Raab, 1978; Grow, 1979; Rosen, 1980; Young et al., 1975), (c) other friends and siblings, and (d) agencies and other groups with which the adolescent has contact.

Although some progress has been made in identifying many and investigating a few potential determinants of decisions to parent or relinquish, several glaring weaknesses exist in the literature. First, the description of how such decisions are made is unspecified. Researchers of adolescent pregnancy have only infrequently attempted to investigate the machinations of decision making (see Bracken, Klerman, & Bracken, 1978, and Jorgensen & Sonstegard, 1984, for noteworthy exceptions). Most research on adolescent pregnancy, consequently, has been atheoretical. Second, when theories have been considered, they have generally considered the impact on the adolescent but not on her family. Research is needed to investigate decision making by pregnant adolescents as family stress. Third, these problems are compounded for investigations that study adoption, which is statistically infrequent and has traditionally been shrouded in secrecy. Sample sizes in studies of relinquishment decisions by adolescent mothers have generally been small (cf. McLaughlin et al., 1987, $N = 269$), geographically limited, and lacking in experimental or statistical control. Fourth, due to small sample sizes in adoption studies, it has been difficult to contrast comparable groups on their decision making. When contrasts have been made, groups often differ widely. For example, Sandven and Egeland (1985) compared black girls who shared parenting with their families of origin, those who temporarily relinquished their babies to someone else to raise (while retaining legal custody), and those who moved out of the family home to assume exclusive parenting. Their sample apparently included only one girl who decided on formal legal adoption — a finding with black adolescents that is frequently replicated (e.g., Bachrach, 1986; Michaels & Fanelli, 1986; Wolf, 1983). In a second recent example, McLaughlin et al. (1978) compared relinquishers with parenters, but apparently included adolescents who remained within their family of origin and those who established their own household within both groups (parenters and adopters). Clearly, the family of origin is expected to be more influential in and affected by the decisions of adolescents who remain at home than by the decisions of adolescents who move out of their families of origin. In the following sections of this review, research on intrapersonal and interpersonal determinants of the relinquishmment decision is examined.

Intrapersonal Factors in Parenting/Relinquishing Decision Making

There are four potential areas in which the decision making of the adolescent might be affected by her intrapersonal characteristics. Research support for each of the areas has been variable. Some areas have yet to be addressed in empirical studies. One area is the girl's perceived ability to mother. Presumably, girls evaluate their fitness to mother when deciding whether to relinquish or parent their child and that evaluation is part of their decision about who will parent their child. The second area involves their attitudes toward the baby, including their expectations about what the baby will be like, their evaluation of the rewards and costs that the baby will provide them, their considerations of the welfare of the baby, their moral beliefs concerning abortion, adoption and family, and their consideration of other extra-family members who might want to adopt. The third area involves the sexual history of the girl — including her experience with previous pregnancies and her evaluation of herself as a potential sexual partner both with and without a baby that she is rearing. Fourth, the girl's race exerts a substantial effect on her decision making because the cultural expectations are widely diverse across races and ethnic backgrounds.

Perceived ability to mother. Most of the research that has been conducted to differentiate relinquishers and parenters has focused on the differences in maturity between the girls who make different decisions. Almost universally the findings have shown that girls who choose to relinquish their babies for adoption are more emotionally stable than those who choose to parent their babies (Cattel, 1954; Clothier, 1943; Grow, 1979; Herz, 1977; Horn & Turner, 1976; Jacokes, 1965; Levy, 1955; Leynes, 1980; Meyers, Jones & Borgatta, 1956; Scherz, 1947; Vincent, 1960, 1961). Resnick (1984a) has summarized the research in a recent review, so the studies will not be recounted here. All of the twelve studies except Grow's (1979) and Leynes's (1980) are older than ten years.

This has led Michaels and Fanelli (1986) to hypothesize that the results in a more recently selected sample might differ from those in earlier studies because of the changing societal mores, which make it more acceptable to be a single parent today than it was even ten years ago. Michaels and Fanelli (1986) surveyed clients, perused their records, and analyzed counselor notes for 99 adolescents who sought counseling and supportive services from an expectant parents' service in a medium sized metropolitan area in New York state. Of the 99, 42 ultimately decided to have their babies adopted, which is far above the national average. The girls were mostly white and lower-middle SES. They were comparatively well-educated (mean of 11.3 years). Most were primaparous. Michaels and Fanelli found, as they had hypothesized, that the emotional stability of parenters and relinquishers were statistically equal. They attributed this to the recent liberalization of societal mores. Given the consistency of previous research, though, it is more likely that their findings were due to the nature of their sample. Their clients differed from national averages in a number of striking ways. They were fairly old (mean 17.8 years), well-educated, and either pre-disposed toward adoption or counseled strongly toward that alternative (given the large number of girls who placed their children for adoption). At present, the best assumption still appears to be that relinquishers will generally be more emotionally mature and stable than parenters — probably for a variety of reasons.

Another consistent finding across a variety of research studies is that relinquishers generally have completed more education than parenters (Alan Guttmacher, 1981; Bachrach, 1986; Festinger, 1971; Grow, 1979; Sandven & Egeland, 1985). Again, Michaels and Fanelli (1986) found no differences between relinquishers and parenters, but their entire sample was highly educated and mature relative to those samples in earlier research. Generally, the tendency for relinquishers to be more educated is consistent with speculations by Resnick (1984a) and Musick, Handler, and Waddill (1984) that the girl who relinquishes her baby might be at a higher level of cognitive development. According to Piaget and Inhelder (1969), this might suggest that girls who opt to relinquish their children might use formal operational thinking more than girls who opt to parent their babies. Perhaps, when a girl is confronted by the very "concrete" stimulus of seeing her pregnancy become increasingly visible, it is hard for the girl who reasons more frequently in concrete operational thought to ignore the physical reality in order to imagine herself not being attached to the child. For the more cognitively mature girl, who engages in less concrete operational thought and more formal operational thought, it is easier to imagine relinquishing the child.

Besides cognitive and emotional maturity, girls who relinquish their children for adoption have been found to have better self-esteem (Blum & Resnick, 1982) and more internal loci of control (Blum & Resnick, 1982; cf. Sandven & Egeland, 1985) than girls who elect to parent their children. Finally, Leynes (1980) found that girls who elected to relinquish their babies for adoption generally were more mature in their ability to communicate with their parents than girls who parented their children. That is unfortunate, considering that girls who elect to parent are often highly involved with the parents in rearing the new child.

Overall, despite a few discordant findings, the picture that emerges is that girls who relinquish their children are usually more mature emotionally, cognitively, psychologically, and interpersonally than girls who elect to parent their children. As is true throughout this review, however, there are undoubtedly subgroup differences within both the relinquishers and parenters. For example, parenters who are older and who move from their families of origin and establish their own households to rear their new babies — whether they marry or not — might be expected to be equally (or more) mature as many relinquishers. Furthermore, many parenters continue with their educations and have high educational and occupational aspirations. Despite the disadvantage relative to their peers of having an infant, these girls will often succeed with their aspirations (see Anthony & Cohler, 1987). Such girls differ markedly from girls who are generally unsuccessful at academic pursuits and who use parenting as an excuse for discontinuing their educations. Future research should give more attention to investigating the differences in the subgroups within relinquishers and parenters.

The decision making in adolescent pregnancy is dependent on economics. Several analyses of the economics of childbearing have been done (Card & Wise, 1978; Espenshade, 1980; Kasun, 1984; Kramer, 1975; Leibowitz, Eisen, & Chow, 1984; Mondy, 1985; Moore & Caldwell, 1977; Moore & Hofferth, 1981; Mueller, 1972; Ross & Sawhill, 1975). Relinquishment of the baby for adoption has generally been found to be associated with higher SES families and parenting associated with expectations of drawing welfare, AFDC, or medical insurance covering child care (see Musick et al., 1984; Resnick, 1984a, 1984b). Further, relinquishment has led to more employability of adolescent mothers than parenting, even when prior employability and SES were controlled (McLaughlin et al., 1987).

Ambitious plans for the future by pregnant girls have consistently been related to choosing to relinquish their child for adoption rather than to parent the child. For example, Michaels and Fanelli (1986) found that relinquishers expressed more intent to return to or continue high school (see also Eisen & Zellman, 1984) and to go to college than parenters. Relinquishers also more frequently expressed the intent to graduate from college (Bachrach, 1986) or obtain a professional or advanced degree (Sandven & Egeland, 1985) than parenters. More relinquishers than parenters were enrolled in school at the time of the studies (Festinger, 1971; Grow, 1979; McLaughlin et al., 1987; Musick et al., 1984; cf. Michaels & Fanelli, 1986, who did not find differences between relinquishers and parenters on current school attendance). Three important interrelated areas have received scant attention from both researchers and theoreticians. The girls' attitudes about motherhood should be expected to differentiate between parenters and relinquishers. For example, some girls hold the belief that motherhood makes a woman complete or that children will cure loneliness or fill unmet needs for a love object. Others believe that adoption is morally wrong (Musick et al., 1984) and that once a teen has become pregnant it would be irresponsible for the teen to shirk her duty as a mother. On the other side of the coin, many girls believe that motherhood is a thankless duty and should be postponed or avoided as long as possible or only undertaken under ideal conditions.

A second interrelated area involves the girl's knowledge that motherhood involves enormous sacrifices on behalf of the child. To the extent that the adolescent is aware that she is likely going to have to forego sleep, freedom to date whom and when she wishes, graduation with her high school class (Blum & Resnick, 1982), or free interaction with her usual peer group, she should be expected to choose relinquishment over parenting.

Third, the girl's assessment of her mothering skills might be expected to play a role in her decision whether to parent or relinquish her child. Many girls have extensive experience caring for infants and preschool age children through babysitting or caring for younger siblings. Some girls have little ability to deal with crying babies (Kirkland, 1983; Kirkland et al., 1983; Thomas & Chess, 1981) or they become frustrated in the face of daily calamities. They have little knowledge of childrearing techniques, child care, or nutrition (see Roosa, 1986 for a review). Many who elect to parent their children depend on and expect aid from their own parents in rearing the children and learning mothering skills.

Attitudes toward the baby. What the girl believes about the baby is undoubtedly important to her decision about whether she will assume the role of parent after the birth of the child. However, like her beliefs about herself as a mother, her attitudes toward the child have been rarely explored by researchers studying the parenting/relinquishing decision. Such attitudes include expectations about the baby's health, intelligence and attractiveness, the reward value of the baby for the adolescent, the expected costs to the adolescent in both the event of parenting and placing for adoption, the considerations of the overall welfare of the baby, the considerations of people who want to adopt but are not related to the adolescent, and the moral beliefs of the adolescent about abortion, adoption, and the family.

Of these attitudes, the only one to receive empirical attention in the literature to date involves the moral beliefs of the adolescent. Grow (1979) found that parenters generally believed abortion to be morally justifiable more than relinquishers. Festinger (1971) found that parenters held more traditional views about the family than relinquishers. Grow's research took place before the full impact of the *Roe v. Wade* decision was felt, so many of the girls who did not wish to raise a child but were unable to obtain an abortion resolved their pregnancy through having the child but then placing it for adoption.

More recent research is not expected to show the same results as Grow's (1979) research. Traditional family values might be related to the decision to parent. One thing that might stimulate adolescents to express more traditional family values is the bonding they feel to the preborn baby. Bibring and Wallerstein (1976) and Cranely (1981) have both hypothesized a pre-birth attachment of the young mother for the fetus. Michaels and Fanelli (1986) have found that parenters have more contact with the baby in the hospital than relinquishers, which supports Klaus and Kennell's (1976) theory of maternal-child bonding. On the other hand, the results could be explained by assuming the decision to parent or relinquish was made prior to the baby's birth and the parenters were simply availing themselves of current hospital practices that allowed frequent maternal-child contact.

Girl's sexual history. Little mention has been made of the girl's previous history with pregnancy. Girls who have been pregnant before are going to be influenced by the decisions they made at that time and by their subsequent reactions to those decisions. Previous abortions or spontaneous miscarriages might promote a sense of loss in girls and make them more susceptible to having the child on a repeat pregnancy. Further, girls who have already had one child and are rearing it themselves will be likely to have another. This is supported by much research on age of pregnancy and fertility (Baldwin, 1976; Bumpass & Sweet, 1972; Card & Wise, 1978; Furstenberg, 1976a; McCarthy & Menken, 1979; Millman & Hendershot, 1980; Moore & Waite, 1981; Mott, 1986; O'Connell & Rogers, 1984; Wilson & Myers, 1984). In one study that compared the fertility of relinquishers and parenters, McLaughlin et al. (1987) studied the effects of the decision on subsequent fertility. They found that parenters tended to marry more, conceive a second child more quickly, and have children closer together than relinquishers. Apparently, the relinquishment decision has an effect on later child-bearing, but it has yet to be established whether previous child conception and the decision about pregnancy resolution has an impact on the subsequent decision about relinquishment.

Race. Race has a large impact on the decision about relinquishment. Black parents rarely relinquish their children for formal adoption (Bachrach, 1986; Fischer, 1971; Hill, 1971; Jones, 1975; Ladner, 1977; Martin & Martin, 1978; Michaels & Fanelli, 1986; Musick et al., 1984; Palmer, 1981; Sandven & Egeland, 1985; Sharrar, 1971; Stack, 1971; Stokes & Greenstone, 1981; Wolf, 1983; Zelnick & Kanter, 1978). Many of the black adolescents who do not wish to raise their children opt for informal adoption in which the child is reared by someone else, but the adolescent retains legal custody of the child. In addition, the family network is highly involved in childrearing in black communities.

One recent study by Sandven and Egeland (1985) compared 54 black urban adolescents who each raised her child herself within the family of origin, those who moved out of the family and raised the child, and those who used informal adoption. (Only one adolescent relinquished her child through formal adoption.) The group that raised their children themselves divided into two subgroups — those who were independent but accepted help from relatives and those who were rebellious and had little initial desire for pregnancy. The group of adolescents who shared parenting with others in their family tended to stay in school longer and had better relationships with their mothers than other groups. They also were more satisfied with their pregnancies. The group that used informal adoption was generally composed of younger girls who experienced higher stress and more school-related problems than did other girls. Overall, all girls recognized their pregnancy late (at least second trimester) and few girls expressed a desire to marry within the next five years.

In a large study of the economics of pregnancy decision making, Leibowitz, Eisen, and Chow (1984) surveyed 297 California teenagers aged between 13 and 19 who were pregnant for the first time between 1982 and 1984. Their sample included both Anglo- and Mexican-American girls. They found that the Mexican-American girls were more likely than the Anglo-American girls to carry their pregnancies to term. They also found that the Roman Catholicism of the girls was not responsible for the propensity to carry to term (see also Westoff & Ryder, 1977), but the cultural differences between Anglo- and

Mexican-American girls was an influential factor in the decision. Currently, some funded studies are in progress that investigate Mexican-Americans (Becerra, two studies) and Puerto Ricans (Gutierrez).

Summary of intrapersonal factors. Most of the research that has investigated the intrapersonal factors associated with the decision to parent or relinquish the child has investigated the emotional, cognitive, psychological and interpersonal maturity of the girl. Except for a few instances, that research has not been voluminous (see Resnick 1984a for a review). There are important deficits in the research in terms of investigating the attitudes of the adolescents toward themselves as mothers and toward their babies. These cognitive factors have been almost entirely neglected in research. In addition, the cognitive process involved in the decision making has not been investigated at all for the relinquishment decision. Studies of decision making on abortion versus childbearing suggest that investigation of decision making processes might be fruitful (Bracken et al., 1978).

One study has given careful attention to decision making in pregnant adolescents (Resnick, 1987). Adolescent mothers who relinquished their babies (n=60) were matched with adolescent mothers who parented their babies (n=60) according to age, marital status, ethnicity, number and age of offspring, and agency used. Most adolescents in both groups reported that friends or family members had become pregnant during adolescence. Parenters reported this more frequently than relinquishers. Relinquishers (73%) were more likely to be exposed to adoption among friends or family than were parenters (63%), but relinquishers were two times as likely to report that the friend or family member had had a positive experience with the adoption than were parenters. In addition, respondents' sisters who had become pregnant as adolescents and had relinquished their child for adoption were almost five times as prevalent for relinquishers as for parenters. Also, relinquishers were more likely to be advised by the putative father to place the child for adoption than were parenters. Resnick (1987) suggests that the stimulus of living in an environment conducive to adoption prompts the adolescent to relinquish her child. Further, adolescents presumably operate from a limited informational base; thus friends and other models are especially influential.

An alternative interpretation of the data might suggest the problem solving theory is employed by the adolescent. One way that people often solve problems in ways that are less complete than using optimization strategies (Janis & Mann, 1977) is to use "availability heuristics". An availability heuristic is a vivid cognitive representation of how to behave in a situation that is readily available. It engulfs the cognitive field, so to speak, in a similar way that in stimuli control explanations, such as used by Resnick, stimuli engulf the physical stimulus field.

Resnick also compared relinquishers and parenters on the effects of the decision. He found that relinquishers experienced more postdecisional distresses, more sense of loss and more guilt (see Burnell & Norfleet, 1979; Deykin et al., 1984; Panner et al., 1978; Rynearson, 1982 for other reports of psychological problems in relinquishers). On the other hand, relinquishers also experienced less restriction in their daily activities and more closeness to their parents than did parenters.

Both relinquishers and parenters who were dissatisfied with their original decision were asked what decision they would make if they were able to make the decision again. Of the relinquishers, two-thirds said they would parent and one-third were unsure; none said they would abort. Of the parenters, about half said they would abort; over one-fourth said they would relinquish the child for adoption; 17 percent said they were unsure. Overall, over half of the adolescents — regardless of group — had been either physically or sexually abused as children.

Even though there is a need to better understand the cognitions of the pregnant adolescent and her decision making, the understanding cannot be complete without placing the decision within the interpersonal context that the adolescent faces. The following sections of the present review summarize the research dealing with interpersonal factors involved in adolescent decision making.

Interpersonal Factors in the Relinquishment Decision: Putative Father

Besides the girl's mother, the putative father of the baby is thought to be the most influential person in the girl's decision making (Rosen & Benson, 1982). Given recent court decisions that give fathers the right of adopting their child when he or she is unwanted by the girl, the role of the opinions of the putative father might conceivably become even more important in the future. Generally, the amount of influence that the putative father is likely to have will depend on three major factors: the closeness of the emotional relationship between the girl and the putative father, the girl's expectations about the future or lack of future of the relationship with him, and the influence attempts made by him.

Closeness of emotional relationship. Generally, the closer the emotional relationship between the girl and the putative father, the more influence he has on the girl's decision. Gabbard and Wolff (1977) and Musick et al. (1984) found that a close relationship led to more influence. Grow (1979) found that when the girl became pregnant by her steady boyfriend, she more often made the decision to parent the child than to place him or her for adoption. Previous research has not investigated the effects of pregnancy by rape, casual sex, or incest in the relinquishment decision — probably because rates of abortion are very high in those cases.

Expectation for a continuing relationship. A number of researchers have found that the girl's expectation for a continuing or deepening relationship between her and the putative father is related to the decision to parent the child rather than to place for adoption (Grow, 1979; Michaels, 1984; Michaels & Brown, 1982; Michaels & Fanelli, 1986). It is even conceivable that the baby can be used as a lever by the adolescent to persuade the boy to marry her (see Resnick, 1987), although this is probably rarer now than ten years ago.

Influence attempts by the father. Generally, research on influence attempts by the father of the baby have simply investigated whether the father prefers that the adolescent relinquish or parent the child. The common finding is that the girl usually acts in accord with the wishes of the baby's father. This is especially true if the girl intends to parent (Rosen, 1980). There is a need to determine how the putative fathers are involved in the decision making. Do they casually proffer suggestions, or are they involved to the extent that they might use threats and overt coercive strategies to influence the girl's decision? Given that romantic relationships are often unstable and highly emotional during adolescence, there is likelihood that either the girl or the putative father could employ coercive strategies of influence — expecially to the extent that they are empowered by having a close emotional relationship initially.

Interpersonal Factors in the Relinquishment Decision: The Family Constellation

Most adolescents are still part of their families. Adolescent pregnancy is consequently a family affair. Decisions by the girl are, of necessity, strongly affected by the family because the decisions strongly affect the entire family. The family constellation is the framework within which interpersonal interactions around the decisions occur. Of primary importance is the relationship between the parents of the adolescent. Several researchers have shown that the presence of both mother and father in the home (Grow, 1979; McLaughlin et al., 1987) and the mother and father's commitment to a stable, long-term relationship (Michaels & Fanelli, 1986) affect the girl's decision to relinquish or parent her child. In each case, strong family ties are associated with relinquishment rather than parenting. One might speculate on a number of reasons to explain these findings. For example, single parent families create financial strains that the adolescent might resolve through parenting her child and receiving public financial assistance. Or perhaps a stable, intact family might be unwilling to broaden its boundaries through the inclusion of another child. All reasons are highly speculative at present. Empirical investigation is needed to determine *why* strong family ties are related to relinquishment decisions rather than parenting decisions.

Of the family members, the girl's mother has consistently been found to be the most influential family member. Young, Berkman, and Rehr (1975) reported on 48 pregnant teenagers. They found that 90% of the daughters brought their babies to live in the family home (see also Grow, 1979). Of the 48, four-fifths of the daughters identified their mothers as being the most significant person in their lives. Clapp and Raab (1978) followed up unmarried adolescent mothers. They recommended that parental influence, norms, and values regarding adoption decision making be studied. Resnick (1984b) studied 32 relinquishers and 12 parenters. He found that relinquishers were more likely than parenters to have a close relationship with their mothers. Rosen (1980) studied 432 girls younger than 18 who were unmarried when they became pregnant. Girls completed anonymous questionnaires prior to abortion or delivery. Rosen found that only 12% consulted their mothers when they thought they might be pregnant. After confirming their pregnancies, 56 percent involved their mothers in future decision making. This was most true for whites who adopted out (79%) and least true for whites who parented (40%). Whites who aborted (54%), blacks who parented (55%), and blacks who aborted (61%) involved their mothers over half of the time. In cases of abortion and adoption, mothers were consulted more than male partners; in cases of parenting, male partners were consulted more than mothers. The fathers of the adolescents and the adolescents' girlfriends were consulted less than the adolescents' mothers. Generally, white adolescents rated their mothers as most influential when they relinquished their children and black adolescents rated their mothers as most influential when they aborted. Male partners were most influential for white parenters.

The father is somewhat influential whenever the mother is. Rosen found that whenever girls consulted their mothers, they also tended to consult their fathers, but not as frequently. In addition, fathers were perceived to have less influence than mothers on the girls' decisions.

The life stage of the parents is assumed to have some bearing on the girl's decision, presumably because the parents will exert some persuasive pressure on the girls based on the family situation. For example, if the parents are aging, they are unlikely to want to assume the role of primary caretakers for their daughter's baby. Further, if the parents have launched most or all of their children except the adolescent who has become pregnant, they will likely be unwilling to start a "new" family. If the parents are highly involved in their careers, they also might be unlikely to take on surrogate parenting responsibilities.

The presence of others in the home might predispose the family to be more or less accepting of a new member. For example, a retired grandparent (great-grandparent of the new baby) might have abundant time to give to helping the adolescent raise her infant, or might, as likely, require extra time and energy from family members that would reduce the likelihood that a new baby would be accepted within the family constellation. The presence of a younger sibling, especially very young siblings, might predispose the family to be willing to accept the new infant, for the new baby would fit easily into the lifestyle of the family with other young children; or, as likely, the presence of young siblings might already occupy the family's resources. The presence of other adolescents or near adolescents might provide an ample supply of child care resources for the new baby. Each of the above is speculative. It is likely that situations will be perceived differently in families with different demands and resources.

Existing demands in the family. The addition of a child to the family structure greatly increases the time and energy required of the family members. In addition to child care duties that are shared within the family, the adolescent who parents must be given training to function as a mother. Most of this instructional burden falls to the adolescent's mother. Consequently, it is crucial to understand the nature of the current demands on the family's resources. The family might face a variety of pressures from school, work, or social groups. Financial pressures on the family might include large debts or difficulties supplying the basics of life — food, shelter, and clothing. Individual members of the family might have personal problems that create strains in the family. For example, alcohol or drug abuse (Sandven & Egeland, 1985), and chronic or frequent depression, tax the family's coping capabilities. Finally, high levels of ongoing conflict in the family, whether between spouses, parent-child dyads, or siblings, create an exhausting environment for the family. Adding another child to environments already overburdened with demands on physical and psychological resources can create high stress in the family (McCubbin & Patterson, 1983).

Existing resources. Balanced against existing demands, however, are the family's resources for coping with them. Financial resources include the assets and the incomes of all family members. Time is another precious commodity that can help the family cope (LaRossa, 1983). Finally, emotional energy is important for dealing with the crises that occur in normal adolescence and those compounded by the loss of the baby through adoption or the presence of the new baby if the girl decides to parent. The long-lasting crisis of pregnancy and birth is likely to deplete the family's finances, time and emotional energy, leaving them vulnerable to stress during the post-delivery period.

Religious climate in the family. No research has investigated the religious climate in the families of pregnant adolescents during the relinquishment decision (cf. the large amount of research on religious environment during the abortion decision). Religion might have important effects on how the entire family adjusts to the crisis. Several aspects of the religious environment are important. The religious beliefs of family members and the intensity with which they pursue their beliefs in daily life are important because differences in intensity or content of beliefs might bespeak conflict in one fundamental part of family life. In addition, the religious beliefs of the parents might determine their attitudes towards sexual behavior in their adolescents. Premarital intercourse might be described as sin within a family. Serious divisions and feelings of betrayal might exist between the adolescent and her parents because of the pregnancy. Religious beliefs might also influence the parents' attitudes toward forgiveness and acceptance of the adolescent. Family values about adoption (Clapp & Raab, 1978) might be influenced by religious beliefs. Finally, the adolescent's religious convictions might help her forgive herself and adjust more quickly than she might without religious beliefs. Again, such reasoning is highly speculative and has not been investigated empirically.

Perceptions of desire for another child. Several researchers have found that the adolescent's parents might encourage her to have and rear the child because they want a grandchild or are unwilling to give up their grandchild for adoption (Leynes, 1980; Rosen, 1980; Young, Berkman,

& Rehr, 1975). In some cases, the adolescent's parents offer help with child rearing (Young et al., 1975) or financial support (Michaels & Fanelli, 1986). Indeed, the perceived helpfulness of the adolescent's parents in providing emotional support generally has been found to encourage the adolescent to parent her child (Eisen & Zellman, 1974; Grow, 1979; Michaels & Fanelli, 1985; Rosen, 1980; Young et al., 1975).

Perception of family environment. In making her decision about parenting or relinquishing her child, the adolescent must consider the family environment into which she might introduce the child or prevent the child from entering. Generally, three elements of the family situation are relevant: family communication, intimacy-love-mutual support, and conflict. Grow (1979) found that good communication in families of origin was related to the decision to relinquish. Parents of teens who relinquish have also been found to be more intimate with each other (Resnick, 1984b; Smith, 1977) than have parents of girls who parent.

Perhaps the area that has been most researched, though, concerning the family environment has been the power dynamics in the family. Michaels and Fanelli (1986), who surveyed 57 parenters and 42 relinquishers, most of whom were older adolescents (mean age 17.8 years), found that about 40 percent of the adolescents reported that their parents did not try to influence them at all. In only one-eighth of the cases did the adolescents report that their parents did not care about the outcome of the pregnancy. In about 15 percent of the cases, adolescents reported strong parental influence attempts including explicit threats, such as telling the adolescent that she would have to leave home if she did not comply. Of the parents who did try to influence their daughters, there was no relationship between the parents' desired outcome and the actual outcome decided by the adolescent. The stronger the adolescent's parents apparently felt about the decision, the less well the adolescent functioned. Of course, cause and effect are impossible to determine in that analysis. It could be that strong parental preferences created conflict in the adolescent, or that troubled adolescents' parents become more involved in the decision making. Young et al. (1975) found that the degree of open conflict between parents was related to their ability to influence their daughters. Conflict between parents and their daughters also has been found to affect the parents' ability to influence their daughters (Sandven & Egeland, 1985; Young et al., 1975).

Perception of disruption in the family caused by parenting or relinquishing. Although no research has explicitly addressed the question with the relinquishment decision, Worthington and Buston (1986) and Worthington (1987) have proposed that disruptions in time schedules and in relationship rules will affect the course of family crises. It is suggested that disruption is generally seen as negative by most families; thus it is considered a cost in evaluating the merits and costs of alternatives.

Summary of the effects of family relationships. Despite the centrality of the family to understanding decision making in adolescents, especially early and middle adolescents, the dynamics of the family around the decision to parent or relinquish have been largely uninvestigated. Research concerning the family has most often involved structural characteristics of the family and differences or similarities of opinions between the parents and the adolescent. No research has been conducted on specifically *how* parents try to influence their daughters and what methods of influence are effective or provoke rebellion. The decision about relinquishment occurs over a protracted period of time, thus allowing a great deal of flexibility in using influence attempts. There is a need to catalogue the influence attempts and to determine whether influence attempts increase in coerciveness over the time throughout the pregnancy. Further, the role of communication and mutual supportiveness as it relates to effective influence has yet to be determined. Research on family variables related to adolescent decision making has generally not been driven by theory. It is crucial to understand these influence attempts in light of both decision making theory and family stress theory.

Interpersonal Factors in the Relinquishment Decision: Other Support Systems

Peers. Substantial research has addressed the question of which are more influential in decision making by adolescents: parents or peers. Early research generally posed hypothetical situations and asked adolescents to whom they would turn for advice (Brittain, 1963; Emmerich, 1978). More recently, research has dealt with actual decisions and has asked adolescents to nominate individuals to whom they would turn for help (see Blyth, Hill & Thiel, 1982; Keats et al., 1983). Research has generally shown that the content of the decision has important implications for whom adolescents ask for assistance. Generally, adolescents seek help from peers on present-time, lifestyle and easier decisions and seek help from parents on future-oriented, moral, and more difficult decisions. Age and sex have been found to influence adolescents' choices of whom to consult (Emmerich, 1978; Floyd & South, 1972).

In pregnancy-resolution decision making, it would generally be hypothesized that peers would be less influential than parents — except for the male partner when the adolescent decides to parent the child. In Rosen's (1980) study, she evaluated the influence of the adolescent's mother versus the adolescent's best friend. In all cases, she found the mother to be more influential except in instances in which white girls decided to parent their child (no differences). Resnick (1987 in progress) has found that the presence of siblings or close friends who have also become pregnant as adolescents influences pregnant teenagers in their choice between relinquishment and parenting. Relinquishers tended to have more friends or siblings who had adopted out their child or who had had better experiences with relinquishment than did parenters. Resnick interprets this as due to the limited informational base that the adolescents have for decision making and due to the powerful environmental influence of living in a world that accepts relinquishment. It is expected that when adolescents are substantially influenced by their siblings or by close female friends, it is because of the closeness of the interpersonal relationship. Research is needed to investigate this hypothesis.

Others. Other support groups can be influential in helping a girl make emotion-laden decisions. The girl might be closely affiliated with church groups, athletic teams, grandparents, or colleagues at work. Individuals in each group — e.g., pastor or youth leaders, coach, employer — might have respect from the adolescent and might be able to influence her decisions. Little research has been done to date on extra-family group influence, except for the potential influence of public or private agencies and their counselors. Michaels and Fanelli (1986) report that when agencies offer support to the girl for relinquishing the child, the adolescent is more likely to relinquish than if the agency does not offer support. Musick et al. (1984) reports that little agency support is typically available for relinquishment. They speculate that counselors might be embarrassed to suggest adoption because they know that adoption is not popular with most girls. Sandven and Egeland (1985) reported that many of the black, urban adolescents in their sample sought counsel from doctors or nurses. Baptiste (1986) has suggested that family counseling in pregnancy-related decisions is becoming more appropriate. He makes suggestions for how to counsel families. Several funded studies are now underway that investigate the attitudes of agency counselors toward adoption and parenting the child (e.g., Mech, Kallen).

Summary. It is generally recognized that most of the influence on teenagers concerning relinquishment will come from family members and the putative father. Consequently, the research concerning influence has largely been concerned with those two groups. Because of the political ramifications of agency counseling, though, a number of recent studies have investigated the influence of agency counselors on the decisions of adolescents.

CONCLUSION

Research on decision making by pregnant adolescents is at a rudimentary level. Despite the existence of five theoretical schools of decision making theories, little empirical investigation has related decision making theory to adolescent pregnancy. Most research has concerned determinants for various decisional outcomes. There are several large needs for future research in adolescent decision making:

1. to relate research to theory,
2. to explore the *process* of decision making, and
3. to investigate the impact by and on the family during decision making by pregnant adolescents.

BIBLIOGRAPHY
CHAPTER 9

Adams, B. N. (1964). Structural factors affecting parental aid to married children. *Journal of Marriage and the Family, 26,*327-331.

Adler, A. (1939). *Social interest.* New York: Putnam.

Adler, N.E. (1975). Emotional responses of women following therapeutic abortion. *American Journal of Orthopsychiatry, 15,* 446-454.

Adler, N.E. (1976). Sample attribution in studies of psycho-social sequelae of abortion: How great a problem? *Journal of Applied Social Psychology, 6,* 240-257.

Adler, N. (1979). Abortion: A social psychological perspective. *Journal of Social Issues, 35,* 100-119.

Adler, N.E. (1981). Sex roles and unwanted pregnancy in adolescent and adult women. *Professional Psychology, 12,* 56-66.

Ainslie, G. (1975). Specious reward: A behavioral theory of impulsiveness and impulse control. *Psychological Bulletin, 82,* 463-496.

Ajzen, I., & Fishbein, M. (1980). *Understanding attitudes and predicting social behavior.* Englewood Cliffs, N.J.: Prentice-Hall.

Alan Guttmacher Institute (1976). *11 million teenagers.* New York: Planned Parenthood Federation of America.

Anthony, E.J., & Cohler, B.J. (Eds.) (1987). *The invulnerable child.* New York: Guilford.

Ashton, J.R. (1979). Patterns of discussion and decision making amongst abortion patients. *Journal of Biosocial Science, 12,* 247-259.

Bachrach, C.A. (1986). Adoption plans, adopted children and adopted mothers. *Journal of Marriage and the Family, 48,* 243-253

Balakrishnan, T.R.; Shan, R., Allingham, J.D., & Kantner, J.F. (1972). Attitudes toward abortion of married women in metropolitan Toronto. *Social Biology, 19,* 36-42.

Baldwin, W.H. (1976). *Adolescent pregnancy and childbearing — growing concerns for Americans.* Population Reference Bureau 31 (September). Washington, D.C.: Population Reference Bureau.

Baldwin, W., & Cain, V.S. (1980). The children of teenage parents. *Family Planning Perspectives, 12,* 34-43.

Baptiste, D.S., Jr. (1986). Counseling the pregnant adolescent within a family context: Therapeutic issues and strategies. *Family Therapy, 13,* 161-176.

Barglow, P.; Bornsetin, M.B.; Exum, D.B.; Wright, M.K., & Visotsky, H.M. (1967). Some psychiatric aspects of illegitimate pregnancy during early adolescence. *American Journal of Orthopsychiatry, 37,* 266-267.

Becerra, R. (In progress — funded by the Office of Adolescent Pregnancy). *Sexual behavior among Mexican adolescents: A followup.* School of Social Welfare, University of California at Los Angeles, California.

Becerra, R. (In progress — funded by the Office of Adolescent Pregnancy). *Sex and pregnancy among Mexican-American adolescents.* School of Social Welfare, University of California at Los Angeles, California.

Bernstein, R. (1971). *Helping unmarried mothers.* New York: Associated Press.

Bibring, G.L., & Wallerstein, A.F. (1976). Psychological aspects of pregnancy. *Clinical Obstetrics and Gynecology, 9,* 357-371.

Blum, R., & Resnick, M. (1982). Adolescent sexual decision-making: Contraception, pregnancy, abortion, motherhood. *Pediatric Annual, 11,* 797-805.

Blyth, D.A.; Hill, J.P., & Thiel, K.S. (1982). Early adolescents' significant others: Grade and gender differences in perceived relationships with familial and nonfamilial adults and young people. *Journal of Youth and Adolescence, 11,* 425-450.

Bolton, F.G., Jr. (1980). *The pregnant adolescent: Problems of premature parenthood.* Beverly Hills, CA: Sage.

Bouvier, L.F., & Rao, S.L. (1975). *Socioreligious factors in fertility decline.* Cambridge, Mass.: Ballinger Publishing.

Bracken, M.B.; Hachamovitch, M.D., & Grossman, A. (1974). The decision to abort and psychological sequelae. *The Journal of Nervous and Mental Disease, 15,* 154-162.

Bracken, M., & Kasl, S. (1975). Delay in seeking induced abortion: A review and theoretical analysis. *American Journal of Obstetrics and Gynecology, 121,* 1008-1019.

Bracken, M.; Klerman, L.; & Bracken, M. (1978). Coping with pregnancy resolution among never married women. *American Journal of Opthopsychiatry, 48,* 320-334.

Brittain, C.E. (1963). Adolescent choices and parent-peer cross pressures. *American Sociological Review, 28,* 358-391.

Brody, H.; Meikle, S., & Gerritse, R. (1971). Therapeutic abortion: A prospective study. *American Journal of Obstetrics and Gynecology, 109,* 347-352.

Bumpass, L.L., & Sweet, J.A. (1972). Differentials in marital instability: 1970. *American Sociological Review, 37,* 754-766.

Burnell, G.M., & Norfleet, M.A. (1979). Women who place their infants up for adoption: A pilot study. *Parent Counseling and Health Education, 16,* 169-176.

Card, J.J., & Wise, L.L. (1978). Teenage mothers and teenage fathers: The impact of early child-bearing on the parents' personal and professional lives. *Family Planning Perspectives, 10,* 199-205.

Cattel, J.P. (1954). Psychodynamic and clinical observations in a group of unmarried mothers. *American Journal of Psychiatry, 111,* 337-342.

Chilman, C.S. (1980). Social and psychological research concerning adolescent childbearing: 1970-1980. *Journal of Marriage and the Family, 42,* (November), 793-805.

Clapp, D.F., & Raab, R.S. (1978). Follow-up of unmarried adolescent mothers. *Social Work, 23,* 149-153.

Clary, F. (1982). Minor women obtaining abortions: A study of parental notification in metropolitan area. *American Journal of Public Health, 72,* 283-285.

Clayton, R.R., & Tolone, W.L. (1973). Religiosity and attitudes toward induced abortion: An elaboration of the relationship. *Sociological Analysis, 34,* 26-39.

Clothier, F. (1943). Psychological implications of unmarried parenthood. *American Journal of Orthopsychiatry, 13,* 531-549.

Cobliner, W. (1974). Pregnancy in the single adolescent girl: The role of cognitive functions. *Journal of Youth and Adolescence, 3,* 69-76.

Cohen, S. & Wills, T.A. (1985). Stress, social support, and the buffering hypothesis. *Psychological Bulletin, 98,* 310-357.

Controneo, M., & Krasner, B. (1977). A study of abortion and problems in decision making. *Journal of Marriage and Family Counseling, 3,* 69-76.

Cranley, M.S. (1981). Development of a tool for the measurement of maternal attachment during pregnancy. *Nursing Research, 30,* 281-284.

David, H. (1972). Abortion in psychological perspective. *American Journal of Orthopsychiatry, 42,* 61-68.

De Amicis, L.A.; Klorman, R.; Hess, D.W., & McAnarney, E.R. (1981). A comparison of unwed pregnant teenagers and multigravid sexually active adolescents seeking contraception. *Adolescence, 16,* 11-20.

Deykin, E.Y.; Cambel, L., & Patti, P. (1984). The post adoption experience of surrendering parents. *American Journal of Orthopsychiatry, 54,* 271-280.
Ebaugh, H.R.F., & Haney, C.A. (1980). Shifts in abortion attitudes: 1973-1978. *Journal of Marriage and the Family, 42,* 491-499.
Eisen, M.; Zellman, G.L.; Leibowitz, A.; Chow, W.K., & Evans, J.R. (1983). Factors discriminating pregnancy resolution decisions of unmarried adolescents. *Genetic Psychology Monographs, 108,* 69-95.
Eisen, M., & Zellman, G.L. (1984). Factors predicting pregnancy resolution decision satisfaction of unmarried adolescents. *Journal of Genetic Psychology, 145,* 231-239.
Elkind, D. (1967). Egocentricism in adolescence. *Child Development, 38,* 1025-1034.
Emmerich, H.J. (1978). The influence of parents and peers on choices made by adolescents. *Journal of Youth and Adolescence, 7,* 175-180.
Espenshade, T.J. (1977). The value and cost of children. *Population Bulletin, 32.*
Festinger, L. (1957). *A theory of cognitive dissonance.* Stanford: Stanford University Press.
Festinger, T.B. (1971). Unwed mothers and their decisions to keep or surrender children. *Child Welfare, 50,* 253-263.
Finner, S.L., & Gamache, J.D. (1969). The relationship between religious commitment and attitudes towards induced abortion. *Sociological Analysis, 30,* 1-12.
Fischer, D.D. (1971). Homes for black children. *Child Welfare, 50.*
Fischman, S. (1977). Delivery or abortion of inner city adolescents. *American Journal of Orthopsychiatry, 47,* 127-133.
Fishman, S.H. (1975). The pregnancy resolution decision of unwed adolescents. *Nursing Clinics in North America, 10,* 217-227.
Floyd, H.H., & South; D.R. (1972). Dilemma of youth: The choice of parents or peers as a frame of reference for behavior. *Journal of Marriage and the Family, 34,* 627-634.
Forrest, J.; Sullivan, E., & Tietze, C. (1979). Abortion in the United States, 1977-1979. *Family Planning Perspectives, 11,* 329-341.
Frankl, V. (1967). *Psychotherapy and existentialism.* New York: Simon & Schuster.
Freeman, E.W. (1977). Influence of personality attributes on abortion experiences. *American Journal of Orthopsychiatry, 47,* 503-513.
Friedman, A.S. (1971). *Therapy with families of sexually acting out girls.* New York: Springer.
Fromm, E. (1950). *Psychoanalysis and religion.* New Haven: Yale University Press.

Furstenberg, F.F., Jr. (1976a). The social consequences of teenage parenthood. *Family Planning Perspectives, 8,* 148-164.

Furstenberg, F. (1976b). *Unplanned parenthood: The social consequences of teenage childbearing.* New York: Free Press.

Gabbard, G.O., & Wolff, J.R. (1977). The unwed pregnant teenager and her male relationship. *Journal of Reproductive Medicine, 19,* 137-140.

Gispert, M., & Falk, R. (1976). Sexual experimentation and pregnancy in young black adolescents. *American Journal of Obstetrics and Gynecology, 126,* 459-466.

Granberg, D., & Granberg, B. (1980). Abortion attitudes, 1965-1980: Trends and determinants. *Family Planning Perspectives, 12,* 251.

Grisso, T., & Vierling, L. (1978). Minor's consent to treatment: A developmental perspective. *Professional Psychology, 9,* 412-427.

Group for the Advancement of Psychiatry. (1986). *Crises of adolescence. Teenage pregnancy: Impact on adolescent development.* New York: Brunner/Mazel.

Grow, L.J. (1979). Today's unmarried mothers: The choices have changed. *Child Welfare, 58,* 363-371.

Gutierrez, M.J. (In progress — funded by the Office of Adolescent Pregnancy). *Premarital sexual relations among Puerto Rican youth.*

Hanson, M.W. (1978). Abortion in teenagers. *Clinical Obstetrics and Gynecology, 21,* 1175-1190.

Harris, R., & Mills, E. (1985). Religion, values, and attitudes toward abortion. *Journal for the Scientific Study of Religion, 24,* 119-236.

Hatcher, S. (1976). Understanding adolescent pregnancy and abortion. *Primary Care, 3,* 407-425.

Hedderson, J.; Hodgson, M.B., & Crowley, T. (1974). Determinants of abortion attitudes in the U.S. in 1974. *Cornell Journal of Special Relations, 9,* (Fall).

Hedderson, J., & Hodgson, L. (1976). *Recent changes in Catholic women's attitudes toward abortion.* Paper presented at the meeting of the Population Association of America, Montreal.

Henshaw, S.K.; Binkin, N.J.; Blaine, E., & Smith, J.C. (1985). A portrait of American women who obtain abortions. *Family Planning Perspectives, 17,* 90-96.

Hertel, B.; Hendershot, G.E., & Grimm, J.W. (1974). Religion and attitudes toward abortion: A study of nurses and social workers. *Journal for the Scientific Study of Religion, 13,* 23-34.

Herz, D.G. (1977). Psychological implications of adolescent pregnancy: Patterns of family interaction in adolescent mothers-to-be. *Psychosomatics, 18,* 13-16.

Hill, R. (1949). *Families under stress,* New York: Harper and Brothers.

Hill, R.B. (1971). *The strengths of black families.* New York: Emerson Hall Publishers.

Horn, J., & Turner, R. (1976). MMPI profiles among subgroups of unwed mothers. *Journal of Consulting and Clinical Psychology, 44,* 25-33.

Huckeba, W.M., & Mueller, C.P. (1987). *Systematic analysis of research on psycho-social effects of abortion reported in referred journals 1966-1985.* Unpublished report by the Family Research Council to Office of Population Affairs, Department of Health and Human Services. (Published report on this research is in this "Values and Public Policy" volume, page 77.)

Hudson, J.M., & Gray, W.M. (1986). Formal operations, the imaginary audience and the personal fable. *Adolescence, 21,* 751-877.

Hunt, J.M. (1982). Toward equalizing the developmental opportunities of infants and preschool children. *Journal of Social Issues, 38,* 163-191.

Hutchins, F.L. (1978). Teenage pregnancy and the black community. *Journal of National Medical Association, 70,* 857-859.

Illsley, R., & Hall, M.H. (1976). Psychosocial aspects of abortion: A review of issues and needed research. *Bulletin of World Health Organization, 53,* 83-106.

Jacokes, L.E. (1965). MMPI prediction of the unwed mother's decision regarding child placement. *Journal of Clinical Psychology, 21,* 280-281.

Janis, I.L., & Mann, L. (1977). *Decision making: A psychological analysis of conflict, choice, and commitment.* New York: Free Press.

Jones, L.W. (1975). *Informal adoption in black families in Lowndes and Wilcox County, Alabama.* Tuskegee, AL: Tuskegee Institute.

Jorgensen, S.R., & Sonstegard, J.S. (1984). Predicting adolescent sexual and contraceptive behavior: An application and test of the Fishbein model. *Journal of Marriage and the Family, 46,* 43-55.

Kahneman, D. (1973). *Attention and effort.* Englewood Cliffs, NJ: Prentice-Hall.

Kahneman, D., & Tversky, A. (1984). Choices, values, and frames. *American Psychologist, 39,* 341-350.

Kasun, J.R. (1984). Teenage pregnancy: Media effects versus facts. In F. Glahe and J. Peden (Eds.) *American family and the state.* San Francisco: Pacific Institute for Public Policy Research.

Keats, J.A.; Keats, D.M.; Biddle, B.J.; Bank, B.J.; Hauge, R.; Wan-Rafaei, & Valantin, S. (1983). Parents, friends, siblings and adults: Unfolding referent other importance data for adolescents. *International Journal of Psychology, 18,* 239-262.

Kent, I (1977, Sept.). *Emotional sequelae of therapeutic abortion.* Paper presented at the 17th annual meeting of the Canadian Psychiatric Association, Saskatoon, Canada.

Kirkland, J. (1983). Infant crying — problems that won't go away! *Parents' Centre Bulletin, 96* (Summer), 17.

Kirkland J.; Deane, F., & Brennan, M. (1983). About Cry SOS, a clinic for people with crying babies. *Family Relations, 32,* 537-543.

Klaus, M.J., & Kennell, J.H. (1976). *Maternal-infant bonding: The impact of early separation or loss on family development.* St. Louis: Mosby.

Klein, L. (1978). Antecedents to teenage pregnancy. *Clinical Obstetrics and Gynecology, 32,* 1151-1159.

Klerman, L.V.; Bracken, M.B.; Jekel, J.F., & Bracken, M. (1982). The delivery-abortion decision among adolescents. In T.R. Stuart & C.F. Wells (Eds.), *Pregnancy in adolescence: Need, problems, and management.* New York: Van Nostrand Reinhold.

Kramer, M.J. (1975). The incidents of legal abortion among New York City residents: An analysis of socioeconomic and demographic characteristics. *Family Planning Perspectives, 7,* 127-137.

Krumboltz, J.D., & Hamel, D.A. (1977). *Guide to career decision-making skills.* New York: College Entrance Examination Board.

LaRossa, R. (1983). The transition to parenthood and the social reality of time. *Journal of Marriage and the Family, 45,* 579-589.

Lander, J.A. (1977). *Mixed families.* New York: Anchor Press/Doubleday.

Landry, E.; Bertrand, J.; Cherry, F., & Rice, J. (1986). Teen pregnancy in New Orleans: Factors that differentiate teens who deliver, abort and successfully contracept. *Journal of Youth & Adolescence, 15,* 259-274.

Larsen, L.E. (1972). The influence of parents and peers during adolescence: The situation hypothesis revisited. *Journal of Marriage and the Family, 34,* 67-74.

Lazarus, R. S., & Folkman, S. (1984). *Stress, appraisal, and coping.* New York: Springer.

Lee, G.T. (1980). Kinship in the seventies: A decade review of research and theory. *Journal of Marriage and the Family, 42,* 923-934.

Leibowitz, A.; Eisen, M., & Chow, W. (1984). *An economic model of teenage pregnancy decision-making.* (Paper No. 6.009). Austin: The University of Texas, Texas Population Research Center.

Lennard, H., & Bernstein, A. (1970). *Patterns in human interaction.* San Francisco: Jossey-Bass.

Levy, D. (1955). A follow-up study of unmarried mothers. *Social Casework, 36*, 27-33.

Lewis, C.C. (1980). A comparison of minors' and adults' pregnancy decisions. *American Journal of Orthopsychiatry, 50*, 446-453.

Lewis, C.C. (1981). How adolescents approach decisions: Changes over grades seven to twelve and policy implications. *Child Development, 52*, 538-544.

Lewis, C.C. (1987). Minors competence to consent to abortion. *American Psychologist, 42*, 84-88.

Leynes, C. (1980). Keep or abort: A study of factors influencing pregnant adolescents' plans for their babies. *Child Psychiatry and Human Development, 10*, 105.

Litwak, E., & Szeleniyi, I. (1968). Primary group structures and their functions: Kin, neighbors and friends. *American Sociological Review, 34*, 465-481.

Marecek, J. (1987). Counseling adolescents with problem pregnancies. *American Psychologist, 42*, 84-88.

Martin, E.P., & Martin, J.M. (1978). *The black extended family.* Chicago: University of Chicago Press.

Maslow, A.H. (1971). *The farther reaches of human nature.* New York: Viking Press.

May, R. (1953). *Man's search for himself.* New York: Norton.

McCarthy, J., & Menken, J. (1979). Marriage, remarriage, marital disruption and age at first birth. *Family Planning Perspectives, 11*, 21-30.

McCubbin, H.I., & Patterson, J.M. (1983). Family transitions: Adaptation to stress. In H.I. McCubbin and C.R. Figley (Eds.), *Stress and the family Volume I, Coping with normative transitions* (pp. 5-25). New York: Brunner/Mazel.

McLaughlin, S.D.; Manninen, D.L., & Winges, L.D. (1987). *The consequences of the adoption decision* (Final Report to the Office of Adolescent Pregnancy). Seattle, WA: Battelle Human Affairs Research Centers.

Mech, E.V. (1973). Adoption: A policy perspective. In B. Haldwell & H. Riccuiti (Eds.), *Review of Child Development Research*, Vol. III. Chicago: University of Chicago Press.

Melton, G.B. (1981). Children's participation in treatment planning: Psychological and legal issues. *Professional Psychology, 12*, 246-252.

Melton, G.B. (1983). Toward "personhood" for adolescent: Autonomy and privacy as values in public policy. *American Psychologist, 38*, 99-103.

Melton, G.B. (1984b). Developmental psychology and the law: The state of the art. *Journal of Family Law, 22*, 445-482.

Melton, G.B. (1987). Legal regulation of adolescent abortion: Unintended effects. *American Psychologist, 42,* 79-83.
Melton, G.B.; Koocher, G.P. & Saks, M.J. (Eds.). (1983). *Children's competence of consent.* New York: Plenum.
Melton, G.B., & Russo, N.F. (1987). Adolescent abortion: Psychological perspectives on public policy. *American Psychologist, 42,* 69-72.
Meyer, H.J.; Jones, W., & Borgatta, E.F. (1956). The decision by unmarried mothers to keep or surrender their babies. *Social Work, 1,* 103-109.
Michaels, G.Y. (1984, August). *Division of infant caregiving in families with an adolescent mother.* Paper presented at the meeting of the American Psychological Association, Toronto.
Michaels, G.Y., & Brown, R. (1982, August). *A values of children conceptual model for adolescent parenthood.* Paper presented at the meeting of the American Psychological Association, Washington, D.C.
Michaels, G.Y., & Fanelli, J.P. (March 1986). *To keep or place for adoption: Adolescents' pregnancy outcome decisions.* Paper presented at the first biennial meeting of the Society for Research on Adolescence, Madison, WI.
Millman, S.R., & Hendershot, G.E. (1980). Early fertility and lifetime fertility. *Family Planning Perspectives, 12,* 139-140, 145-149.
Mondy, L.W. (1985). Economic considerations in adolescent reproduction. In P. B. Smith & D.M. Munford (Eds.), *Adolescent reproductive health: Handbook for the health professional* (pp. 231-245). New York: Gardner Press.
Moore, K.A., & Caldwell, S.B. (1976). *Out of wedlock pregnancy and childbearing.* Working paper 992-02. Washington, D.C.: The Urban Institute.
Moore, K.A., & Hofferth, S.L. (1980). Factors affecting early family formations: A path model. *Population and Environment, 3,* 73-98.
Moore, K.A.; Hofferth, S.L.; Wertheimer, R.F.; Waite, L.J. & Caldwell, S.B. (1980). Teenage childbearing: Consequences for women, families, and government welfare expenditures. In K. Scott, T. Fields & E. Robinson (Eds.), *Teenage parents and their offspring.* New York: Grune and Stratton.
Moore, K.A. & Waite, L.J. (1981). Marital dissolution, early motherhood and early marriage. *Social Forces, 60,* 20-40.
Moseley, D.T.; Follingstad, D.R., & Harley, H. (1981). Psychological factors that predict reaction to abortion. *Journal of Clinical Psychology, 37,* 276-279.

Mott, F.L. (1986). The pace of repeated childbearing among young American mothers. *Family Planning Perspectives, 18*, 5-12.

Mueller, E. (1972). Economic cost and value of children: Conceptualization and measurement. In J.T. Fawcett (Ed.), *The satisfactions and costs of children: Theories, concepts, methods.* Honolulu: East-West Population Institute.

Musick, J.S.; Handler, A., & Waddelly, K.D. (1984). Teens and adoption: A pregnancy resolution alternative? *Children Today*, 24-29.

National Committee for Adoption (1985). *Adoption factbook: United States data, issues, regulations and resources.* Washington, D.C.: Author.

National Research Council (1987). *Risking the future: Adolescent sexuality, pregnancy, and childbearing.* Washington, D.C.: National Academy Press.

Neisser, U. (1976). *Cognition and reality: Principles and implications of cognitive psychology.* San Francisco: W.H. Freeman and Company.

Nisbett, R.E., & Borgida, E. (1975). Attribution and the psychology of prediction. *Journal of Personality and Social Psychology, 32*, 932-943.

O'Connell, M., & Rogers, C.C. (1984). Out-of-wedlock births, premarital pregnancies and their effect on family formation and dissolation. *Family Planning Perspectives, 4,* 157-162.

Osofsky, J.D., & Osofsky, H.J. (1972). The psychological reaction of parents to legalized abortion. *American Journal of Orthopsychiatry, 42,* 48-60.

Palmer, E. (1981). A community-based comprehensive approach to serving adolescent parents. *Child Welfare, 60,* 191-197.

Panner, R.; Baran, A., & Sorosky, A.D. (1978). Birth parents who relinquished babies for adoption revisited. *Family Process, 17,* 329-337.

Paulker, S. (1969). Girls pregnant out of wedlock. In M. LaBarre and W. LeBarre (Eds.), *Double jeopardy, the triple crisis — illegitimacy today.* New York: National Council on Illegitimacy.

Payne, E.; Kravitz, A.; Notman, M., & Anderson, J. (1976). Outcome following therapeutic abortion. *Archives of General Psychiatry, 33,* 725-733.

Piaget, J. & Inhelder, B. (1969). *The psychology of the child.* New York: Basic Books.

Polanyi, M. (1958). *Personal knowledge: Towards a post-critical philosophy.* Chicago: University of Chicago Press.

Polanyi, M. (1964). *Science, faith and society.* Chicago: University of Chicago Press.

Resnick, M.D. (1984a). Studying adolescent mothers decision making about adoption and parenting. *Social Work, 29,* 5-9.

Resnick, M.D. (October, 1984b). *Adoption and parenting decision-making among adolescent females.* Paper presented at Child Welfare League of American Biennial Conference for Board Leaders and Executives, Minneapolis, MN.

Resnick, M.D. (1987). *Adoption and parenting decision making among adolescent females.* Summary of verbal presentation to Office of Adolescent Pregnancy (Grant APR 000905). Washington, D.C.

Rogers, C.R. (1961). *On becoming a person.* Boston: Houghton Mifflin.

Rogers, J.L.; Phifer, J.F., & Nelson, J.A. (1987). Validity of existing controlled studies examining the psychological effects of abortion. *Perspectives on Science and Christian Faith, 39,* 20-30.

Roosa, M.W. (1986). Adolescent mothers, school drop-outs and school based intervention programs. *Family Relations, 35,* 313-317.

Rosen, R.H. (1980). Adolescent pregnancy decision-making: Are parents important. *Adolescence, 15,* 43-45.

Rosen, R.H. (1982). Pregnancy resolution decisions. In G.L. Fox (Ed.), *The childbearing decision: Fertility attitudes and behavior* (pp. 247-266). Beverly Hills: Sage.

Rosen, R.H. & Benson, T.(1982). The second-class partner: The male role in family planning decisions. In G.L. Fox (Ed.), *The childbearing decision: Fertility attitudes and behavior* (pp. 97-124). Beverly Hills: Sage.

Rosen, R.A.; Martindale, L., & Grisdela, M. (1976). Pregnancy study report. Detroit: Wayne State University.

Ross, H., & Sawhill, I. (1975). *Time of transition: The growth of families headed by women.* Washington, D.C.: The Urban Institute.

Rowe, K.L. (1984, August). *Adolescent contraceptive use: The role of cognitive factors.* Paper presented at the meeting of the American Psychological Association, Toronto, Canada.

Rue, V.M. (1985). Abortion in relationship context. *International Review of Natural Family Planning, 9,* 95-121.

Russo, N.F. (1986). Adolescent abortion: The epidemiological context. In G.B. Melton (Ed.), *Adolescent abortion: Psychological and legal issues* (pp. 40-73). Lincoln: University of Nebraska Press.

Rynearson, E.K. (1982). Relinquishment and its maternal complications: A preliminary study. *American Journal of Psychiatry, 139,* 338-340.

Sandven, K., & Egeland, B. (1985). *Decision-making by black adolescent mothers regarding informal adoption.* Final report Office of Adolescent Pregnancy Programs, NIH, Washington, D.C.

Scherz, F.H. (1947). Unmarried mother's conflict. *Journal of Social Casework, 28,* 57-61.

Sharrar, M.L. (1971). Attitudes of black natural parents regarding adoption. *Child Welfare, 50,* 286-289.

Shusterman, L.R. (1976). The psychological factors of the abortion experience: A critical review. *Psychology of Women Quarterly, 1,* 79-106.

Simon, H.A., & Barenfeld, M. (1969). Information processing analysis of perceptual processes in problems solving. *Psychological Review, 76,* 473-483.

Simon, N.; Senturia, A., & Rothman, D. (1967). Psychiatric illness following therapeutic abortion. *American Journal of Psychiatry, 124,* 97-103.

Smith, E.M., (1973). A follow-up study of women who request abortion. *American Journal of Orthopsychiatry, 43,* 574-585.

Smith, M. (1977). *Unwed pregnant adolescents' relationships with their parents and their decisions to keep or release their babies.* Unpublished master's thesis, Smith College Studies of Social Work, Massachusetts.

Spellacy, W.N.; Mahan, C.S., & Curz, A.C. (1978). The adolescent's first pregnancy: A controlled study. *Southern Medical Journal, 71,* 768-771.

Stack, C.B. (1974). *All our kin.* N.Y.: Harper & Row.

Stokes, J., & Greenstone, J. (1981). Helping black grandparents and older parents cope with child rearing: A group method. *Child Welfare, 60,* 691-701.

Swiger, M.E.; Breslin, R.; Pouzzner, M.N.G.; Quinlan, D., & Blum, M. (1976). Interview follow-up of abortion applicant drop-outs. *Social Psychiatry, 11,* 135-143.

Thomas, A., & Chess, S. (1980). *The dynamics of psychosocial development.* New York: Brunner/Mazel.

Torres, A.; Forrest, J.D., & Eisman, S. (1980). Telling parents: Clinic policies and adolescents use of family planning and abortion services. *Family Planning Perspectives, 12,*(6), 284-292.

Tversky, A., & Kahneman, D. (1974). Judgment under uncertainty: Heuristics and biases. *Science, 185,* 1124-1131.

Tversky, A., & Kahneman, D. (1983). Extensional versus intuitive reasoning: The conjunction fallacy in probability judgment. *Psychological Review, 90,* 293-315.

Ventura, S.J., & Hendershot, G.E. (1984). Infant health consequences of child bearing by teenage and older mothers. *Public Health Report, 99,* 136-146.

Verstaeten, D. (1980). Level of realism in adolescent future time perspective. *Human Development, 23,* 177-191.

Vincent, C.E. (1960). Unwed mothers and the adoption market: Psychological and family factors. *Marriage and Family Living, 22,* 112-118.

Vincent, C. (1961). *Unmarried mothers.* New York: Free Press of Glencoe.

Weithorn, L.A. (1982). Developmental factors and competence to make informed treatment decisions. In G.B. Melton (Ed.), *Legal reforms affecting child and youth services* (pp. 85-100). New York: Haworth.

Weithorn, L.A., & Campbell, S.B. (1982). The competency of children and adolescents to make informed treatment decisions. *Child Development, 53,* 1589-1599.

Westoff, F., & Ryder, N. (1977). *The contraceptive revolution.* Princeton: Princeton University Press.

Williams, D.G. (1982). Religion, beliefs about human life and the abortion decision. *Review of Religious Research, 24,* 40-48.

Wilson, B.F., & Myers, G.C. (1984, May). *Marital pattern variations between Catholics and Protestants.* Paper presented at Population Association of America Annual Meeting.

Winkler, R., & Van Keppel, M. (1984). Relinquishing mothers in adoption: Their long-term adjustment. *Monograph of the Institute of Family Studies* (No. 3) Melbourne, Australia.

Wolf, A.M. (1983). A personal view of black inner-city foster families. *American Journal of Orthopsychiatry, 53,* 144-151.

Worthington, E.L., Jr. (1987). Treatment of families during life transitions: Matching treatment to family response. *Family Process, 26.*

Worthington, E.L., Jr., & Buston, B.G. (1986). The marriage relationship in the transition to parenthood: A review and a model. *Journal of Family Issues, 7,* 443-473.

Worthington, E.L., Jr., & Danser, D.B. (1987). Effects of late adolescents' definition of cohabitation, religious intensity and perceived parent values on their willingness to engage in heterosexual cohabitation. *International Review of Natural Family Planning, 11.*

Young, A.; Beckman, B., & Rehr, H. (1975). Parental influence on the pregnant adolescent. *Social Work, 2,* 387-391.

Zelnik, M.; Kantner, J., & Ford, K. (1981). *Sex and pregnancy in adolescence.* Beverly Hills: Sage.

Zelnik, M., & Kantner, J.F. (1978). First pregnancies to women aged 15-19: 1976 and 1971. *Family Planning Perspectives, 10,* 11-20.

10

"DON'T TELL MY PARENTS" — PARENTS' RIGHTS REGARDING THE PROVISION OF CONTRACEPTIVES TO THEIR CHILDREN

Lynn D. Wardle, J.D. [1]
Professor of Law, J. Reuben Clark Law School
Brigham Young University

> The legal right of a parent to the custody of a child is a dwindling right which the courts will hesitate to enforce against the wishes of the child, the older he is. It starts with a right of control and ends with little more than [a right to give] advice.
> —*Lord Denning.* [2]

INTRODUCTION

The provision of contraceptive information and services to teenagers without the knowledge or permission of their parents is currently a very controversial topic. For more than a decade, the public policy of the United States, as evidenced by the expenditure of substantial amounts of public funds, has been to encourage sexually active teenagers to use contraceptives by facilitating access by all teenagers to contraceptive information, services, and products. [3] To promote the use of contraceptives by sexually active teenagers, Congress has adopted a policy of confidentiality whereby federally-funded family planning clinics are supposed to encourage parental involvement, but are required to guarantee confidentiality to teenagers who receive contraceptive services and products. [4]

This policy has provoked substantial controversy. [5] Moreover, in the past few years the establishment of "School-Based Clinics" (hereinafter "SBCs") in some public schools to facilitate access by sexually active or potentially sexually active teenagers to contraceptives and contraceptive services has generated further controversy. [6] Some people question the wisdom of allowing sexually-active or prospective sexually-active teenagers to obtain contraceptives without requiring parental notification or approval. Others dispute the effectiveness of such programs to curb teenage pregnancy. And many parents believe that the provision of such products or services to their children infringes upon their constitutionally-guaranteed rights to raise their children.

In this paper, I will analyze whether the Constitution of the United States guarantees to parents the right to be notified when third persons (such as educators, doctors, counselors, family planning clinic employees, etc.) provide contraceptive information, products or services to their minor children. I conclude that it does not, but neither does it guarantee to minors the right to not have parents notified. The battle to protect family integrity and to insure that parents are informed of the provision of contraceptives to their children probably should not be fought in the constitutional arena. Rather, it is a policy issue which should be decided by the appropriate representatives of the people, in the legislative and executive departments of federal, state and local governments.

OVERVIEW OF THE PROBLEMS OF TEEN SEXUAL ACTIVITY, TEEN PREGNANCY, AND TEEN CONTRACEPTIVE USE

Before turning to the legal analysis, it is appropriate to put the issues into a factual context to demonstrate the scope of the social problems involved. As Table One shows, approximately 40 percent of teenagers between the ages of 15-19 are "sexually active". More than one million teens become pregnant every year, giving birth to about one-half million children, and leading to about one-half million abortions on teenagers. The percentage of girls aged 15-17 having premarital sexual relations rose from 31.7% in 1971 to 45.2% in 1982. [7]

TABLE ONE
SEXUAL ACTIVITY, BIRTHS AND ABORTIONS AMONG AMERICAN TEENS [8]

Criteria	15-19	15-17	Under 15
# Women	10,000,000 +	—	—
Sexually Active	4,000,000	—	—
# Pregnant	1,000,000 + (13%)	—	30,000
# Of Births *	470,000	—	—
# Of Births O/O/W *	270,000	—	—
# Of Abortions *	449,000	—	—
Abortion Rate/100 A+B	41	42	44

As Table Two shows, 84% of all women under 18 now receive some sex education. But from 33% to 44% of these young women have never received any parental instruction about pregnancy or contraception.

TABLE TWO
Sex Education of Women Under age 18 [9]
(National Survey of Family Growth 1982)

Received instruction re: pregnancy and contraception	68%
Received instruction re: pregnancy only	16%
Received no instruction re: either	16%
Discussion with parent re: pregnancy	67%
Formal Instruction re: pregnancy	81%
Discussion with parent re: birth control	58%
Formal Instruction re: birth control	68%
Formal Instruction re: contraception before 1st coitus	57-65%
Women 15-19 who have had premarital sex	46%

Table Three demonstrates that nine out of ten contraceptive providers do not require parental notification before furnishing contraceptives to 17-year-olds, and 80% of them do not even require parental notification if the teenage recipient is fifteen years old or younger. It also reveals that nearly half of all the teenage contraceptive recipients reported that their parents did not know that they were obtaining contraceptives, including more than one third of the girls aged 15 or younger. Other studies have consistently confirmed that approximately one-half of all teens who seek birth control services do not tell their parents. [10]

TABLE THREE
PARENTAL NOTIFICATION OF TEENAGER'S USE OF ABORTION OR CONTRACEPTIVE SERVICES [11]

Facility Survey:

Percentage Of Facilities Not Requiring Parental Notification

Criteria	Abortion Providers	Contraception Providers
Age 17	70%	90%
Age 16	67%	90%
Age 15 or less	56%	80%
Waiver if Mature	7%	2%
Waiver if Adult Accompany	7%	4%
Waiver if Risk Parental Abuse	10%	3%
Waiver if Court Approval	17%	6%
Waiver if Other Circumstances	4%	3%
No Waiver	5%	2%

TABLE THREE

PARENTAL NOTIFICATION OF TEENAGER'S USE OF ABORTION OR CONTRACEPTIVE SERVICES [11]

Teen Survey (Girls under 18 using facilities):
Parental Involvement

Criteria	Abortions	15 or younger	Contraceptives	15 or younger
Parents *Not* Know	45%	25%	46%	34%
Not Sure	—	5%	5%	—
Parents Would Approve if Know	21%	12%	18%	12%
Parents Would Not Approve	23%	13%	23%	17%
Told Parents Because Clinic Required Parental Notice	2%	2%	1%	2%

Finally, the possibility that providing contraceptives to teenagers might actually lead to more, rather than fewer, teenage pregnancies has not been entirely ignored. The compelling statistical studies by Stan Weed and Joseph Olsen have demonstrated, at least, that such programs have been ineffective in reducing teenage pregnancy and abortion. [12] As Table Four illustrates, their data strongly suggests that the provision of contraceptives to teenagers is directly and powerfully associated with increases in pregnancy and abortion among teenagers.

TABLE FOUR
EFFECT OF PROVIDING FAMILY-PLANNING SERVICES TO TEENAGERS [13]

Projected vs. observed change in pregnancies, births, and abortions (per 1,000 teens)

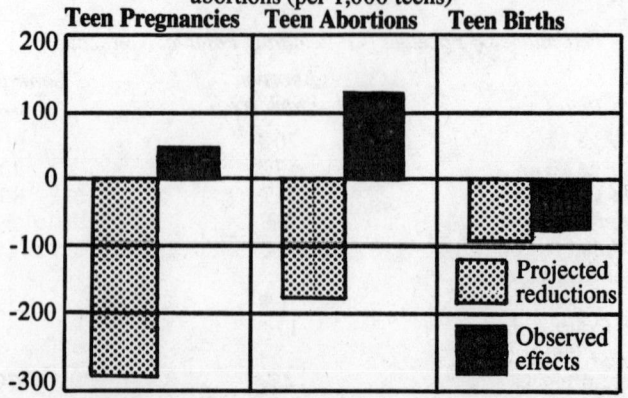

	Teen Pregnancies	Teen Abortions	Teen Births
Projected reductions	-300	-175	-75
Observed effects	+50	+125	-50

The family planning industry has grudgingly acknowledged that there may be a problem. The authors of one article in *Family Planning Perspectives* admitted that "prior exposure to a sex education course is positively and significantly associated with the initiation of sexual activity at ages 15 and 16". [14] These authors also noted: "Adolescent women who have previously taken a sex education course are somewhat more likely than those who have not to initiate sexual activity at ages 15 and 16 (though they are no more likely to do so at ages 17 and 18). [15] Even before the Weed and Olsen studies were published, the authors of the highly publicized National Research Council study, *Risking the Future*, had acknowledged that "more research is necessary". [16]

The recent evaluative evidence justifies substantial concern about the unintended consequences of the current public policy of providing contraceptives to minors without parental notice. Certainly more and immediate investigation to ascertain that the provision of contraceptive services to minors without parental notice is actually increasing teenage pregnancies is imperative.

THE CONSTITUTIONAL RIGHTS OF PARENTS AND MINORS

The topic of teenage sexual activity, pregnancy and access to contraceptive services without parental notice are of profound importance to many individuals, families and to our society as a whole. The issues are of such significance, and feelings about them are so strong, that some people believe that they must be of constitutional dimension.

There is a doctrine of constitutional law that relates to the issue of parental notice of the provision of contraceptives to minor children. It is the doctrine of "privacy". However, the privacy doctrine provides special protections for certain interests and prerogatives of both parents and minors; and on this issue, those interests appear to conflict. Moreover, while many commentators have read the privacy decisions broadly, to define large, generic "zones" of privacy, and there is occasional dicta in some opinions that invites such broad interpretation, the actual holdings of the Supreme Court, and the decisions of most of the lower courts as well, have been relatively specific and restricted. To date, the issue of parental notification has not been and should not be constitutionalized.

Parents' Rights In General

The Constitution of the United States does not explicitly mention parents' rights. Nevertheless, American courts have long recognized that parents are entitled to very broad latitude in raising their children. More than sixty years ago, in *Meyer v. Nebraska*, [17] the Supreme Court of the United States held that the authority of parents to rear their children without coercive interference from the state is one of the unwritten "liberties" protected by the due process clause of the fourteenth amendment. In 1919 the Nebraska legislature had enacted a law prohibiting any person from teaching any subject in any language other than English, or teaching any other modern language than English to students who had not passed the eighth grade. Meyer, a teacher in a school run by the Zion Evangelical Lutheran Congregation, was convicted of violating the law by teaching German (using Bible stories) to a ten-year-old boy who had not passed the eighth grade. [18] The U.S. Supreme Court reversed the conviction. The opinion of the Court did not emphasize the rights that Mr. Meyer had as a teacher or private citizen to teach German, but the rights of the parents of the children to direct the education of their children, and the protection Mr. Meyer enjoyed because he was acting for and as the agent of the parents. Justice McReynolds, writing for the Court, declared that "[w]ithout doubt" among the undefined "liberties" protected by the fourteenth amendment are the rights "to marry, to establish a home and bring up children ..." [19] Corresponding to this right of control, "it is the natural duty of the parent to give his children education suitable to their station in life". [20] The Court acknowledged that Plato and others had advocated that the state should assume the responsibility of raising children, rather than parents, but concluded: "Although such measures have been deliberately approved by men of great genius, their ideas touching the relation between individual and State were wholly different from those upon which our institutions rest..." and it could not be doubted "that any legislature could impose such restrictions upon the people of a State without doing violence to both letter and spirit of the Constitution". [21]

Two years later, in *Pierce v. Society of Sisters*, [22] the Supreme Court again vindicated parental rights when it affirmed that an Oregon law requiring parents of children between the ages of 8-16 to send their children to public school for instruction was unconstitutional. A private military academy and a religious order which operated an orphanage and private school successfully challenged the law in federal court. Justice McReynolds, writing for the Supreme Court, again emphasized the rights of parents in vindicating the position of the private schools.

> [We] think it entirely plain that the Act of 1922 unreasonably interferes with the liberty of parents and guardians to direct the

upbringing and education of children under their control...The fundamental theory of liberty upon which all governments in this Union repose excludes any general power of the State to standardize its children by forcing them to accept instruction from public teachers only. The child is not the mere creature of the State; those who nurture him and direct his destiny have the right, coupled with the high duty, to recognize and prepare him for additional obligations. [23]

The next major case was decided in 1944. In *Prince v. Massachusetts*, [24] the Court extended great rhetorical respect for parental prerogatives in childrearing, but upheld the conviction under Massachusetts child labor laws of a woman who allowed her nine-year-old niece and legal ward to join her in selling religious tracts on public sidewalks. Justice Rutlege, writing for the Court, emphasized family privacy, stating:

It is cardinal with us that the custody, care and nurture of the child reside first in the parents, whose primary function and freedom include preparation for obligations the state can neither supply nor hinder.... And it is in recognition of this that [*Meyer* and *Pierce*] have respected the private realm of family life which the state cannot enter. [25]

"But", the Court further said, "the family itself is not beyond regulation in the public interest..." *Id*. Finding that there were substantial risks of physical and other harm to children from selling religious tracts on busy public streets, the Court upheld the conviction.

In 1972 the Supreme Court reaffirmed the principle of parental freedom from state compulsion in deciding matters involving the education and religion of older adolescents in *Wisconsin v. Yoder*. [26] Three Amish parents who refused to send their fourteen- and fifteen-year-old children to school after they graduated from the eighth grade were convicted of violating Wisconsin's compulsory education law which required parents to keep children in school until the age of 16. Attendance at high school was contrary to Amish beliefs and to the Amish way of life. The Wisconsin Supreme Court reversed the convictions, holding that they violated the first amendment (freedom of religion). The U.S. Supreme Court likewise held that the convictions were invalid, emphasizing parents' rights as well as freedom of religion. Chief Justice Burger, writing for the Court, explained:

There is no doubt as to the power of a State, having a high responsibility for education of its citizens, to impose reasonable

regulations for the control and duration of basic education....
[Likewise,] the values of parental direction of the religious upbringing
and education of their children in their early and formative years
have a high place in our society...Thus, a State's interest in
universal education, however highly we rank it, is not totally
free from a balancing process when it impinges on other fundamental rights and interests such as...the traditional interest of
parents with respect to the religious upbringing of their children
so long as they, in the words of *Pierce*, "prepare [them] for additional obligations". [27]

The Court found that the effect of two additional years of schooling
would contravene the freedom of religion of both the Amish parents
and their children "by exposing Amish children to worldly influences in
terms of attitudes, goals, and values contrary to beliefs...at the crucial
adolescent stage of development..." [28] After finding that the Amish
were remarkably self-reliant, industrious, good citizens and that the
effect of one or two additional years of education would not substantially
further any legitimate state interest, the Court returned to parental
prerogatives.

[T]his case involves the fundamental interest of parents, as
contrasted with that of the State, to guide the religious future and
education of their children. The history and culture of Western
civilization reflect a strong tradition of parental concern for the
nurture and upbringing of their children. This primary role of the
parents in the upbringing of their children is now established
beyond debate as an enduring American tradition.
... To be sure, the power of the parent, even which linked to a free
exercise claim, may be subject to limitation under *Prince* if it
appears that parental decisions will jeopardize the health or safety
of the child, or have a potential for significant social burdens. But
in this case [they do not.] [29]

Likewise, in *Moore v. City of East Cleveland*, [30] the Supreme Court
held that zoning laws could not be written or applied in such a way as to
prevent children and grandchildren from residing in the home of their
mother and grandmother. The Court reversed the conviction of a
woman for violating the housing ordinance of the City of East
Cleveland. Writing for a plurality, Justice Powell reminded that

[a] host of cases...have consistently acknowledged a "private
realm of family life which the state cannot enter".... Of course,

the family is not beyond regulation.... But when the government intrudes on choices concerning family living arrangements this Court must examine carefully the importance of the governmental interests advanced and the extent to which they are served by the challenged regulations. [31]

Additionally, the Supreme Court has held that states may not deprive parents of their parental rights in judicial proceedings without observing substantial procedural protections. These include judicial review of confidential youth correctional files to determine if exculpatory information exists, [32] adherence to the "clear and convincing" standard of proof to terminate parental rights, [33] providing a hearing before terminating the rights of the father of an illegitimate child who had lived with and raised the child, [34] and substantial jurisdictional basis for exercising custody jurisdiction. [35]

The foregoing cases declared and protected the rights of parents to make certain childrearing decisions free from state restriction. However, each case involved a parent-vs.-state conflict. These cases could be read as simply establishing limits to governmental authority as readily as they can be read as establishing constitutionally the "rights" of parents generally.

Minors' Rights In General

Minors are not without rights, even though they are under the tutelage and instruction of their parents. They are, after all, "persons", even if not in the full sense of being the subject of all the legal rights and duties of competent adults. [36] The Supreme Court also has held that minors as well as adults may exercise certain substantive constitutional rights free from state restrictions. For instance, the Supreme Court has recognized the religious liberties of children against state-mandated intrusion. In *West Virginia State Board of Education v. Barnette*, [37] the Court invalidated a state statute which required all school children to salute the flag, including Jehovah's Witnesses who believe as a matter of church doctrine that flag saluting is idolatrous and violates one of the Ten Commandments. The Court concluded: "We think the action of the local authorities in compelling the flag salute and pledge transcends constitutional limitations on their power and invades the sphere of intellect and spirit which is the purpose of the First Amendment of our Constitution to reserve from all official control." [38]

Likewise, in *Tinker v. Des Moines School District*, [39] the Court found that the First Amendment rights of three students had been violated when they were summarily suspended for wearing black armbands to school to protest the Vietnam War. The Court declared: "Students in school as well as out of school are 'persons' under our Constitution. They are possessed of fundamental rights which the State must respect.... In the absence of a specific showing of constitutionally valid reasons to regulate their speech, students are entitled to freedom of expression of their views." [40]

In a series of cases decided during the past two decades the Supreme Court has clarified that minors enjoy the right to be free from invidious discrimination on the basis of illegitimate birth. [41] And *Brown v. Board of Education*, [42] establishes that black children's rights to be free of racial discrimination (especially in educational opportunities) are no different than those of black adults.

Children also are entitled to essentially the same procedural protections against state deprivations of their life, liberty and property as adults. The Court has held that "there is nothing about juvenile or minority status ... that justifies a ... failure to provide the most basic protective safeguards inherent in procedural due process". [43] Thus, in 1967 the Supreme Court held in *In re Gault*, [44] that minors may not be deprived basic procedural protections in juvenile court proceedings. In *Goss v. Lopez*, [45] the Court held that students facing suspension from a state-run school are entitled to certain procedural protections such as prior notice and an opportunity for a hearing. [46]

However, minors do not always enjoy the same procedural or substantive rights as adults. The state's *parens patriae* power and interest in the welfare of minors limit the extent of minors' rights. For instance, in *Ingraham v. Wright*, [47] the Court held that common law restraints upon the infliction of "moderate correction" by means of corporal punishment in school are sufficient, and more formal procedural protections such as notice and prior hearing are not necessary. In *New Jersey v. T.C.O.*, [48] the Court held that the probable cause requirements of the Fourth Amendment do not require exclusion of evidence taken by a school official from a student's purse under less rigorous standards in juvenile court delinquency proceedings. [49] Likewise, in *Prince v. Massachusetts*, the Court also held that "(t)he state's authority over children's activities is broader than over like actions of adults". [50] While recognizing the right of a child to practice her religion, the Court justified the application of a child labor law to prevent a minor adherent of the Jehovah's Witnesses from engaging in public proselyting activities (selling religious tracts), noting:

> It is true children have rights, in common with older people, in the primary use of highways. But even in such use streets afford

dangers for them not affecting adults...What may be wholly permissible for adults therefore may not be so for children, either with or without their parents' presence.

...We think that with reference to the public proclaiming of religion, upon the street and in other similar public places, the power of the state to control the conduct of children reaches beyond the scope of its authority over adults, as is true in the case of other freedoms, and the rightful boundary of its power has not been crossed in this case. [51]

And in *Bethel School District No. 403 v. Fraser*, [52] the Supreme Court held that minors do not enjoy the same latitude of expression under the First Amendment as do adults. [53]

In *Ginsburg* the Supreme Court suggested that if the state is acting as the agent of the parents, it may have more authority to regulate and restrict the actions of minors than it would otherwise have. [54] However, in *New Jersey v. T.C.O.*, [55] the Court emphasized that this notion of "parental delegation" may not be strained to justify all state conduct regarding minors. [56]

Like the parents' rights cases, these minors' rights cases involved "state-vs.-individual" conflicts. And while the state acting as a corporate "parent" may exercise more supervision over the activities of minors, it is clear that there are constitutional limits on state authority. Thus, like the parents' rights cases, the minors' rights cases may tell us more about the limits of state authority than the rights of minors vis-a-vis their parents.

Parents' Rights vs. Minors' Rights in General

Very few cases have come before the Supreme Court of the United States involving direct, actual conflicts between the rights of parents, as parents, to raise their children, and children, as individuals, to be free of parental control. [57] But as a general rule the Court has recognized parental authority even when it conflicts with the opposing desires of their children. For instance, in *Ginsberg v. New York*, [58] the Supreme Court upheld the conviction of a magazine seller for violating a state statute prohibiting the sale of "girlie" magazines to minors under seventeen years of age, even though the magazines were not technically obscene, and adults could buy them. Obviously the minor purchasers wanted to be able to buy the magazines without parental permission; presumably the parents were opposed. In this case the Court suggested that the state could ban the sale because the state was, in a sense, acting as the agent of parents.

> [C]onstitutional interpretation has consistently recognized that parents' claims to authority in their households to direct the rearing of their children is basic in the structure of our society.... The legislature could properly conclude that parents and others... who have this primary responsibility for children's well-being are entitled to the support of laws designed to aid the discharge of that responsibility. [59]

The Court also acknowledged that adequate parental supervision cannot always be provided and that the state also has an independent interest in the well-being of its youth. [60]

Four years later, when this issue was specifically raised in *Wisconsin v. Yoder*, the Court brushed it aside as inconsequential. Justice Douglas, in a separate opinion, dissenting in part, argued that if the Amish youngsters wanted to go to school and their parents were keeping them home against their will, the parents could be convicted of violating the compulsory school attendance law. While the majority did not think it necessary to decide that question, the Court expressed unwillingness to endorse the idea that children could be freed from the restraints of parental direction in matters of education or religion. [61]

In 1979 the Supreme Court directly considered and unequivocally decided a case involving a clear conflict parents' and minors' choices when it reversed a federal district court which had ruled that parents could not commit their children to state mental health facilities for treatment without an adversarial hearing before a formal tribunal. In *Parham v. J.R.*, [62] the Court held that ordinary commitment procedures in which a doctor must approve the parental decision to commit the child are constitutionally sufficient. The Court underscored the general priority of parents' rights when it acknowledged that some minors may object to being committed by their parents for mental treatment, and further admitted that such commitment could detrimentally stigmatize the children. Yet the Court affirmed parental rights in this clear and unavoidable clash of potential interests. Chief Justice Burger's opinion for the Court explained why.

> Our jurisprudence historically has reflected Western Civilization concepts of the family as a unit with broad parental authority over minor children. Our cases have consistently followed that course... Surely, this includes a "high duty" to recognize symptoms of illness and seek and follow medical advice. The law's concept of the family rests on a presumption that parents possess what a child lacks in maturity, experience, and capacity for judgment required

for making life's difficult decisions. More important, historically it has recognized that natural bonds of affection lead parents to act in the best interests of their children.

... That some parents "may at times be acting against the interests of their child" ... creates a basis for caution, but is hardly a reason to discard wholesale those pages of human experience that teach that parents generally do act in the child's best interests. The statist notion that governmental power should supersede parental authority in *all* cases because *some* parents abuse and neglect children is repugnant to American tradition. [63]

Addressing the argument that the earlier Supreme Court parents' rights decisions had involved state-parent conflicts only, and not parent-child conflicts, the Parham Court brushed aside that distinction, declaring:

We cannot assume that the result in Meyer v. Nebraska, supra and Pierce v. Society of Sisters, supra would have been any different if the children there had announced a preference to learn only English or a preference to go to a public rather than a church school. The fact that a child may balk at hospitalization or complain about a parental refusal to provide cosmetic surgery does not diminish the parents' authority to decide what is best for the child. [64]

Justice Stewart's concurring opinion summarized the basic rule succinctly: "For centuries it has been a canon of the common law that parents speak for their minor children. So deeply imbedded in our traditions is this principle of law that the Constitution itself may compel a State to respect it." [65]

Parental authority over minor children is not absolute, however. It is clear that children enjoy some substantive rights or interests which they may assert even against their parents and over parental objection. The categorical right or interest which children may assert against their parents is the right to be free from substantial and immediate risk to their lives or health. In *Prince v. Massachusetts,* while giving a ringing endorsement of parental rights, the Court upheld the conviction of a woman for violation of child labor laws in allowing her nine-year-old niece to sell unpopular religious tracts on public street corners. The Court explained: "It is in the interest of youth itself, and of the whole community, that children be both safeguarded from abuses and given opportunities for growth into free and independent well-developed men and citizens." [66] "Parents may be free to become martyrs themselves.

But it does not follow they are free, in identical circumstances, to make martyrs of their children before they have reached the age of full and legal discretion when they can make that choice for themselves." [67] In *Wisconsin v. Yoder* the Court declared: "To be sure, the power of the parent, even when linked to a free exercise claim, may be subject to limitation under *Prince* if it appears that parental decisions will jeopardize the health or safety of the child, or have a potential for significant social burdens." [68] In *Parham v. J.R.* the Supreme Court noted that past decisions had frequently "recognized that a state is not without constitutional control over parental discretion in dealing with children when their physical or mental health is jeopardized..." [69]

Thus, children do have a right to life and health which may be asserted by or for them against and over the opposition of their parents. But this right is a relatively "protective" right only, comparable to the procedural rights of minors discussed above. These cases do not recognize minors' general "liberties". They do not confer on minors a general right to choose (i.e., exercise judgment, preference, or free will) to behave in some way contrary to parental supervision. Rather, they protect the minors' potential to become mature enough and competent enough to exercise judgment, choice, preference and free will. Presumably the state could act to protect the life or health of a minor even if she *and* her parents objected.

RIGHTS OF SEXUAL PRIVACY
The Abortion Privacy Rights of Minors

Despite general deference to parental authority in parent-child disputes, the Supreme Court has in recent years recognized the constitutional right of minors to make at least one specific, profoundly important decision over parental objection and against parental opposition. That is the abortion decision.

In *Roe v. Wade*, [70] the Supreme Court held that the Constitution shelters an unwritten but fundamental right of privacy which is broad enough to encompass a woman's decision to have an abortion. [71]

Applying strict scrutiny, the Court invalidated a Texas regulation that prohibited all abortions except those necessary to save the life of the mother, indicating that all non-medically-essential regulations of abortion, at least before viability, are unconstitutional. [72] In a concluding footnote, the Court specifically reserved for another day the issue of whether parental consent requirements were permissible. [73]

Three years later, in *Planned Parenthood v. Danforth*,[74] the Supreme Court answered that question when it struck down a Missouri statute that required unmarried minors to obtain parental consent before submitting to an abortion. The majority, per Justice Blackmun, reasoned that

> the State does not have the constitutional authority to give a third party an absolute, and possibly arbitrary, veto over the decision of the physician and his patient to terminate the patient's pregnancy, regardless of the reason for withholding consent.
>
> Constitutional rights do not mature and come into being magically only when one attains the state-defined age of majority. Minors, as well as adults, are protected by the Constitution and possess constitutional rights ....[75]

Recognizing that "the State has somewhat broader authority to regulate the activities of children than adults," the Court rejected the asserted state justification for its "parental veto" statute because it did not believe the statute would "strengthen the family unit" by giving parents "absolute power to overrule" a decision made by a daughter and her doctor to have an abortion. "Neither is it likely that such veto power will enhance parental authority or control where the minor and the nonconsenting parent are so fundamentally in conflict and the very existence of the pregnancy has fractured the family structure."[76] Four justices refused to join in this opinion, and two others (Justices Stewart and Powell) who subscribed to the majority opinion added their concurring opinion emphasizing that the primary defect of the state "lies in its imposition of an absolute limitation on the minor's right to obtain an abortion ..."[77]

Three years later, in *Bellotti v. Baird*,[78] the Supreme Court affirmed the judgment of a federal district court holding as unconstitutional a Massachusetts statute requiring a minor to seek parental consent for abortion and providing that a state court could override a parent's refusal to consent to the abortion, and authorize the abortion, if it found the abortion to be in the best interest of the minor. If the minor were mature, she would still be obligated to convince the state court that the abortion was in her best interests. While eight members of the Court agreed that the statute was invalid under the *Danforth* doctrine, a majority could not agree why.

Justice Powell, writing for a plurality of four justices, carefully reviewed the Supreme Court precedents regarding minor's rights, and identified "three reasons justifying the conclusion that the constitutional rights of children cannot be equated with those of adults: the peculiar vulnerability of children; their inability to make critical decisions in an informed, mature manner; "and the importance of the parental role in child rearing." [79] The extension to minors of procedural protections, including special proceedings in juvenile courts, recognized the unique vulnerability of minors. [80]

> [T]he Court has held that the states validly may limit the freedom of children to choose for themselves in the making of important, affirmative choices with potentially serious consequences. These rulings have been grounded in the recognition that, during the formative years of childhood and adolescence, minors often lack the experience, perspective, and judgment to recognize and avoid choices that could be detrimental to them. [81]

The deeply-rooted tradition of respect for parental authority was also underscored.

> While we do not pretend any special wisdom on this subject, we cannot ignore that central to many of these theories, and deeply rooted in our Nation's history and tradition, is the belief that the parental role implies a substantial measure of authority over one's children. Indeed, "constitutional interpretation has consistently recognized that the parents' claim to authority in their own household to direct the rearing of their children is basic in the structure of our society...."

Properly understood, then, the tradition of parental authority is not inconsistent with our tradition of individual liberty; rather, the former is one of the basic presuppositions of the latter. Legal restrictions on minors, especially those supportive of the parental role, may be important to the child's chances for the full growth and maturity that make eventual participation in a free society meaningful and rewarding. [82]

But the uniqueness of the abortion dilemma necessitated that an exception be made to the general rule of parental control.

> The pregnant minor's options are much different from those facing a minor in other situations, such as deciding to marry. A minor not permitted to marry before the age of majority is required simply to postpone her decision. She and her intended spouse may preserve the opportunity for later marriage should they continue to desire it. A pregnant adolescent, however, cannot

preserve for long the possibility of aborting, which effectively expires in a matter of weeks from the onset of pregnancy. [83]

Thus, writing for four justices, Justice Powell concluded that the Massachusetts statute was defective because it required all minors seeking abortions to first try to obtain parental consent.

We conclude, therefore, that under state regulation such as that undertaken by Massachusetts, every minor must have the opportunity — if she so desires — to go directly to a court without first consulting or notifying her parents. If she satisfies the court that she is mature and well enough informed to make intelligently the abortion decision on her own, the court must authorize her to act without parental consultation or consent. If she fails to satisfy the court that she is competent to make this decision independently, she must be permitted to show that an abortion nevertheless would be in her best interests. If the court is persuaded that it is, the court must authorize the abortion. If, however, the court is not persuaded by the minor that she is mature or that the abortion would be in her best interests, it may decline to sanction the operation. [84]

Justice Stevens, however, writing for four other members of the Court, disagreed with this last point. The Stevens plurality reasoned that the Massachusetts statute was defective because it gave the state court judge "an absolute veto over the minor's decision based on his judgment of her best interest". [85] They would not go so far as to say that parental notification could not be required.

In 1981 the Supreme Court upheld a Utah statute requiring doctors to notify "if possible" the parents of minors seeking abortions. The Court repeated and endowed Justice Powell's analysis in *Bellotti (II)* of the general constitutional validity of "parental notice and consent" requirements, and underscored that the case at bar did not involve a "mature and emancipated" minor, [86] and emphasized that mere notice, giving parents an opportunity to counsel their daughters and consult with their physicians, did not constitute a "veto" of the minor's abortion decision. [87] The Court held that the fact that the requirement of notice to parents may inhibit some minors from seeking abortions is not a valid basis to void the statute..." [88] Justice Stevens added a concurring opinion going further than the five-Justice majority and specifically endorsing the requirement of parental notice even for "mature" minors.

Most recently, in *Planned Parenthood Association v. Ashcroft*, [89] the

Supreme Court upheld a Missouri statute requiring parental or judicial consent for abortions performed on minors. For a plurality of two, Justice Powell wrote:

> [T]he legal standards with respect to parental consent requirements are not in dispute ... A State's interest in protecting immature minors will sustain a requirement of a consent substitute, either parental or judicial. It is clear, however, that "the State must provide an alternative procedure whereby a pregnant minor may demonstrate that she is sufficiently mature to make the abortion decision herself or that, despite her immaturity, an abortion would be in her best interests". [90]

Applying the general principle that "courts should construe a statute to avoid a danger of unconstitutionality", *id.* at 493, the Court held that the Missouri statute conformed to the constitutional standard. Three other Justices agreed that this provision was valid simply "because it imposes no undue burden on any right that a minor may have to undergo an abortion". [91]

In 1988 the Court decided another case dealing with the abortion rights of minors, *Hartigan v. Zbaraz.* [92] That case involved an Illinois statute which required a 24-hour delay between the actual or constructive notification of a parent of a minor's decision to have an abortion and the performance of the abortion. The purpose was to provide a minimum opportunity for actual parent-child consultation (which the parent could waive). In *City of Akron v. Akron Center for Reproductive Health, Inc.*, [93] the Supreme Court held that such "waiting period" requirements are unconstitutional as applied to adult women seeking abortions. In *H.L. v. Matheson,* however, it upheld a requirement of parental notification on the express understanding that it would facilitate parental consultation, which obviously may cause some delay. By a two-to-one vote, a Seventh Circuit appellate court affirmed a district court judgment holding the Illinois law unconstitutional under *City of Akron.* The U.S. Supreme Court affirmed by an equally divided (four-to-four) vote, issuing a short *per curiam* opinion simply announcing the judgment.

Obviously, the cases dealing with minors' rights to have abortions are very controversial and subject to widely varied interpretation. But it appears that at least three tentative conclusions may be drawn:

1. The minor's right to abortion privacy, which she may exercise *against* parental opposition, is substantially related to the uniqueness of her existing pregnancy and the relatively brief period of

time in which an abortion may safely be performed.

2. All of the abortion cases involving minors have involved challenges to state laws restricting the pregnant minor. While some of the laws have assumed the form of mere regulations to support parental authority (such as *H.L.*), most of them have been viewed by a majority of the Court in a different light — i.e., as thinly disguised direct attempts by the *state* to prevent a vulnerable group of individuals from exercising their valuable right to choose to have an abortion. The importance of the "state delegation" language in *Danforth* cannot be overstated: the Court deemed the statute to be an attempt by the state to veto minor's abortion by delegating that unlawful authority to parents.

3. Except in the case of "mature" minors, [94] or when it would be harmful to the minor, parental *participation* in the abortion decision of a minor is constitutionally permissible. The Court has strongly endorsed the principle of parental consultation to the extent it does not constitute parental veto. [95]

The Contraceptive Privacy Rights of Minors

In several cases the Supreme Court has recognized a right of adults to use and have access to contraceptives. In 1965 the Supreme Court invalidated a Connecticut law prohibiting the use of contraceptives by married adults. In *Griswold v. Connecticut*, [96] Justice Douglas, writing for the Court, explained that the law infringed upon a right of marital privacy which was found to emanate from the "penumbras" of certain specific guarantees of the Bill of Rights. The focus of the majority opinion was the need to protect the most "enduring", "sacred", and "noble" [97] institution of society, the "intimate relation of husband and wife", [98] from "destructive" and "repulsive" state intrusion. Four justices (including two dissenters) refused to endorse Justice Douglas' "penumbra" privacy analysis. [99]

Seven years later, in *Eisenstadt v. Baird*, [100] a majority of four Justices invalidated a Massachusetts law that made it a felony for anyone other than a registered doctor or pharmacist to dispense contraceptives and allowed doctors and pharmacists only to distribute contraceptives to married persons, except when necessary to prevent the spread of disease. A doctor who was convicted of violating the law when he gave a contraceptive to a young unmarried woman following an address at a college successfully challenged the law. Without stating that single persons have any fundamental right to engage in nonmarital sexual activity or use contraceptives, the Court held that the Massachusetts law violated the equal protection clause of the Fourteenth

Amendment. Writing for the four-member majority, Justice Brennan rejected the state's claim that the law deterred premarital or elicit sex and furthered public health interests of the state as unfounded and unproven.

[W]hatever the right of the individual to access to contraceptives may be, the rights must be the same for the unmarried and the married alike ... If the right of privacy means anything, it is the right of the individual, married or single, to be free of unwarranted governmental intrusion into matters so fundamentally affecting a person as the decision whether to bear or beget a child. [101]

The Supreme Court has only once discussed a statute restricting the use of or access to contraceptives by minors. In 1977, the Supreme Court invalidated a New York statute making it a crime for anyone but a pharmacist to distribute contraceptives to persons 16 or under, for anyone to advertise or display contraceptives or for anyone to distribute contraceptives to minors under age 16. In *Carey v. Population Services International*, [102] Justice Brennan, writing for a majority, found the prohibition against advertising and the restriction that only pharmacists distribute contraceptives to be unconstitutional under the plain principles of *Griswold* and *Eisenstadt*. [103] But he could not muster a majority to support his analysis of the provision forbidding the sale of contraceptives to minors under 16. Writing for only four members of the Court, Justice Brennan reasoned that "the right of privacy in connection with decisions relating to procreation extends to minors as well as adults". [104] Since the state may not restrict access to contraceptives by adults, he reasoned, *"a fortiori"* it may not restrict minors' access to contraceptives. [105] Justice Brennan rejected the idea that a state could adopt a policy imposing unwanted teenage pregnancy as a punishment for fornication. [106] And since the state conceded that "there is no evidence that teenage extramarital sexual activity increases in proportion to the availability of contraceptives", he rejected the argument "that juvenile sexual activity will be deterred by making contraceptives more difficult to obtain". [107]

However, a majority of the Supreme Court refused to endorse Justice Brennan's analysis. Justices White and Stevens separately agreed that the prohibition against distribution of contraceptives was unconstitutional, emphasizing that the state had failed to prove that the prohibition against distribution of contraceptives to minors deterred any minors from engaging in sexual relations. [108] But they explicitly rejected as "frivolous" the idea that minors had a constitutional right "to put contraceptives to their intended use". [109] Justice Stevens also emphatically distinguished the abortion cases. [110] Justice Powell likewise separately agreed that the law restricting sale of contraceptives to minors under 16 was unconstitutional. He, like Justice Stevens, found the law to be defective because it would prevent married minors from buying contraceptives from anyone but a pharmacist and because it would even prevent parents from distributing contraceptives to their own children. [111] But Justice Powell strongly endorsed other state regulations including parental consultation requirements. [112] Chief Justice Burger and Justice Rehnquist dissented, the latter filing an opinion emphatically endorsing the propriety of state legislation designed to "discourage unmarried minors under sixteen from having promiscuous sexual intercourse with one another". [113]

In the decade since *Carey* was decided, the Supreme Court has not considered further the question of minor's rights regarding the use of contraceptives. The multiple opinions in *Carey* have spawned a kaleidoscope of theories and approaches, but no clear constitutional doctrine. [114]

Lower Courts and Commentators: Legislative Policy Not Constitutional Doctrine

While a majority of the Supreme Court has never held that the Constitution protects the right of minors to obtain or use contraceptives without parental notification, several commentators have expressed that opinion. [115] And more than a dozen federal courts have invalidated statutes protecting parental involvement in the provision of contraceptives to minors. From this one might draw the conclusion that the lower courts have been convinced that mandatory parental notice of the provision of contraceptives to minors is unconstitutional. But that is not so. The rulings of most of the lower courts have been much narrower. Few have even addressed this constitutional issue, and some of the courts that have reached the privacy issue have had before them parental *consent* requirements, not parental *notice* requirements. When the courts have considered the constitutionality of parental notice, more of them have indicated that it is constitutionally permissible than have concluded that it is not.

The most prominent parental notice cases involved the so-called "squeal rules", promulgated in January 1983, by the Department of Health and Human Services. Those regulations required parental notification when prescription contraceptives were provided to minors by federally-funded family planning clinics. [116] Within two weeks, the regulations had been enjoined by two different federal district courts for essentially the same reasons, and by the end of the year, both injunctions had been affirmed by two separate federal courts of appeals. [117] All four courts held that the regulations were invalid because they were inconsistent with the Congressional language and intent of Title X. [118] The courts found that the language of the statute and the legislative history indicated that, while Congress wanted minors to be encouraged to consult with their parents concerning contraceptives, it had rejected amendments to require parental notification. [119] And in both cases the courts found that the primary effect of the proposed "squeal rules" would be to deter adolescents from using family planning clinics and significantly increase the incidence of teenage pregnancies, abortions and births in America, thus frustrating the intent of the legislation. [120] These factual findings rested upon the failure of the DHHS to factually support its position and on "substantial statistical and medical documentation" [121] provided by Planned Parenthood and state family planning agencies. [122] Since the Department of Health and Human Service was only authorized to enact regulations consistent with the legislation enacted by Congress, the "squeal rule" regulations were invalid. None of the four courts analyzed whether the parental notice requirement would violate any constitutional privacy rights of minors; the sole basis for the opinion and judgment in each case was statutory.

The decision of the four federal courts in the so-called "squeal rule" cases is typical of the decision of most of the federal courts that have addressed this issue in that it was predicated solely on statutory grounds. The issue of parental notification of, or participation in, the provision of contraceptives to their minor children has been addressed by the lower federal courts in thirteen different reported decisions since 1975 in eight separate cases. [123] In eight of the thirteen decisions, the federal courts based their judgments exclusively on statutory grounds. [124] In two other cases, the courts based their decisions on both statutory and constitutional grounds. [125] In three reported decisions, the lower federal courts addressed based their judgments solely upon the constitutional issue. [126]

Twice lower federal courts have invalidated on unconstitutional grounds state statutes or regulations protecting parental participation when contraceptives are provided to their minor children. [127] Both cases were decided by federal district courts sitting in Utah. But in both cases, the court had already found the state statutes to be invalid because they were preempted by federal statutes or regulations. And one of these cases, in dicta, supports the position that parental notification does not violate the constitutional privacy rights of minors.

In *T-H- v. Jones*, [128] three-judge federal district court held that a Utah statute requiring parental consent before distributing contraceptives to minors was preempted by federal law when applied to federal positions, and violative of the privacy rights of minors. But the court also suggested that parental notification would not violate the right of privacy of minors. [129] Moreover, one of the members of the three-judge panel strenuously dissented from the conclusion of the majority that even parental consent was unconstitutional. And the Supreme Court subsequently affirmed the decision of the three-judge court solely on statutory grounds, explicitly declining to endorse the lower court's holding that parental consent prior to the provision of contraceptives to minors is unconstitutional. [130]

Four lower court decisions indicate that mandatory parental notification would not violate the constitutional rights of a minor seeking contraceptives. In addition to the dicta of the three-judge district court in *T-H- v. Jones* distinguishing parental notification from parental consent, the federal district court in Michigan twice, separately, upheld the claims of and granted relief to parents who urged that the practice of state and state-funded family planning clinics of distributing contraceptives to minors without parental notification or consent violated the fundamental constitutional rights of parents. And on appeal the Sixth Circuit held that the Constitution does not mandate either parental notification or teenager confidentiality.

In March 1977, the district court in *Doe v. Irwin* [131] carefully and thoroughly considered the claim to privacy rights of minors as well as the interests of the state and the rights of parents, and concluded that the failure of state family planning agencies to notify parents before providing contraceptives to minors unconstitutionally infringed on parents' rights. The case involved a suit by parents whose minor, unemancipated daughter was given prescriptive and nonprescriptive contraceptives, without their knowledge or consent, by a state-funded and county-administered family planning clinic. The plaintiffs sought a declaration judgment that the clinic policy of distributing contraceptives to minors without parental notification or consent violated the constitutional rights of the parents, as well as an injunction against enforcement of the policy. District Judge Fox concluded that "parents have a constitutionally protected right to participate in the very important decisions of their minor, unemancipated children as to whether or not to initiate sexual activity or to undertake the substantial medical risks of certain contraceptives". [132] The district court considered the center's practice of not notifying parents to be tantamount to "totally exclud(ing) the parents of the child from ... a momentous decision." [133] Accordingly, it granted the relief sought by the parents.

After the Supreme Court decided *Carey*, the U.S. Court of Appeals for the Sixth Circuit vacated and remanded the case for reconsideration in light of *Carey*. [134] A few months later, district court rendered another opinion reaffirming the earlier order and opinion and reemphasizing that the constitutional rights of privacy of parents prohibited state actors from providing contraceptives to minors without parental notification. [135]

In 1980, however, a unanimous panel of the court of appeals for the Sixth Circuit reversed in a concise and decisive opinion. [136] The court acknowledged that parents have a constitutional right to raise their children, including the right to inculcate moral values, and noted that while the Supreme Court had not indicated whether parental notification regarding the provision of contraceptives was constitutionally permissible, at least one other district court, in addition to the court below, had concluded that it was allowable. [137] But the key to the disposition of the case at bar was that the state did not require or prohibit anything. In *Meyer, Pierce, Yoder* and *Prince* the state actually required or prohibited certain conduct. But Michigan had imposed no compulsory requirements or prohibitions. Thus, parents in Michigan "remain(ed) free to exercise their traditional care and custody and control over their own emancipated children". [138] The court noted that

> [T]here was no evidence the parents are excluded from any decisions or supplanted by the activities of the [state-funded family planning clinic]. The uncontradicted evidence was that personnel of the Center encouraged minors to involve their parents in their decisions concerning sexual activity and birth control, and even offered to help bring the parents into discussions of these subjects. [139]

The appellate court emphasized that the question was not whether a state could require or prohibit parental notification, since the state in this case did neither. "Rather it is *whether the Constitution requires such a condition*... [I]t is clearly a matter for the state to determine whether such a requirement is necessary or desirable ... There is no basis for a federal court to impose conditions in the absence of an overriding constitutional requirement." [140]

Perhaps the most notable aspect of the Sixth Circuit opinion in *Doe v. Irwin* is the subsequent history of the opinion. Since it deals directly with an issue that has been very controversial, and a subject that has been written upon so extensively and litigated rather frequently in the seven years since the opinion was rendered, it is surprising to find that the opinion has *never been cited* by another federal court. Obviously, both sides of the controversy — those who argue for a constitutional right of minors to get contraceptives without parental participation, as well as those who argue for a constitutional right of parents to be notified of the provision of contraceptives to their minor children — are dissatisfied with this Sixth Circuit opinion which says quite plainly that this is not a controversy for which the Constitution mandates any particular resolution. Sixth Circuit emphasized that the role of the courts is not to make the policy for the people under the guise of declaring constitutional rights.

CONSTITUTIONAL ANALYSIS

The Sixth Circuit was right. The United States Constitution does protect certain fundamental rights. Some of those rights are not spelled out in detail in the text of the Constitution or its amendments. There is a constitutional right of privacy that does protect certain specific acts, decisions, and relationships — even though the term "privacy" and many of those acts or relationships are not described specifically anywhere in the Constitution. The problem with the constitutional right of privacy, however, is that it means all things to all people. When courts are asked to interpret the right of privacy to strike down state policy, there is a great risk of overreaching — reading into the Constitution one's own policy preference in the name of identifying and defending unwritten constitutional rights. That is the primary error that was made by the Supreme Court in the abortion cases. [141] The error is the error of overreaching — going beyond the legitimate judicial function of interpreting the Constitution and getting into the legislative function of establishing public policy on controversial contemporary issues.

Regrettably, some people who genuinely are upset by the excesses and extremes of some of the privacy cases have been drawn into a constitutional tug-of-war regarding what the policy of the law should be. They see the contest to be how the courts should interpret the Constitution to set public policy on this and other controversial contemporary issues. However, they fail to appreciate that there is a more important, preceding question. That is whether the courts should be setting policy at all. Ironically, by overlooking the question of who (what branch of government) should set the policy, and focusing on what they believe the policy should be — and arguing for that policy to be implemented as a constitutional right — they have legitimated the very mistake of the courts they have found to be so objectionable.

The solution to bad judicial legislation is not more judicial legislation. The remedy is not to substitute a conservative agenda of judicial policy making for the current liberal agenda. In the first place, it won't work. The people who will decide what the "judicial policy" should be — lawyers and judges as a group — hold much more liberal opinions regarding public and private morals than do the American people as a whole. More importantly, however, the constitutional system of checks and balances allocates the responsibility for establishing public policy on such issues as contraceptives and minors to the other branches — the politically accountable branches. The courts are not authorized by the Constitution to create new constitutional rights or abolish old constitutional liberties. The limited but powerful role of the court to ascertain constitutional rights not expressly identified in the constitution should not be misappropriated to achieve a short-cut advantage in settling politic questions like this.

In the face of mounting empirical evidence, not to mention common sense and experience, the overriding wisdom and value of parental notification before contraceptives are provided to minors is becoming increasingly apparent, and the tragic absurdity of not notifying parents is becoming undeniably clear. The policy choice is clear. It must be recognized for exactly what it is — a policy choice, not a constitutional issue. That distinction should be emphasized, and the diverting claims of unwritten judge-made constitutional policy determinations must be repudiated. Then the pros-and-cons, the facts-and-fictions of parental participation can be squarely addressed. The real policy issue is: What should the policy of a state, an agency, a program be regarding parental notification? What does the evidence show? What does the public support? Those issues should be addressed cleanly and clearly as policy questions, and not buried in or disguised as constitutional doctrines.

CONCLUSION

The issue of parental notification of the provision of contraceptive information and services to teenagers is of profound importance to our country, its future, its families and its teenagers. But the Constitution does not provide the answers to all important questions. Just because the issue is of compelling importance does not necessarily mean that the Constitution compels any particular resolution of the controversy. The fact that some resolutions would violate the Constitution (e.g., if contraceptives were provided by the state only to black teenagers but not to white teenagers, or if they were made available only to Protestants but not Catholics) does not mean that the Constitution mandates a specific resolution to the policy issue. Parental notification is neither mandated nor prohibited by the Constitution.

It would be unwise and unwarranted to interpret the Constitution as either mandating or prohibiting parental notification. Until the evidence of the effects (both intended and unintended) of the current policy of not requiring parental notification of the provision of contraceptives to minors is seen, it would be foolish and premature to set public policy in constitutional cement. Moreover, until a real constitutional consensus for a public policy, for or against parental notification, is established, i.e., until the constitutional text, tradition or precedents clearly demonstrate a genuine and permanent constitutional consensus on the issue, it would be irresponsible for courts to interpret the Constitution to dictate a particular public policy on the matter.

While this analysis will disappoint some, it should encourage all. It means that claims of the family-planning industry that the Constitution prohibits parental notification can and should be exposed as fraudulent. It also means that persons who believe that parents should be notified must put their beliefs into action, and work to make local, state and national programs concerning teenage pregnancy reflect the policy of parental notice. For ultimately, the Constitution does provide, indirectly, the solution to this controversy, but it is not an easy solution. It is self-government, participatory democracy. And that solution puts the burden on the people to make the law be what they believe it should be, by persuading their elected representatives to require parental notification, or by replacing them with persons who will do so. The constitutional solution is political responsibility, not judicial irresponsibility.

END NOTES — CHAPTER 10

1. Professor of Law, Brigham Young University. Parts of this paper were presented at a National Meeting on School-Based Health Clinics in Washington, D.C., March 24, 1987, sponsored by the National Conference of Catholic Bishops, United States Catholic Conference, and Catholic Charities USA.
2. *Hewer v. Bryant*, [1969] 3 All E.R. 578, 572.
3. "By 1980, nearly three times as many black teenagers and almost 17 times as many white teenagers received family-planning services from organized programs as in 1969." Olsen & Weed, Effects of Family-Planning Programs for Teenagers on Adolescent Birth and Pregnancy Rates, 20 *Fam. Perspective* 153, 154 (1986). "In 1971 the annual national expenditure (federal, state and local money) for [family-planning] clinics was $11 million, and 300,000 of their clients were teen-agers. By 1981, the numbers were $442 million and 1.5 million clients." Weed, Curbing Births, Not Pregnancies, *The Wall Street J.*, Oct. 14, 1986, at 36, col. 4 (Both reprinted by Family Research Council, 1986).
4. *See infra*, Part IV C (discussing "squeal rule" cases).
5. See generally, Children Having Children, *Time Magazine*, 1988, at 78; Bennett, Sex and the Education of Our Children, *America*, Feb. 14, 1987 at 120; Bennett, Why Johnny Can't Abstain, *Nat'l Rev.* July 3, 1987, at 36; Goldberg, Values and Key Factor in Teen-Age Pregnancy, *Ed. Week*, Jan 21, 1987, at 5; Bowen, Teenage Sexual Activity: Postponement As a Viable Alternative *J. Fam. & Cult.*, Autumn 1986, at 1; Dawson, The Effects of Sex Education on Adolescent Behavior, 18 *Fam. Planning Perspectives* 162 (1986); Politz, et al, Sex Education and Family Planning Services for Adolescents in Foster Care, 19 *Fam. Planning Perspectives* 18 (1987); Silver, et al, Banners to Contraceptive Services, 19 *Fam. Planning Perspectives* 94 (1987).
6. *See generally* Kenney, School-Based Clinics: A National Report,

18 *Fam. Planning Perspectives* 44 (1986); Zabin et al, Evaluation of Pregnancy Prevention Program for Urban Teenagers, *18 Fam. Planning Perspectives* 119 (1986); Sex and Schools, *Time Magazine*, Nov. 24, 1986, at 54; Glasow, School-Based Clinics Promote Abortion in *Window on the Future* 121 (D. Andrusko, ed., 1987); see also papers presented at National Meeting on School-Based Health Clinics, Mar. 23-24, 1987, sponsored by the U.S. Catholic Conference Department of Education et al.; Report on School-Based Clinics, Arch diocese of Boston (undated); Glasow, Abortion and the Rise of School-Based Clinics, *Nat'l Rt. to Life News*, Sept. 11, 1986, at 1; id, (Part II), *Nat'l Rt. to Life News*, Sept. 25, 1986, at 6; id (Part III), *Nat'l Rt. to Life News*, Oct. 9, 1986, at 1; Glasow, School-Based Clinic Supporters Remain Confident Despite Mounting Opposition, *Nat'l Rt. to Life News*, Oct. 24, 1986, at 1.

7. S. Hoffereth et al., Premarital Sexual Activity Among Teenage Women Over The Past Three Decades, 19 *Fam. Planning Perspectives* 46 (1987).

8. I National Academy of Sciences, *Risking The Future: Adolescent Sexuality, Pregnancy And Child Bearing*. 51-52, 65 (C. Hayes, ed., 1987).

9. Dawson, The Effects Of Sex Education On Adolescent Behavior, 18 *Fam. Planning Perspectives*, 162, 169 (1986).

10. *See also* Rosen, Benson & Stack, Help or Hinderance: Parental Impact on Pregnant Teenagers' Resolution Decision, 31 *Fam. Rev.* 271 (1982) (43% Secret abortions). R. Mnookin, *In the Interests of Children*, 158 ("over one-half" get secret abortions).

11. A. Torrez, J. Forrest & Eisman, Telling Parents: Clinic Policies And Adolescents' Use Of Family Planning And Abortion Services, 12 *Fam. Planning Perspectives* 284 (1980).

12. *See* Olsen & Weed, *supra* note ; Weed & Olsen, Effects of Family-Planning Programs on Teenage Pregnancy — Replication and Extension, 20 *Fam. Perspective*, 173 (1986); Weed, *supra* note at 36 col. 4 (Research Reprinted by Family Research Council, 1986).

13. Weed, Curbing Births, Not Pregnancies, *The Wall Street J.*, Oct. 14, 1986, at p.36, col. 4 (Research Reprint by Family Research Council, 1986).

14. W. Marsiglio & F. Mott, The Impact Of Sex Education On Sexual Activity, Contraceptive Use And Premarital Pregnancy Among American Teenagers, 18 *Fam. Planning Perspectives*, 151, 158 (1986).

15. *Id.*

16. Critics of family planning programs suggest that the availability of contraceptives services has caused higher rates of sexual activity, unintended pregnancy, abortion, and births to unmarried teenagers.

Indeed, the period of significant increase in teenage sexual activity during the 1970's was paralleled by significant growth of the availability of contraceptive services for both adult women and adolescents. However, whether there is a causal connection or whether both trends were responses to the same changing social context and mores is unclear. Using data for California, Kasun (1982) concluded that increased spending on contraceptive services led to increased levels of sexual activity and, as a result, increased pregnancies, abortions, and births outside marriage. However, as Hofferth (vol. II: Ch. 9) points out, associations do not show causation, and Kasun (1982) did not control for initial differences between California and the rest of the United States ....

In contrast, Moore and Caldwell (1977) found no association between the availability of family planning services and the probability that an adolescent girl would initiate sexual intercourse, net of other factors (age, socioeconomic status, family structure, urban/rural residence, religiousness, birth cohort). However, as Hoffereth (vol. II: Ch. 9) concludes, "more research is needed on this issue". I National Research Council, *Risking The Future: Adolescent Sexuality, Pregnancy And Child Bearing* 165,(1987)at 165. *See also* Dawson, The Effect of Sex Education On Adolescent Behavior, 18 *Fam. Planning Perspectives* 162, 169 (1986) (could find correlation between sex education and sexual activity of teens only for 14-year-olds in limited circumstances).

17. 262 U.S. 390 (1923).
18. Today the fact that he taught from the Bible would be more disturbing to some.
19. *Id.* at 399.
20. *Id.* at 400.
21. *Id.* at 402.
22. 268 U.S. 510 (1925).
23. *Id.* at 534-35.
24. 321 U.S. 158 (1944).
25. *Id.* at 166.
26. 406 U.S. 205 (1972).
27. *Id.* at 213, 214.
28. *Id.* at 218.
29. *Id.* at 223, 234.
30. 431 U.S. 494 (1977).
31. *Id.* at 499.
32. Sylvania v. Ritchie, 1075 Ct. 989 (1987).
33. Santosky v. Kramer, 455 U.S. 745 (1982).

34. Caban v. Mohammed, 441 U.S. 380 (1978); *see also,* Quillion v. Walcott, 434 U.S. 246 (1978).
35. May v. Anderson, 345 U.S. 528 (1953).
36. Justice Douglas suggested that the term "person" includes all individuals who "are humans, live and have their being," Levy v. Louisiana, 391 U.S. 68, 70 (1968) (speaking of illegitimate children). Even Justice Blackmun, who rejected the personhood of the unborn generally, Roe v. Wade 410 U.S. 113, 158, 162 (1972) has emphasized that minors who do not enjoy full legal rights are persons and may claim certain fundamental constitutional rights. Planned Parenthood v. Danforth, 428 U.S. 52, 74 (1976). *See infra* notes 74-77 and accompanying text.
37. 319 U.S. 624 (1943).
38. *Id.* at 642.
39. 393 U.S. 503 (1969).
40. *Id.* at 511.
41. See, e.g., Levy v. Louisiana, 390 U.S. 68 (1968); Weber v. Aetna Casualty Insurance Co., 406 U.S. 164 (1972); Trimble v. Gordon, 430 U.S. 762 (1977); Mill& v. Habluetzel, 456 U.S. 91 (1982); Pickett v. Brown, 462 U.S. 1 (1983).
42. 347 U.S. 483 (1954).
43. Hafen, Privacy and Protection: The Risks of Children's Rights, 63, *A.B.A.J.* 1383, 85 (1977).
44. 387 U.S. 1 (1967).
45. 419 U.S. 565 (1975).
46. *See also* Breed v. Jones, 421 U.S. 512 (1975) (minor enjoys "double jeopardy" clause protection); In re Winship, 397 U.S. 358 (1970) (proof beyond a reasonable doubt); Gallegos v. Colorado, 370 U.S. 1209 (1962) (protection against coerced confessions).
47. 430 U.S. 651 (1977).
48. 469 U.S. 325 (1985).
49. *See generally* Hafen, Children's Liberation and the New Egalitarianism: Some Reservations About Abandoning Youth to Their "Rights", 1976 *B.Y.U.L.Rev.* 605, 33-37, 44-48
50. Prince v. Massachusetts, 321 U.S. at 168.
51. *Id.* at 169-70.
52. 106 S. Ct. 3159 (1986).
53. *Id.* at 3164-65 (upholding suspension of high school student for speech filled with offensive sexual innuendos nominating student body office candidate). *See also* Board of Education v. Pico, 457 U.S. 853

(1982) ("all members of the court, otherwise sharply divided, acknowledged that the school board has the authority to remove [from a school library] books that are vulgar." 106 S. Ct at 3165).

54. 390 U.S. at 639.

55. 469 U.S. 325 (1985).

56. In *T.C.O.* a 14-year-old girl had been found by a teacher smoking in a restroom at school. She was taken to the Principal's office where she denied using cigarettes at all. Over her objections, her purse was taken and searched by an Assistant Vice Principal. In addition to cigarettes, the purse contained a quantity of marijuana, a pipe, plastic bags, many one dollar bills, a list of students who owed her money, and two incriminating letters. This evidence was admitted in a juvenile court delinquency proceeding against her. The New Jersey Supreme Court reversed her adjudication as delinquent because the search of her purse violated the Fourth Amendment. The U.S. Supreme Court reversed and held that the probable cause requirements of the Fourth Amendment do not apply as strictly to children at school as in other contexts. But the Court flatly rejected the school's sweeping argument that the Fourth Amendment did not apply at all because the school officials were merely acting as agents of parents.

[P]ublic school officials do not merely exercise authority voluntarily conferred on them by individual parents; rather, they act in furtherance of publicly mandated educational and disciplinary policies. In carrying out searches and other disciplinary functions pursuant to such policies, school officials act as representatives of the State, not merely as surrogates for the parents, and they cannot claim the parent's immunity from the strictures of the Fourth Amendment.

Id. at 336-37.

57. The potential for conflict between parents and children has been present in most parents' rights cases. That is, the children in *Meyer* may not have wanted to learn German; the children in *Pierce* may not have wanted to attend public schools, etc. The fact that for half a century the Court never addressed the potential conflict underscores the pervasiveness of the assumption of parental prerogatives. *See infra* note 64 and accompanying text.

58 310 U.S. 629 (1968).

59. *Id.* at 639.

60. *Id.* at 640.

61. Our holding in no way determines the proper resolution of possible competing interests of parents, children, and the State in an

appropriate state court proceeding in which the power of the State is asserted on the theory that Amish parents are preventing their minor children from attending high school despite their expressed desires to the contrary. Recognition of the claim of the State in such a proceeding would, of course, call into question traditional concepts of parental control over the religious upbringing and education of their minor children recognized in this Court's past decisions. It is clear that such an intrusion by a State into family decisions in the area of religious training would give rise to grave questions of religious freedom comparable to those raised here and those presented in *Pierce v. Society of Sisters* ...

Id. at 231.
62. 442 U.S. 584 (1979).
63. *Id.* at 602.
64. *Id.* at 603-04.
65. 442 U.S. 621
66. 321 U.S. at 165.
67. *Id.* at 170.
68. 406 U.S. at 223, 234. (Quere—Might not some people view parental refusal to allow a child to engage in sexual activity with condoms or other contraceptives while a teenager to "have a potential for significant social burdens"?)
69. 442 U.S. at 603.
70. 410 U.S. 113 (1973).
71. *Id.* at 153.
72. 410 U.S. at 163.
73. *Id.* at 165 n. 67.
74. 428 U.S. 52 (1976).
75. *Id.* at 74.
76. *Id.* at 75.
77. *Id.* at 90.
78. 43 U.S. 662 (1970).
79. *Id.* at 634.
80. *Id.*
81. *Id.* at 635.
82. *Id.* at 638-39.
83. *Id.* at 642.
84. *Id.* at 647-48.
85. *Id.* at 654.
86. *Id.* at 405.
87. *Id.* at 411.
88. *Id.* at 413.

89. 462 U.S. 476 (1983).
90. *Id.* at 490-91.
91. *Id.* at 505 (O'Connor, J., concurring in part joined by White, J., and Rehnquist, J.).
92. Sup. Crt. No. 85-673 S.Ct. (Dec. 14, 1987). The decisions below are Zbaraz v. Hartigan, 584 F. Supp. 1452 (N.O.Ill. 1984), *aff'd.* 763 F.2d 1532 (7th Cir. 1986).
93. 462 U.S. 416 (1983).
94. Interestingly, even Justice Powell, who championed the "mature minor" notion, admitted he was not sure how the term should be defined. *See Bellotti*, 443 U.S. at 643 n. 23 (Powell, J., plurality opinion).
95. *H.L.*, 450 U.S. at 410, 412.
96. 381 U.S. 479 (1975).
97. *Id.* at 486.
98. *Id.* at 482.
99. *Id.* at 499 (Harlan, J., concurring in judgment); *id.* at 502 (White J., concurring in judgment); *id.* at 507 (Black, J., dissenting); *id.* at 527 (Stewart, J., dissenting).
100. 405 U.S. 438 (1972).
101. *Id.* at 453.
102. 431 U.S. 684 (1977).
103. *Id.* at 689-91.
104. *Id.* at 693.
105. *Id.* at 694 (Brennan, J.).
106. *Id.* at 695 (Brennan, J.).
107. *Id.* (Brennan, J.).
108. *Id.* at 703 (White, J., concurring); *id.* at 715 (Stevens, J., concurring).
109. *Id.* at 703 (White, J., concurring); *id.* at 713 (Stevens, J., concurring).
110. *Id.* at 703 (Stevens, J., concurring).
111. *Id.* at 707-08 (Powell, J., concurring); *id.* at 713 (Stevens, J., concurring).
112. *Id.* at 709 (Powell, J., concurring).
113. *Id.* at 719 (Rehnquist, J., dissenting).
114. I believe that six points will ultimately prove to be essential to the constitutional doctrine of minors' privacy rights to use contraceptives.
 1. Regardless of whether minors have a constitutional right to engage in sexual activity, some of them are going to do so, and the Court will assess the reasonableness of any restriction as against this group of teens.

2. The Court is very concerned about the injuries (unintended pregnancies) these teens will incur if denied access to contraceptives. Justice Stevens compared denying teens the use of contraceptives to denying them the use of motorcycle helmets. "One need not posit a constitutional right to ride a motorcycle to characterize such a restriction as irrational and perverse." Carey, 431 U.S. at 715 (Stevens, J.).

3. Development of empirical data strongly supporting the relationship between increased teenage pregnancy and access of teens to contraceptives is imperative for opponents of teenage contraceptive use. Without such data it will be *impossible* to distinguish *Carey*. So critical was such quantitative proof that it was mentioned in three separate opinions. *Id.* at 695 (Brennan, J.); *id.* at 703 (White, J., concurring); *id.* at 715 (Stevens, J., concurring).

4. The test for determining whether a law restricting the sexual privacy rights of teenagers is constitutional "is apparently less rigorous than the 'compelling state interest' test applied to restrictions on the privacy rights of adults. Even Justice Brennan so acknowledged. *Id.* at 693 n. 15 (Brennan, J.)

5. There may be greater constitutional protection for the privacy of a pregnant teen seeking an abortion than for an unpregnant teen seeking to use contraceptives. "The options available to the already pregnant minor are fundamentally different from those available to its nonpregnant minors." *Id.* at 713 (Stevens, J., concurring).

6. Nevertheless, it is unlikely that any absolute parental *consent* requirement restricting distribution of contraceptives to minors will be upheld. That is the implication of *Carey*, where the judgment was 7-2, even though there was no majority opinion on the subject. Some *Bellotti*-type alternative to parental *consent* probably will be necessary for the same practical reasons Justices Powell and Stevens alluded to in *Bellotti.*

115. *See generally*; Note, The Squeal Rule: Statutory and Constitutional Implications—Burdening the minor's Right of Privacy, 1984, *Duke J.* 1325 (1984); Utah Legislative Survey, 1984, *Utah L. Rev.* 145, 196-202; note, Minors' Right of Privacy: Access to Contraceptives Without Parental Notification, *J. Juv. L* 238 (1983); Compare Developments in the Law: The Constitution and the Family, 93, *Harv. L. Rev.* 1156, 1372-77 (1980); note, Parental Consent and Privacy Rights of Minors: The Contraception Controversy, 88 *Harv. L. Rev.* 1001 (1975).

116. 42 C.F.R. 59.5 (1983).

117. New York v. Schweiker 557 F. Supp. 354 (S.D.N.Y. 1983), *aff'd sub nom* New York v. Heckler, 719 F.2d 1191 (2d Cir. 1983); Planned Parenthood Federation of America v. Schweiker, 559 F. Supp. 658 (D.D.C. 1983), *aff'd sub nom.* Planned Parenthood Ass'n v. Heckler, 712 F.2d 650 (D.C. Cir. 1983).

118. 42 U.S.C. 300 et seq (1981).

119. *New York,* 557 F. Supp. 360, 719 F.2d at 1196; *Planned Parenthood,* 559 F. Supp. at 669, 712 F.2d at 655-64.

120. *New York,* 557 F. Supp. at 359, 719 F.2d at 1194; *Planned Parenthood,* 559 F. Supp. at 666.

121. *New York,* 557 F. Supp. at 359.

122. Planned Parenthood, 559 F. Supp. at 663, 64 n. 11; *id.* at 666; Note, The Squeal Rule: Statutory Resolution of Constitutional Implications—Burdening the Minor's Right of Privacy, 1984, *Duke L.J.* 1325, 33 n. 50; *See also* Note, Minors' Right of Privacy: Access to Contraceptives Without Parental Notification, 7 *J. Juvenile L.* 238 (1983).

123. The issue has also arisen in some state courts. For instance, in *Doe v. Planned Parenthood Association, 29 Utah 2nd 356, 510 P.2d 75, app. dism'd for want of juris. and cert. denied,* 414 U.S. 805 (1973) (rejecting claim of teenager and her class that government-funded planning clinic must provide contraceptives to minors without parental notice or consent). The same statutes were involved in federal litigation later. See *infra.* note 125.

124. In addition to the four "squeal rule" cases described *supra,* notes 116 through 123, *see:* Doe v. Picket, 480. Sup. 1218. (S.D.W.VA. 1979) (holding West Virginia Department of Health policy of denying contraceptive services to minors who do not have parental *consent* violative of and preempted by Title X [family planning], Title IV-A [A.F.D.C.], Title XIX [Medicaid], Title XX [family planning]); Planned Parenthood Association v. Dandoy, 635 F.Sup. 184 (D. Utah 1986) (holding Utah law requiring prior written consent of minor's parent or guardian before contraceptive services are provided to unmarried minors is violative of and preempted by Title XIX [Medicaid]), *Aff'd,* 810 F.2d 984 (10 cir. 1987) (Utah parental consent requirement violates and is preempted by Title XIX [Medicaid]); Jane Doe's 1 through 4 v. Utah Department of Health, 776 F.2d 253 (10 Cir. 1985) (affirming injunction against enforcement of Utah parental consent requirement is violative of Title X [public health service family planning]).

125. T-H- v. Jones, 425 F. Supp. 873 (D. Utah 1975) (holding Utah

regulations requiring parental consent for the provision of contraceptives to minors violative of and preempted by federal law — Title IV-A [AFDC] and Title XIX [Medicaid], as well as unconstitutionally infringing on the privacy of minors), *aff'd on statutory grounds only*, 425 U.S. 986 (1976); Planned Parenthood Association v. Matheson, 582 F. Supp. 1001 (D. Utah 1983) (holding Utah law requiring parental notification before provision of contraceptives to minors inconsistent with and preempted by Title IV-A [AFDC], Title X [public health family planning], Title XIX [Medicaid] and also violative of minors' rights of privacy).

126. Doe v. Irwin, 428 F. Sup. 1198 (W.D. Mich. 1977) (holding that the distribution under color of state law of contraceptive devices to minors without parental knowledge or consent violates the constitutional rights of parents), *vacated and remanded for reconsideration*, 559 F.2d 1219 (6th Cir. 1979), *judgment reentered and confirmed*, 441 F. Supp. 1247 (W.D. Mich. 1977) (again concluding that the provision of contraceptives to minors without notification or consent of parents violates the constitutional rights of parents), *rev'd* 615 F.2d 1162 (6th Cir. 1980) (holding that the voluntary provision to willing minors of contraceptives without parental notification does not violate any constitutional rights), *cert. denied*, 449 U.S. 829 (1980).

127. *T-H- v. Jones, supra.* note 125; Planned Parenthood Association v. Matheson, *supra.* note 125.

128. 425 F. Sup. 873 (D. Utah 1975).

129. "[W]e hold that the state may not enforce the choice of parents that conflict with a minor's constitutional right of free access to birth control information and services. This is not to say, of course, that the state may not require notification of parents or guardians before minors receive such services." *Id.* at 882. It may have been improper for the three-judge district court in *T-H- v. Jones* to reach the constitutional issue. Previously the same statute had been attacked by the same class in a state court, and the statute had been upheld against claims of privacy by the state's Supreme Court. Even if the privacy right was not expressly raised in that case, the doctrine of claim preclusion would prevent the parties in the first case (and those in privity with them) from "splitting" his or their cause of action and challenging the same statute on another theory a little later.

130. *T-H- v. Jones*, 425 U.S. 986 (1976).
131. 428 F. Supp. 1198 (W.D. Mich. 1977).
132. 428 F. Supp. at 1209-10.
133. 428 F. Supp. at 1210; *id.* at 1211, 12, 14.

134. *Doe v. Irwin*, 559 F.2d 1219 (6th Cir. 1977).
135. *Doe v. Irwin*, 441 F. Supp. 1247 (W.D. Mich. 1977).
136. *Doe v. Irwin*, 615 F.2d 1162 (6th Cir.) *cert. denied* 449 U.S. 829 (1980).
137. 615 F.2d at 1167, 68.
138. *Id.* at 1168.
139. *Id.* at 1168 n.2.
140. *Id.* at 1169 (emphasis added).
141. *See generally*, L. Wardle & M. Wood, *A Lawyer Looks At Abortion* (1982).

11

THE BENEFITS OF LEGISLATION REQUIRING PARENTAL INVOLVEMENT PRIOR TO ADOLESCENT ABORTION

Everett L. Worthington, Jr., Ph.D.
Associate Professor of Psychology
Virginia Commonwealth University

D.B. Larson, M.D., M.S.P.H.
M.W. Brubaker, J.D.
M.W. Colecchi, B.S.
J.T. Berry, M.S.
D. Morrow, M.S.

INTRODUCTION

Throughout the United States, a number of states have enacted or are considering legislation that requires that the parents (or one parent) of a pregnant minor be notified prior to performance of an abortion on the adolescent. Some states have statutes that require parental or judicial consent for the abortion. Where the requirement is one of parental consent, the United States Supreme Court has held (*Bellotti v. Baird*, 1979) that if the state chooses to require parental consent, it must provide some means by which a mature minor, or a minor whose best interest would be served by an abortion, may avoid the parental consent requirement. The Court has specifically upheld a confidential judicial-bypass procedure as an adequate alternative to the parental consent requirement in *Planned Parenthood v. Ashcroft* (1983).

Where the issue is parental notification, however, the Court has never held that any alternative to the parental notice requirement is necessary. The Court upheld a Utah notice statute that had no bypass mechanism, but the scope of that decision was narrow and did not answer the question as to the definition of a "mature minor" or what constitutes being in the "best interest" of minors (*H.L. v. Matheson*, 1981). The Court is reviewing in the present term (with a decision probably rendered by the time of publication) the decision of the Seventh Circuit Court of Appeals invalidating the 24-hour waiting period in the Illinois parental notice law (*Zbaraz v. Hartigan*, 1986). The lower federal courts have been generally reluctant to support parental involvement statutes, whether they contain notice or consent requirements. The recent decision in *Hodgson v. Minnesota* (1986) is a relevant illustration. In *Hodgson*, Federal District Court Judge Donald Alsop invalidated the Minnesota parental notice law, even though it had a judicial-bypass provision. Judge Alsop heard five weeks of testimony from judges, lawyers, counselors, physicians, and abortion clinic operators before he concluded that the "[d]efendants offered the court no persuasive testimony upon which to base a finding that ... [the] law enhances parent-child communications, or improves family relations generally". This decision clearly lays down a gauntlet for all states to consider, even though the scope of the decision is currently limited to Minnesota.

Recently, some psychologists have argued that legally mandating parental or judicial involvement prior to abortion decisions by early, middle, and late adolescent girls (a) has unintended negative effects for some girls (Interdivisional Committee on Adolescent Abortion, 1987; Melton, 1987), (b) at best is costly and purposeless (Melton, 1987), and (c) is based on assumptions that are unsupported by extant research (Interdivisional Committee on Adolescent Abortion, 1987; Lewis, 1987; Maracek, 1987; Melton, 1987).

Legislation mandating parental or judicial involvement prior to abortion decisions by adolescents rests on three assumptions about the psychological aspects of abortion. First, minors have been assumed to be vulnerable to harmful sequelae of abortion. Second, minors have been presumed to make less reasoned decisions than adults, even with medical consultation. Third, more minors are thought to benefit from parental consultation than are harmed by it. The validity of each assumption has been challenged by the Interdivisional Committee on Adolescent Abortion (1987) of the American Psychological Association.

Against this backdrop, this chapter summarizes evidence on adolescent abortion. Much of this evidence supports the position that parental involvement legislation is beneficial for the adolescent, her parents, her family life, her physician and (perhaps) even for society. We realize this may be a minority position within the American Psychological Association, but we think it to be a reasonable alternative nonetheless. We offer this paper in the spirit of stimulating reasonable debate on this important social issue.

PRIMARY ORIENTING ASSUMPTION

Perhaps the fundamental disagreement undergirding the issue of mandated parental involvement in adolescent pregnancy decision making is between individual liberty and communal responsibility. The issue is, of course, not that simple. Tension is inevitably created by attempts to reconcile the two political ideologies. Opponents of parental involvement legislation (e.g. Interdivisional Committee on Adolescent Abortion, 1987; Lewis, 1987; Maracek, 1987; Melton, 1987; Melton & Russo, 1987) tend to focus almost exclusively on the individual adolescent. Other people or social units are considered to be ancillary, superfluous, or downright harmful to the adolescent's presumed rights. Research evidence is typically adduced to bear on this *a priori* political position. Although research is generally treated fairly, the underlying assumption that individual liberty is the penultimate relevant value shapes the choice of research examined and results in a limited examination of the issue—the case *against* parental involvement.

In this paper, we take a different assumption as the foundation for examining adolescent pregnancy. We affirm an adolescent's involvement in decisions about her pregnancy and assume that other social units, such as parents, have a responsibility and thus a right to contribute to those decisions. With adolescent pregnancy considered in a social and familial context, "data" in addition to those considered by the Interdivisional Committee become relevant for evaluation. As a consequence, it will be argued that not only will most pregnant adolescents benefit from parental involvement in decisions regarding abortion versus bearing to term, but also parents and the family as a unit will benefit.

In providing a case *for* parental involvement, we hope to enrich the literature in this area by providing a counterpoint against which to evaluate the previously mentioned reviews.

BENEFICIAL FOR THE ADOLESCENT

Helps the Adolescent Make Decisions

Adolescent's capability of reasonable decision making — the conflict. Several people have been found by legislators and by the courts to have rights and responsibilities associated with adolescent pregnancy. For example, grandparents of a teen's baby — even the parents of the putative father — may be required to support the child based on laws passed recently in Hawaii and Wisconsin. In addition, the courts have ruled that the baby's father has rights in adoption (see *Stanley v. State of Illinois* and *Caban v. Mohammed*).

Opponents of parental notification legislation usually argue that the adolescent alone should be allowed to make her own decisions about whether to remain pregnant or abort. Leaving aside all arguments about whether the fetus is human or not and thus also has rights, and leaving aside questions about maternal and paternal grandparents' rights (Donovan, 1986) and even about the father's rights (Shostak, McLouth, & Seng, 1984), let us consider the ability of the adolescent to make responsible decisions about either aborting or bearing her child to term.

One mistake that it is possible to make is to treat all adolescents as if they were equally capable and responsible at making wise, reasoned decisions in a time of crisis. There is undoubtedly a range of capability (Hatcher, 1976). Opponents of parental notification legislation claim that essentially all adolescents are mature enough to make a responsible decision about aborting or not aborting. In fact, the American Psychological Association's Brief in *Thornburgh v. American College of Obstetricians and Gynecologists* claims "that there is no empirical basis for concluding that minors fourteen and older are less capable of making informed decisions than adults" (quoted in Interdivisional Committee on Adolescent Abortion, 1987, p. 77). These conclusions rest largely on research evaluated by Lewis (1987). Contrary to the above quoted conclusion in APA's Brief, Lewis's (1987) review suggests that decision making differs substantially across adolescence and between adolescence and adulthood. She suggests that decision making *performance* differs across adolescence even though decision making *competence* might not.

Proponents of legislation mandating parental involvement are equally guilty of over-generalization. They have claimed that few (if any) adolescents are capable of making decisions regarding abortion without the aid of their parents. Debate is typically characterized by polarization instead of compromise. One reason that the sides talk at cross purposes is because they use the word "capability" differently.

Piagetian conception of "capability" of reasoned decision making. Piaget and Inhelder (1969) have described the mental capabilities of children and how their capabilities change as they age (see Keating, 1980, for a recent review). Most pre-teens generally are capable of thought involving concrete operations. Concrete operations involve thinking about specific objects and specific situations. Thinking is governed primarily by what is sensed in the child's immediate environment. When an adolescent uses concrete operational thinking, she will have difficulty anticipating the future and examining the logical consequences of her decisions. Her thinking will generally be egocentric, meaning that she usually fails to consider options from perspectives of others in making her decisions (Elkind, 1967).

At about the age of 11 or 12, the young adolescent's capability of formal operational thought emerges. Formal operations involve thinking about objects and situations symbolically. Logic can be applied to understanding the likelihood of future consequences of events.

"Capability" of reasoned decisions in emotionally charged, real-life circumstances. Once a person becomes capable of formal operational thought, he or she does not forever abandon concrete operational thought. Fully mature adults, in their forties or fifties, still engage in some concrete operational thought (Keating, 1980). Although able to foresee some of the logical consequences of their actions, even fully mature adults do not always consider the future consequences of an act, or they may consider the consequences inadequately. They are ruled by immediate circumstances in surprisingly many decisions (see Janis & Mann, 1977, for extensive evidence). Keating (1980) and Siegler and Richards (1982) have shown that neither the majority of adolescents nor of adults actually use formal operations consistently.

Emotionality can interfere with logic. Janis and Mann (1977) clearly show that emotionally "hot" decisions are different than those that are emotionally "cool". Thus, adolescents (and adults) who are capable of logical decision making in laboratory tests are not necessarily capable of making logical decisions in real-life crises. The evidence usually used to support the belief that adolescents are "capable" of making reasoned decisions concerning abortion has been (a) collected at times of low or no emotional arousal and (b) framed in ways that elicit logical (formal operational) responses from participants.

The main question, then, is not whether early, middle, or late adolescents are capable of formal operational thought in a Piagetian sense, but rather how frequently (relative to adults) do they engage in formal operational thought during emotionally charged real-life dilemmas involving the necessity of rapid decision making? That question, unfortunately, has not been researched.

Evidence concerning differences in actual decision making by adolescents and adults. There is substantial evidence that adolescents differ across the adolescent years and differ from adults in the ways they actually make decisions (as opposed to a lack of differentiation in Piagetian capabilities for logical decision making).

1. Younger adolescents consult different people for advice than do older adolescents and adults (Ashton, 1979; Clary, 1982; Lewis, 1980; Rosen, 1980; Torres, Forrest, & Eisman, 1980). The relative influence of parents and peers changes with age and topic area (Larsen, 1972).
2. Adolescents and adults have differed in their abilities to view situations from the perspective of others. For example, 52 two-parent families with an adolescent between 13 and 16 took Rest's (1979) Defining Issues Test concerning moral decision making three times — once as they would complete it themselves and once each as if they were the other two members in the family (Whitbeck & Mullis, 1987). Adults were better able to take the perspective of others than were adolescents.
3. Adolescents at varying ages between 15 and adulthood consider different factors in their pregnancy decisions (Hatcher, 1976) and in their consideration about their potential for child rearing (Leibowitz, Eisen, & Chow, 1984; Lewis, 1980; Musick, Handler, & Waddill, 1984).
4. In decision making instances, adolescents have been found to consider future solutions and goals less often than adults (Rowe, 1984; Verstraeten, 1980).
5. Adolescents have differed from adults in their consideration of future consequences in some hypothetical dilemmas. For example, Lewis (1981) found that adolescents' consideration of the consequences of cosmetic surgery increased with age. Eisen, Zellman, Leibowitz, Chow, & Evans (1983) concluded that many teens did not have the ability to reason abstractly or foresee future consequences in many sexual decisions. This is not a universal finding (see Lewis, 1987, for a review).
6. Adolescents delay decision making more than adults (Bracken & Kasl, 1975; Russo, 1986).

"Good" decision making. The foregoing differences in decision making across adolescence and between adolescents and adults suggest that adolescents and adults may differ in the quality of their decision making. It is difficult to obtain agreement among researchers on what "good" decision making is. The theory of Janis and Mann (1977) is probably the most widely accepted theory of decision making. It suggests that effective decision making processes are more important than decisional outcomes in determining "good" decision making. To that end, good decision making (a) seeks multiple perspectives, (b) understands multiple perspectives, (c) considers potential costs and

benefits about all reasonable alternatives (not just the first alternatives that are considered), (d) identifies future solutions and goals, (e) considers consequences or outcomes, and (f) does not result in long delays or procrastination in making decisions. Furthermore, good decision making is not prematurely foreclosed (through "satisficing" or hasty, impulsive decision making). By the criteria (a through f) set forth by Janis and Mann (1977), the above six points of evidence (1 through 6) support the belief that older adolescents and adults engage in "better" decision making than do younger adolescents. Evidence for differences between adults and late adolescents is more equivocal.

Parental involvement helps adolescents make "better" decisions. Thus, based on the foregoing reasoning and findings, we conclude that legislation requiring parental involvement with adolescents helps the adolescent, especially the early adolescent, make better decisions about how to resolve her pregnancy. First, the adolescent is required to take at least 24 hours to consider the decision to abort, rather than respond immediately to the often demand-laden situation of finding she is pregnant while at a clinic that does abortions. Cobliner (1974) suggests that pregnant adolescents are particularly vulnerable to immediate situational cues in making pregnancy resolution decisions. Such responsiveness to immediate cues might eliminate reasoned decision making.

Second, notifying parents involves them in the decision making. Most parents are more experienced decision makers than their teenage daughter (see points 1 through 6 above). Even though they will likely experience the girl's pregnancy as stressful, and thus consider their own wishes and fears (in addition to their daughter's), they will have had more experience in making decisions under emotional strain and will presumably be more likely to carefully consider a variety of options than will the adolescent.

Third, they will supply other points of view for the adolescent to consider in her decision, which will broaden the adolescent's understanding of the ramifications of her decision.

Fourth, parents will be available to correct any misapprehensions that their daughter might have and to challenge erroneous beliefs (Maracek, 1987). One especially important erroneous belief that would be corrected is that parents will reject the adolescent because of her pregnancy. In fact, parents usually react less negatively than adolescents anticipate (Clary, 1982; Furstenberg, 1976; Maracek, 1987).

Opponents of legislation requiring parental notification have voiced concern that the parent will intervene and either decide the fate of the pregnancy for the adolescent or pressure the adolescent to decide as *they* want her to. Undoubtedly that can occur. However, opponents usually fail to mention that whomever the adolescent tells about her pregnancy — parents, siblings, the baby's father or her girl friends (Rosen, 1980) — will almost invariably have a point of view which they will communicate to the girl, and the girl will inevitably feel pressure from the important people in her environment. In fact, the girl will feel some pressure to consider parents' views whether or not she consults them (Lewis, 1980). Yet, the girl often thinks the parents' views will be less accepting than they actually are (Furstenberg, 1976). Even counselors, who usually try to avoid influencing the outcome of the adolescent's decision, will often be perceived as exerting pressure. For instance, Maracek (1987) suggested that "the counselor's efforts to explore difficulties with the client's choice and to suggest other alternatives may be experienced by the client as pressure to do things the counselor's way" (p. 91).

Most parents will *not* automatically intervene and make the girl's decision for her. This happens in a small minority of instances, and when it does, it can cause negative reactions to abortion such as guilt, post-decisional regret and psychological problems (Adler & Dolcini, 1986; Barglow et al., 1967; Bracken, Hachamovitch, & Grossman, 1974) and to childbirth (Adler & Dolcini, 1986). Usually, parents are the most able to understand the capabilities of their daughter and should be the best qualified to determine her decision making ability (Baptiste, 1986; Cotroneo & Krasner, 1977; Rue, 1985). Further, they will be most likely to stick with her after the decision.

Although little research has assessed other friends or extended family, one study did examine the adolescents' male partners. Milling (1975) interviewed over four hundred male partners at a clinic that performed abortions. About two-thirds of the relationships failed within months of the abortion. Counselors in one or two visits, teachers unprepared for such conflict-ridden decisions, and adolescent friends will generally be less able to discern the adolescent's maturity accurately due to restrictions in the time, their own skills, or their immaturity, respectively.

In summary, most adolescents facing pregnancy-related decisions can be assisted in these emotional decisions by adults. Furthermore, under most circumstances, the parents are the most qualified to help because they know the adolescent best and because they will share with their daughter the consequences of her decision.

The Girl Gains Support for Her Ordeal

Most teenage girls, when they become pregnant, feel guilty, ashamed, and anxious. They are usually afraid to tell their parents, fearing that their parents will become angry. They are usually correct. If parents are informed that their child is pregnant, most (but not all) Caucasian parents initially become angry (Musick, Handler, & Waddill, 1984; Osofsky & Osofsky, 1978), which often provokes an emotional family crisis. Generally, there will be turmoil after the discovery of a pregnancy (see Bernstein, 1971). Bolton (1980), after performing a major review of research on adolescent pregnancy, concluded, "the total picture of the familial response to the pregnancy event spans the full range of positive and negative attitudes ..." (p. 115).

It is misleading, though, to consider the initial reaction to the adolescent's announcement of her pregnancy as the full parental response to the crisis. According to a major research-based theory of crisis (McCubbin & Patterson, 1983), the degree of family crisis depends on three factors: the nature of the event (pregnancy), the perception of the seriousness of the event, and the degree to which it threatens the survival of the family and the resources of the family. While the decision about abortion or childbearing is being made, the family might simultaneously experience both mutual support and conflict (Adler, 1981; Figley, 1983; Swigar et al., 1976).

McCubbin and Patterson (1983) have conducted and reviewed substantial research that argues that the resolution of the crisis depends on other factors besides the initial reaction. A crisis can lead to successful or unsuccessful adaptation. Most crises are successfully resolved. The degree of resolution of a crisis depends on three additional factors, which are more important to the family's ultimate functioning than is the parent's initial reaction to the crisis. The first additional factor is the accumulation of multiple simultaneous stressors. The cumulative stress influences the magnitude of the crisis. The second crucial factor is the family members' perceptions of the crisis as it unfolds and as they try to cope with it. The third factor is the extent of family adaptive resources, which include the degree to which the family is able to support each other fiscally, physically, and emotionally, plus the other resources and social support that the adolescent and her family receives from extra-familial sources (such as church groups, close friends, or peer support groups).

There is substantial evidence that most parents will support their daughters during an adolescent pregnancy. Barglow et al. (1967)

described a pattern of family reaction throughout the entire pregnancy. Adolescents experienced initial turmoil, but soon expressed anticipation of the birth and a uniform resistance to separation from the infant. In most cases Barglow et al. found this to parallel the attitude of their families. This same pattern was found by Friedman (1966) and Smith (1975): "After a preliminary period of disequilibrium, there seems to be a more stable period when both mother and daughter begin to take steps toward solving some of the problems of pregnancy (Smith, 1975, p. 279). In a separate study, Bowerman, Irish, and Pope (1966) found that before the birth of an adolescent's child, two-thirds of the white respondents and four-fifths of the black respondents felt that the adolescent's child belonged to the entire family. Other studies have found that only a small number of mothers of the adolescents felt that the baby should be relinquished for adoption (Lander, 1971; Rains, 1971). Although some parents will convey subtle messages of blame to the adolescent throughout her pregnancy (Osofsky, Hagen, & Wood, 1968) in general at least two-thirds of the families strongly support each other and participate with the pregnant adolescent in attachment to the new child — prior to its birth. Thus, the data from several independent sources show that families pull together in times of crisis in substantially over half of the cases (see also, Baptiste, 1986; Bolton, 1980; Litton-Fox, 1980; Raymond, Slaby, & Lieb, 1975).

One of the primary mechanisms that adults use to cope with the stress of pregnancy and childbirth is to seek social support (Levitt, Weber, & Clark, 1986). This is done first in the context of the immediate family; next, by involving the extended family; finally, by reaching out to peers (Belsky & Rovine, 1984; Miller & Sollie, 1980). Social support by family members during crisis is even more important for the pregnant adolescent than for pregnant adult women, since adolescents are generally more financially, physically, and emotionally tied to their parents than are adults (Adams, 1964; Lee, 1980; Litwak & Szeleniyi, 1969).

Social support from the family is crucial in how adolescents cope, whether they abort or have an extended pregnancy. For example, a variety of reviewers have shown that the adolescents who experience the most stress and emotional upheaval after an abortion are the very ones who experience problems if they carry to term — those who are *not* loved and supported by their parents (Adler, 1976, 1981; Bolton, 1980; Illsley & Hall, 1976; Melton, 1987; Olson, 1980; Rue, 1985; Shusterman, 1976).

An adolescent who is afraid to consult her parents prior to an abortion and who is supported by legislation to the extent that she need not consult them probably will not consult them. She thus compounds her dearth of social support. Ultimately, she must either (a) keep her pregnancy and abortion secret from her parents, which can cause guilt and anxiety that her parents might somehow discover the secret, or (b) tell her parents that not only did she become pregnant, but she also made an important life decision without notifying them. We propose that the potential for parent-adolescent alienation is usually greater from not informing parents than from informing them.

The implication of these findings is directly relevant to parental involvement legislation. Adolescents who seek abortion without prior parental involvement may be classed as (a) those whose parents truly would not support them or (b) those whose parents would support them (see Adler & Dolcini, 1986; Ashton, 1979; Torres, Forrest, & Eisman, 1980).

Most adolescents who truly lack parental support will experience distress whether or not parents are informed of an impending abortion. If they have an abortion without involving their parents (because no parental involvement law is operative), then those adolescents are likely to have trouble coping with abortion (Adler, 1976, 1981; Alder & Dolcini, 1986). If they are (by law) forced to notify their parents and their parents do not support them, they likely will have difficulty in bearing the child to term.

On the other hand, many other adolescents seek abortion without prior parental involvement, but the parents would have ultimately supported the adolescent's decision to abort (Ashton, 1979; Torres et al., 1980). Such adolescents would be helped by passage of parental involvement legislation. Many teens fear telling their parents about their pregnancy, overestimating the effect of their parents' anger and underestimating the parents' supportiveness. With parental involvement legislation, those girls can discover their mistaken perception of their parents' reactions. Without parental involvement legislation, those girls who opt for abortions out of a mistaken perception of their parents' reactions deprive themselves of their parents' support during their crisis — the most powerful and permanent social support they have — and will either (a) erect a wall of guilt and secrecy between themselves and their parents or (b) later reveal to their parents that they not only got pregnant but also made a unilateral abortion decision.

Failure to consider the social supportive role of families is also relevant to some of the arguments advanced by Judge Alsop in *Hodgson v. Minnesota*. Judge Alsop heard testimony from judges, who claimed

(a) that the girls who petitioned for judicial bypass of parental notification were generally mature and that the immature almost never petitioned, (b) that most girls who petitioned were approved almost perfunctorily, and (c) that girls who petitioned were apprehensive about their court appearance. The weakness in Judge Alsop's method is his failure to include control groups. Thus, it should be noted that Judge Alsop did not interview families of girls who would have aborted without parental notification, but according to this statute notified their parents and subsequently found their parents to be supportive. Judge Alsop also interviewed clinic counselors (who could hardly be considered objective, given their pro-abortion-related employment) who testified about cases in which parental notification "disrupted and harmed families" (p. 37). Again, such a causal statement by clinic counselors is improper without proper controls. The clinic counselor cannot know whether the adolescent and her family would be more or less traumatized by an abortion without parental notification.

HELPFUL FOR THE ADOLESCENT'S PARENTS

Over half of all pregnant adolescents currently notify their parents of their pregnancies (Lewis, 1987; Rosen, 1980). The parents of the other half of the population, though, are not currently involved in the adolescent's decision making, even though they will be primarily responsible for any medical or psychological expenses that result from or follow the abortion. Abortion is an operation that frequently may have both short-term and long-term sequelae (Adler, 1981; Bolton, 1980; Bulfin, 1979; Cates, et al., 1983; Hall & Zisook, 1983; Kent, 1980; Kuman & Robson, 1978; Sanberg, 1980; Spaulding & Cavernar, 1978; Tishler, 1981). For example, after abortion women have been found to be at risk for psychotic reactions (David, Rasmussen, & Holst, 1981; Spaulding & Cavernar, 1978), anniversary suicides years later (Tishler, 1981), depression and anxiety (Kuman & Robson, 1978), grief and mourning (Horowitz, 1978; McAll & Wilson, 1987), loneliness (Robbins & DeLamater, 1985), and other psychological effects—not to mention the potential risks of physical injury. It is contestable whether the effects of abortion or childbearing are more serious (for reviews see Adler, 1976; Huckeba & Mueller, 1987; Illsley & Hall, 1976; Rogers, Phifer, & Nelson, 1987; Rue, 1985; Shusterman, 1976), despite the claim of the Interdivisional Committee on Adolescent Abortion of the APA (1987) that "there is no research evidence to support [the assumption that the] risks of abortion are substantially greater than the psychological risks that arise in the decision required when a minor carries a fetus to full term," (p. 74). In one of the better designed community-based studies with high statistical power, David, Rasmussen, and Holst (1981) obtained data on subsequent psychiatric hospitalization for 71,378 women carrying to term and 27,234 women aborting in Denmark. For teens, the psychiatric hospitalization rate was 11.4 per 10,000 for women aborting and 6.2 per 10,000 for women giving birth.

Because parents are held legally responsible for the health of their children, most states require that parents of unemancipated adolescent minors give written permission for medical personnel to dispense medication or administer even routine medical care. However, many states do not require that physicians inform parents prior to abortion. This is usually justified by the assumption that the girl has a right to make her own decisions about her own body. Yet, when an adolescent has a fever or headache at school, the school nurse cannot dispense aspirin without the parent's approval. The fever or the headache is clearly a physical symptom, yet a minor adolescent is not permitted to make independent decisions about the symptom and must wait for relief until the parent's permission is obtained.

Parents might derive several other benefits from being informed prior to their adolescent daughter's abortion, though research has not tested these potential benefits. First, informed parents can provide support and nurturing for each other as well as for their daughter. Second, the communication between parents and daughter might be enhanced. In fairness, communication might also be destructive. The relative frequency of both positive and negative communications and the impact of communication on parents and adolescent have not been investigated empirically, though they have been the subject of conjecture among pro-life and pro-choice advocates. Third, the possibility exists that informed parents will experience a greater sense of input and more perceived control than uninformed parents — especially when the uninformed parents are subsequently told about the abortion.

HELPFUL FOR FAMILY UNITY

A number of researchers argue that out-of-wedlock pregnancy contributes to increased family estrangement unless the family is involved (Baptiste, 1986; Hanson, 1978; Johnson & Szurke, 1952; Rue, 1985; Young, Beckman, & Rehr, 1975). For example, Baptiste (1986) lists six reasons for family involvement with adolescent pregnancies:

1. *The family's need to deal with its pervasive sense of failure precipitated by the pregnancy* ...
2. *Family members' needs to clarify their different views about the pregnancy and the unborn baby* ...
3. *The need for the adolescent and her parents to resolve any conflict existing prior to the pregnancy, especially those resulting from the pregnancy situation* ...
4. *The importance of maintaining and/or improving communication in a crisis situation for the adolescent and her family* ...
5. *Parents' need to maintain their relationship while they "parent" their daughter through the crisis of pregnancy* ...
6. *Parents' and adolescent's need to resolve developmental independency-dependency issues.* (italics Baptiste's, 1986, pp. 168-169).

Not all adolescent pregnancies are motivated by the same factors (Cheetham, 1977); however, one common finding is that a substantial number of adolescents use sexual behavior (and often pregnancy) as a manipulative power tactic against their parents (Friedman, 1971; Group for Advancement of Psychiatry, 1985; Klein, 1978, Paulker, 1969). When the adolescent uses her sexual power unilaterally by becoming pregnant, she sets up or increases conflict in her family, which has been associated with high rates of distress and with problems in self-esteem among adolescents (Montemayor, 1983). The pregnant adolescent who then decides to abort without consulting her parents compounds the power struggle by making another emotion-laden decision without consulting her parents. This especially exacerbates the problem if the abortion later becomes known and its revelation as a *fait accompli* is used to hurt the parents. Furthermore, if the parent-adolescent conflict is unresolved and the adolescent has an abortion, she may become pregnant again, and might have a repeat abortion (Henshaw, Binkin, & Smith, 1985).

In sum, family involvement in decisions about abortion or bearing to term can promote increased family unity in two ways. First, it will allow the family to deal with some of the underlying issues that might have been involved in the original pregnancy. By dealing with the issues, the chances that the adolescent will have a repeat pregnancy will be reduced. Secondly, in families where the girl might have opted for a secret abortion, the compounding of problems (secret pregnancy and secret abortion) is avoided.

HELPFUL FOR PHYSICIANS

The physician confronted by a pregnant adolescent who wishes to obtain an abortion is in a no-win position. Except for physicians who categorically refuse to perform abortions or those who perform them frequently, the usual physician must exercise clinical judgment based on available information to make the best decision possible with his or her patient. The fundamental difficulty in decision making when the adolescent desires that the abortion be kept secret from her parents is that the physician usually has information that comes only from the adolescent — who has a vested interest in what the decision is. The desire to keep the abortion hidden from parents might cause the adolescent to either lie or tell only the part of the truth that she thinks supports her decision. It has already been pointed out that the typical early or middle adolescent is likely to engage in concrete operational thinking, which is characterized by focus on immediate rather than long-term consequences and which rarely considers the effects of her decisions from the perspectives of significant others.

Without being able to obtain information from the adolescent's parents, the physician has only the girl's opinion about what her parents' reactions are likely to be. The girl focuses on the fear that her parents are not likely to be supportive — a fear that is unfounded on reality in many (if not most) cases — and a fear of loss of control if she and her parents jointly make a decision. If parents were consulted, the physician might have a more accurate indication about their reactions and supportiveness.

In addition, the adolescent might not have accurate information about medical problems that have existed in her childhood. Her parents will be more likely to recall relevant medical information from the adolescent's childhood.

Of course, not all physicians might appreciate the requirement that parents be notified. For some, it will mean a decrease in the number of abortions they perform or a decrease in the number of patients they will see, although this group is the vast minority. Abortions are cost-effective procedures. It is often easier to deal solely with the girl, who gives a relatively consistent story about what she wants, than to deal with a family, in which the family members might disagree about the desired outcome of the pregnancy. Thus, most physicians will experience a quandary, uncertain about whether the benefits of more varied and possibly more accurate information outweigh the costs of complying with a law with which some may not even agree.

HELPFUL TO SOCIETY

Some opponents of parental involvement legislation fear that passage of such legislation would increase the number of births to teens (and decrease abortions). They believe that babies born to teens involve costs to society, which nonparents must help bear (and consequently should have a right to help decide). Analyses of the economic societal costs and benefits of teenage pregnancy usually depend on what assumptions are made by analysts. For example, Mondy (1985) calculates that societal costs due to adolescent pregnancy outweigh societal benefits. Kasun (1984), in a powerful analysis, considers variables not considered by Mondy. Specifically, Kasun enumerates many benefits stemming from the children born to adolescent mothers. For instance, children born to adolescent parents were found to have somewhat less academic aptitude in high school than did other children, but this difference was not characteristic of children of teens when similar family background was considered. Those children of adolescents were followed up at age 30. At that age, they were earning as much as children born to older parents (Card, 1981). Based on current rates of spending for Aid to Families with Dependent Children and on anticipated table income earned by the children of teen mothers (discounted to present value), Kasun (1984) estimated a substantial public benefit rather than public cost for teenage pregnancy.

Finally, passage of legislation requiring parental involvement prior to adolescent abortion would communicate a clear societal message to custodial parents that their involvement with their daughter is both valued and expected when their adolescent becomes pregnant.

SUMMARY

Adolescent pregnancy, whether it terminates in abortion or childbirth, is stressful. When adolescents elect to have abortions without informing their parents — whether they do it through misunderstanding of their parents' potential acceptance, or through the use of power — they deny themselves one of their best resources for coping with the crisis of unexpected pregnancy and with the predisposing and precipitating circumstances that led to the pregnancy. In families that are truly unsupportive — which cannot usually be accurately determined through understanding the perception of the adolescent alone — the stress on the family and the adolescent will be great and of about equal severity whether or not the pregnancy is terminated through abortion. For families in which the adolescent is mistaken about her family supportiveness, the research shows that the adolescent will benefit, the parents of the adolescent will benefit, the family unity of the adolescent will benefit, and the physician will benefit from involving the parents in the decision about abortion or bearing to term.

BIBLIOGRAPHY — CHAPTER 11

Adams, B.N. (1964). Structural factors affecting parental aid to married children. *Journal of Marriage and the Family, 26*, 327-331.
Adler, N.E. (1976). Sample attribution in studies of psycho-social sequelae of abortion: How great a problem? *Journal of Applied Social Psychology, 6*, 240-257.
Adler, N.E. (1981). Sex roles and unwanted pregnancy in adolescent and adult women. *Professional Psychology, 12*, 56-66.
Adler, N.E. & Dolcini, P. (1986). Psychological issues in abortion for adolescents. In G.B. Melton (Ed.), *Adolescent abortion: Psychological and legal issues* (pp. 74-95). Lincoln: University of Nebraska Press.
APA (1987). APA Brief in *Thornburgh v. American College of Obstetricians and Gynecologists* (excerpts). *American Psychologist, 42*, 77-78.
Ashton, J.R. (1979). Patterns of discussion and decision making amongst abortion patients. *Journal of Biosocial Science, 12*, 247-259.
Baptiste, D., Jr., (1986). Counseling the pregnant adolescent within a family context: Therapeutic issues and strategies. *Family Therapy, 13*, 163-176.
Barglow, P.; Bornstein, M.B.; Exum, D.B.; Wright, M.K., & Visotsky, H.M. (1967). Some psychiatric aspects of illegitimate pregnancy during early adolescence. *American Journal of Orthopsychiatry, 37*, 266-267.
Bellotti V. Baird (1979). 443 U.S. 622.
Belsky, J., & Rovine, M. (1984). Social-network contact, family support, and the transition to parenthood. *Journal of Marriage and the Family, 46*, 455-462.
Bernstein, R., (1971). *Helping unmarried mothers.* New York: Association Press.
Bolton, F.G., Jr. (1980). *The pregnant adolescent: Problems of premature parenthood.* Beverly Hills, CA: Sage.

Bowerman, C.E.; Irish, D.P., & Pope, H. (1966). *Unwed motherhood — personal and social consequences.* Chapel Hill: University of North Carolina Institute for Research in the Social Science, 1963-1966.

Bracken, M.B.; Hachamovich, M.D., & Grossman, A. (1974). The decision to abort and psychological sequelae. *The Journal of Nervous and Mental Disease, 15,* 154-162.

Bracken, M., & Kasl, S. (1975). Delay in seeking induced abortion: A review and theoretical analysis. *American Journal of Obstetrics and Gynecology, 121,* 1008-1019.

Bulfin, M. (1979). A new problem in adolescent gynecology. *Southern Medical Journal, 72*(8), 967-968.

Cates, W., Jr.; Schulz, K.F. & Grimes, D.A., et al. (1983). The risks associated with teenage abortion. *New England Journal of Medicine, 309,* 621-627.

Card, J.J. (1978). *Long-term consequences for children born to adolescent parents.* Palo Alto, CA: American Institute for Research.

Cheetham, J. (1977). *Unwanted pregnancy and counseling.* London: Routedge & Kegan Paul. (Boston: Henley).

Clary, F. (1982). Minor women obtaining abortions: A study of parental notification in a metropolitan area. *American Journal of Public Health, 72,* 283-285.

Cobliner, W. (1974). Pregnancy in the single adolescent girl: The role of cognitive functions. *Journal of Youth and Adolescence, 3,* 17-29.

Cotroneo, M. & Kasner, B. (1977). A study of abortion and problems in decision making. *Journal of Marriage and Family Counseling, 3,* 69-76.

David, H.P.; Rasmussen, N.K., & Holst, E. (1981). Postpartum and postabortion psychotic reactions. *Family Planning Perspectives, 13,* 88-92.

Donovan, P. (1986). Will grandparent liability help curb teenage pregnancy? *Family Planning Perspectives, 18,* 264-268.

Eisen, M.; Zellman, G.L.; Liebowitz, A.; Chow, W.K., & Evans, J.R. (1983). Factors discriminating pregnancy resolution decisions of unmarried adolescents. *Genetic Psychology Monographs, 108,* 69-95.

Elkind, D. (1967). Egocentricism in adolescence. *Child Development, 38,* 1025-1034.

Figley, C.R. (1983). Catastrophes: An overview of family reactions. In C.R. Figley and H.I. McCubbin (Eds.), *Stress and the family: Volume II, Coping with catastrophe.* New York: Brunner/Mazel.

Friedman, H.L. (1966). The mother-daughter relationship: Its potential in the treatment of young unwed mothers. *Social Casework, 47,* 502-506.

Friedman, A.S. (1971). *Therapy with families of sexually acting out girls.* New York: Springer.

Furstenberg, F.F., Jr. (1976). *Unplanned parenthood: The social consequences of teenage childbearing.* New York: The Free Press.

Group for the Advancement of Psychiatry (1986). *Crises of adolescence: Teenage pregnancy: Impact on adolescent development.* New York: Bunner/Mazel.

H.L. v. Matheson(1981). 450 U.S. 398.

Hall, C., & Zisook, S. (1983). Psychological distress following therapeutic abortion. *The Female Patient, 8* (March, 34/47 34/48).

Hanson, M. (1978). Abortion in teenagers. *Clinical Obstetrics and Gynecology, 21,* 1173-1190.

Hatcher, S. (1976). Understanding adolescent pregnancy and abortion. *Primary Care, 3,* 407-425.

Henshaw, S.; Binkin, E.B., & Smith, J.C. (1985). A portrait of American women who obtain abortions. *Family Planning Perspectives, 17,* 90-96.

Hodgson v. Minnesota (1986). No. 3 81 Civ 538 (D. Minn. Nov. 6, 1986).

Horowitz, N.H. (1978). Adolescent mourning reaction to infant and fetal loss. *Social Casework, 59,* 551-559.

Huckeba, W.M., & Mueller, C.P. (1987). *Systematic analysis of research on psycho-social effects of abortion reported in referred journals 1966-1985.* Unpublished report by the Family Research Council to Office of Population Affairs, Department of Health and Human Services. (Published report on this research is in this "Values and Public Policy" volume, page 77.)

Illsley, R., & Hall, M.H. (1976). Psychosocial aspects of abortion: A review of issues and needed research. *Bulletin of World Health Organization, 53,* 83-106.

Interdivisional Committee on Adolescent Abortion (1987). Adolescent abortion: Psychological and legal issues. *American Psychologist, 42,* 73-78.

Janis, I.L., & Mann, L. (1977). *Decision making: A psychological analysis of conflict, choice, and commitment.* New York: Free Press.

Johnson, A.M., & Szurek, S.A. (1952). The genetics of antisocial acting out in children and adults. *Psychoanalytical Quarterly, 21,* 323-343.

Kasun, J.R. (1984). Teenage pregnancy: Media effects versus facts. In F. Glahe and J. Peden (Eds.) *American family and the state.* San Francisco: Pacific Institute for Public Policy Research.

Keating, D. (1980). Thinking processes in adolescence. In J. Adelson (Ed.), *Handbook of adolescent psychology* (pp. 211-246). New York: Wiley.

Kent, I. (1980). Abortion as profound impact. *Family Practice News*, June, 80.

Klein, L. (1978). Antecedents to teenage pregnancy. *Clinical Obstetrics and Gynecology, 32*, 1151-1159.

Kumar, R., & Robson, K. (1978). Previous induced abortion and antenatal depression in priparae: Preliminary report of a survey of mental health in pregnancy. *Psychological Medicine, 8*, 711-715.

Ladner, J.A. (1971). *Tomorrow's tomorrow: The black woman.* Garden City, NJ: Doubleday.

Larsen, L.E. (1972). The influence of parents and peers during adolescence: The situation hypothesis revisited. *Journal of Marriage and the Family, 34*, 67-74.

Lee, G.T. (1980). Kinship in the seventies: A decade review of research and theory. *Journal of Marriage and the Family, 42*, 923-934.

Leibowitz, A.; Eisen, M., & Chow, W. (1984). *An economic model of teenage pregnancy decision making.* (paper No. 6.009). Austin: The University of Texas, Texas Population Research Center.

Levitt, M.J.; Weber, R.A., & Clark, M.C. (1986). Social network relationships as sources of maternal support and well-being. *Developmental Psychology, 22*, 310-316.

Lewis, C.C. (1980). A comparison of minors' and adults' pregnancy decision. *American Journal of Orthopsychiatry, 50*, 446-453.

Lewis, C.C. (1981). How adolescents approach decisions: Changes over grades seven to twelve and policy implications. *Child Development, 52*, 538-544.

Lewis, C.C. (1987). Minors' competence to consent to abortion. *American Psychologist, 42*, 84-88.

Litton-Fox, G. (1980). Teenage sexuality and the family. *Change*, Spring, 9.

Litwak, E., & Szeleniyi, I. (1969). Primary group structures and their functions: Kin, neighbors and friends. *American Sociological Review, 34*, 465-481.

Maracek, J. (1987). Counseling adolescents with problem pregnancies. *American Psychologist, 42*, 84-88.

McAll, K., & Wilson, W.P. (1987). Ritual mourning for unresolved grief after abortion. *Southern Medical Journal, 80*, 817-821.

McCubbin, H.I. & Patterson, J.M. (1983). Family transitions: Adaptation to stress. In H.I. McCubbin and C.R. Figley (Eds.), *Stress and the family: Volume I, coping with normative transitions* (pp. 5-25). New York: Brunner/ Mazel.

Melton, G.B. (1987). Legal regulation of adolescent abortion: Unintended effects. *American Psychologist, 42*, 79-83.
Melton, G.B., & Russo, N.F. (1987). Adolescent abortion: Psychological perspectives on public policy, *American Psychologist, 42*, 69-72.
Miller, B.C. & Sollie, D. (1980). Normal stresses during the transition to parenthood. *Family Relations, 29*, 459-465.
Milling. E. (1975, April). The men who wait. *Woman's Life*, 48-49; 69-71.
Mondy, L.W. (1985). Economic considerations in adolescent reproduction. In P. B. Smith and D.M. Munford (Eds.), *Adolescent reproduction health* (pp. 231-245). New York: Gardner Press.
Montemayor, R. (1983). Parents and adolescents in conflict: All families some of the time and some families most of the time. *Journal of Early Adolescence, 3*, 83-103.
Musick, J.S.; Handler, A., & Waddill, K.D. (1984). Teens and adoption: A pregnancy resolution alternative? *Children Today*, 24-29.
Olson, L. (1980). Social and psychological correlates of pregnancy resolution among women: A review. *American Journal of Orthopsychiatry, 42*, 48-60.
Osofsky, H.J.; Hagen, J.W., & Wood, P.W. (1968). A program for pregnant school girls — some early results. *American Journal of Obstetrics and Gynecology, 100*, 1020.
Osofsky, J.D., & Osofsky, H.S. (1978). Teenage pregnancy: Psychological considerations. *Clinical Obstetrics and Gynecology, 21*, 1161-1173.
Paulker, S. (1969). Girls pregnant out of wedlock. In M. LaBarre and W. LeBarre (Eds.), *Double jeopardy, the triple crisis — illegitimacy today.* New York: National Council on Illegitimacy.
Piaget, J., & Inhelder, B. (1969). *The psychology of the child.* New York: Basic Books.
Planned Parenthood of KC v. Ashcroft (1983). 462 U.S. 476.
Rains, P. (1971) *Becoming an unwed mother.* Chicago: Aldine/Atherton.
Raymond, M.; Slaby, A., & Lieb, J. (1975). *The healing alliance.* New York: Norton Co.
Rest, J.R. (1979). *Development in judging moral issues.* Minneapolis: University of Minnesota Press.
Robbins, J.M., & DeLamater, J.D. (1985). Support from significant others and loneliness following induced abortion. *Social Psychology, 20*, 92-99.
Roe v. Wade (1973). 410 U.S. 113, 93 S. Ct. 705.

Rogers, J.L.; Phifer, J.F., & Nelson, J.A. (1987). Validity of existing controlled studies examining the psychological effects of abortion. *Perspectives on Science and Christian Faith, 39,* 20-30.

Rosen, R.H. (1980). Adolescent pregnancy decision-making: Are parents important? *Adolescence, 15,* 43-45.

Rowe, K.L. (1984, August). *Adolescent contraceptive use: The role of cognitive factors.* Paper presented at the meeting of the American Psychological Association, Toronto, Canada.

Rue, V.M. (1985). Abortion in relationship context. *International Review of Natural Family Planning, 9,* 95-121.

Russo, N.F. (1986). Adolescent abortion: The epidemological context. In G.B. Melton (Ed.), *Adolescent abortion: Psychological and legal issues* (pp. 40-73). Lincoln: University of Nebraska Press.

Sanberg, E. (1980). Psychology of abortion. In *Comprehensive Handbook of Psychiatry,* (3rd ed.). New York: Kaplan & Friedman Publishers.

Schostak, A.; McLouth, G., & Seng, L. (1984). *Men and abortions: Lessons, losses, and love.* New York: Praeger.

Shusterman, L.R. (1976). The psychological factors of the abortion experience: A critical review. *Psychology of Women Quarterly, 1,* 79-106.

Siegler, R., & Richards, D. (1982). The development of intelligence. In R. Sterngerg (Ed.), *Handbook of human intelligence* (pp. 493-559). New York: Cambridge University Press.

Smith, E.W. (1975). The role of the grandmother in adolescent pregnancy and parenting. *Journal of School Health, 24,* 278-283.

Spaulding, J., & Cavernar, J. (1978). Psychoses following therapeutic abortion. *American Journal of Psychiatry, 135,* 364-365.

Swigar, M.E.; Breslin, R.; Pouzzner, M.G.; Quinlan, D., & Blum, M. (1976). Interview follow-up of abortion application drop-outs. *Social Psychiatry, 11,* 135-143.

Thornburgh v. American College of Obstetricians and Gynecologists (1986). 106 S. Ct. 2169.

Tishler, C.L.; McKenry, P.C., & Morgan, K.C. (1981). Adolescent suicide attempts: Some significant factors. *Suicide and Life Threatening Behavior, 11,* 86-92.

Torres, A.; Forrest, J.D., & Eisman, S. (1980). Telling parents: Clinic policies and adolescents' use of family planning and abortion services. *Family Planning Perspectives, 12,* 284-292.

Verstraeten, D. (1980). Level of Realism in adolescent future time perspective. *Human Development, 23,* 177-191.

Whitbeck, D.A., & Mullis, R.L. (1987). Parent and adolescent perspective taking. *Family Perspective, 21,* 39-47.

Wisconsin v. Yoder (1972). 406 U.S. 205, 92 S. Ct. 1526 (1972).
Young, A.; Beckman, B., & Rehr, H. (1975). Parental influence on the pregnant adolescent. *Social Work*, 2, 387-391.
Zbaraz v. Hartigan (1976). 763 F. 2d 1532 (7th Cir. 1985), *Cert. granted*, 55 U.S.L.W. 3247 (U.S. Oct. 14, 1986) (No. 85-673).

12

FATHERS AND TEENAGERS: SOCIAL FACTS AND BIBLICAL VALUES

Stephen M. Clinton, Ph.D.
Director, International Leadership Council

INTRODUCTION

The purpose of this paper is to investigate the empirical information available from studies done since 1980 regarding the relationship between fathers and teenagers in the United States, and to seek to make public policy recommendations for this area in light of specific biblical values.

Section I will focus on the empirical data for both behavior and attitudes of fathers and teenagers. Many studies have linked teenage behavioral problems to young people's early family life and the effects of divorce or parental absence. The discussion will include two-parent homes and single-parent homes. One factor which has not been extensively studied is the role of the father in establishing and maintaining the cohesiveness of the home and the effect of the father on adolescent development. Many personal and social problems continue to rise among teens, even though the number of divorces has leveled off in the U.S. since 1982 (Beal, 1987).

Section II will discuss values derived from the Bible regarding families, especially fathers' duties toward their children and the role of parental influence on developing young people. Positive values exist which can give direction to efforts at meeting the problems identified in Section I. These social and moral values are trans-cultural and are derived from biblical values in the Judeo-Christian heritage. The social and moral values can be taught and practiced without necessarily involving the spiritual beliefs and religious activities of any particular religion or denomination.

In Section III suggestions will be made regarding public policies in light of Sections I and II. The nature of governmental influence in family life is examined. The government has both direct and indirect influence on families already. Possible steps for positive influence will be suggested.

I. EMPIRICAL STUDIES

This discussion will be based on studies done in the late 1970's and in the 1980's. Teenage personal problems and anti-social behavior have risen quickly in the last ten years. When asked why teens break down, Billy Graham (1987) said, "I am convinced the basic answer lies in the rapid and severe erosion of family life today. The family is one of the most fundamental means God uses to communicate with us and shape us." Much earlier, Lyndon B. Johnson, at the Commencement Address at Howard University (June 4, 1965), said, "... unless we work to strengthen the family, to create conditions under which most parents will stay together — all the rest: schools, and playgrounds, and public assistance, and private concern, will never be enough to cut completely the circle of despair and deprivation." Thus, for twenty years it has been accepted in wide public circles that the family is in crisis.

What is family life like right now in the 1980's? There are 63 million families in the U.S. (NYT, Sept. 17, 1986). Eighteen million families are headed by single parents, mostly mothers (NYT, Feb. 19, 1986). Greif (1985) found that single-father families account for only 600,000 families. The number of these single-father families has tripled since 1970. According to Dornbush (1985), one child in five in the U.S. now lives with a single parent. Fifty percent of all poor families are headed by a single woman. 49.4% of mothers with a child less than one year old are working part- or full-time (NYT, March 16, 1986).

According to the New York Times (June 8, 1986), 40% (700,000) of the children in the New York City live in poverty. In the nation as a whole, 20% of the children live in poverty. On July 12, 1986, the New York Times reported that the persistent high divorce rate is leading to widespread child neglect because of emotional and economic stress, rather than because of lack of concern.

1,100,000 teenage girls will become pregnant this year. 400,000 of these will have abortions and 600,000 will keep their babies. But 80% of those who keep their babies will drop out of school, and 70% will go on welfare. 60% of all pregnant girls will be pregnant again within two years. 60% of those who get married will be divorced within five years (Kessler, 1987).

In spite of these terrible statistics, a Harris poll (1980) showed that 96% of Americans put "have a good family life" at the top of their goals (NYT, Sept. 25, 1986). 63% of college freshmen agreed. In a Gallup poll, "a good family life" was the number one social value (The Family, 1986).

A. Teen Behavior

Olson reported (1983) that teens (adolescents) said they had a hard time communicating with both parents. Responding mothers thought they communicated effectively. Dads knew there wasn't good communication. Mothers tended to be more open (ie., willing) in their communication. It was noted that parents saw the greatest stresses with teens as (1) increased outside activities and (2) financial load. Teens saw greatest stresses with parents as (1) day-to-day hassles, and (2) pressure to do well in school. The three greatest stresses on the whole family during years with teens were (1) finances, (2) marital satisfaction, and (3) family accord. However, Hagestad et al. (1984) found that 90% of responding mothers claimed their relationship with their teens was as good after a divorce as before; 58% of the responding fathers said it was as good; 68% of teens said it was worse.

According to Bell & Avery (1985), even in two-parent families, if there were four or more children, a third or fourth girl reported less father closeness. Middle boys (second of three children or third of four children) have more problems with both parents.

Strommen and Strommen, in *Five Cries of Parents* (1985) reported that 2/3 of 9th graders placed "make my own decisions" at the top of their list of desires for their family. A study of 10,467 parents showed that 20% were not happy in their marriages (9th graders noticed this far more than 5th graders did). If the child felt like an emotional orphan, 60% considered suicide. 58% of 5th graders felt they could talk over their problems with parents; 37% of 9th graders felt that they were able to. 2/3 of parents and 9th graders would have liked to talk over the problems, but few did so. 53% of teens spent less than 30 minutes per day with their fathers. 39% of teens felt their parents were too strict.

They also found that verbal affection daily from parents decreased from 61% of mothers and 40% of fathers in 5th grade to 37% of mothers and 24% of fathers in 9th grade.

Strommen and Strommen also noted that over 2/3 of parents responding identified religion/faith as most important or one of the most important factors in life. Half of teens gave the same response. 3/4 of parents wanted to help children grow in faith. But teens reported (68%) that faith or religion was discussed once or twice a month at most. 60% of teens didn't know what to believe about God. Only 46% of teens rated church or synagogue as very important. When asked who they would turn to in a family crisis, 27% of the mothers responding and 31% of the fathers said they would seek help from the clergy. The second category of persons to turn to was chosen by 16% of the mothers responding and 26% of the fathers — no one. The third category was chosen by 17% of the mothers and 14% of the fathers - medical doctors.

Rekers (1985) said that 70% of mothers resented the time they had to spend with young children. A two-year study with teens concluded that 90% of daily verbal inputs were negative (parents, schools, peers).

These statistics look very bad for the family; however, not all families are even fortunate enough to have two parents present. Judith Wallerstein, reporting on a ten-year study (The Family, 1986), concluded that divorce can so disturb youngsters that they become psychologically unable to live happy lives as adults.

Joe Frost, of Stanford University, reported in 1985 (The Family) that children in single-parent families headed by a mother had higher arrest rates, more disciplinary problems in school, and a greater tendency to smoke and run away from home than did their peers who lived with both natural parents — no matter what their income, race, or ethnicity.

John Guidubaldi, of Kent State, noted "far more detrimental effects of divorce on boys than on girls" (The Family, 1986).

Late adolescent children from single-parent families (the parents are divorced, separated or one is dead) have been found to show significantly lower self-esteem, decreased feelings of self-satisfaction and reduced feelings of personal worth (Beissenger, 1976, in Beal, 1987). Dornbusch (1985) reported that teen boys in single mother and mother-stepfather situations had a higher indication of deviance. Natural parents together have always had the lowest score for deviance for either sex child. Mothers heading households were much more likely to allow a child to make his own decisions (for better or for worse).

A seven-year study was done in Seattle and Denver on the effects of receiving welfare. Dissolution of marriages was 36% higher for whites receiving the benefits than for those who did not, and 42% higher for blacks (The Family, 1986).

If the rate of family fragmentation had not increased, there would have been 4.2 million households below the poverty line in 1980, instead of the 6.2 million which were actually in poverty then (The Family, 1986).

For children, the key determinant of poverty was whether they live in an intact family. Between 1960 and 1985, poverty among children in two-parent families decreased almost by half. Among minorities, intact families have attained incomes much nearer the national average (The Family). The formation of households without bread-winners, usually through illegitimacy and often through desertion, is the root of child poverty in America. This is the brutal fact: only one-fifth of children are in single-parent families, but they make up over one-half of all children in poverty (The Family, 1986).

Armand Nicholi (Changes in the American Family, nd) reported that over a million children a year are involved in divorce cases. He says that 13 million children under the age of 18 (over one-half of all U.S. children) have one or both parents missing, and that within three years after the divorce decree, half the fathers never see their children.

A fifteen-year study of several hundred young men who dropped out of Harvard showed two characteristics: (1) a marked isolation and alienation from their parents, especially their fathers, and (2) an overwhelming apathy and lack of motivation (Nicholi). He added, "The majority underlying difficulty found was the absence of the father from the home" (Kessler, 1987).

Glen and Kramer (1985) found that male teens have an immediately difficult time coping with divorce; females have a more difficult time longer range.

Dr. Urie Bronfenbrenner told a Senate committee that " ... the junior high years are probably the most critical to the development of a child's mental health. It is during this period of self-doubt that the personality is often assaulted and damaged beyond repair" (Dobson, Kessler, 1987).

Josh McDowell, who has spoken to millions of teens, reported one occasion when "I had forty-two personal appointments with junior high and high school students who wanted counseling. I asked each one of these kids, 'Can you talk with your father?' Only one said yes" (Kessler, 1987).

A study in the Archives of General Psychiatry (Nicholi, nd) showed that the periodic absence of the father in 200 children's cases had the same emotional results as the death of the father would have had.

Several other studies bear on the absence or inaccessibility of the father, and all point to the same conclusions: A father absent for long periods contributes to (a) low motivation for achievement, (b) inability to defer immediate gratification for later rewards, (c) low self-esteem, and (d) susceptibility to group influence and to juvenile delinquency (Nicholi, nd).

The effects of divorce on children was reported in 1980 by Wallerstein and Kelley. The initial reaction of over 90% of the children was "an acute sense of shock." Half of the children feared being abandoned forever by the parent who left. One-third feared being abandoned by the custodial parent. Five years after the divorce, 37 percent of the children were moderately to severely depressed ... and their unhappiness was greater at five years than it had been at one and a half years after the divorce (Nicholi).

In contrast to this, some families are doing well and the children appear to be making the adjustment to adult life successfully. Barnes & Olson (Parent-Adolescent Communication, *ERIC*) say that parents report few problems communicating with teens. (Teens report problems in general and especially with fathers.) But families with good parent-child communication had high levels of family cohesion, adaptability and satisfaction.

Studies have shown significant correlations linking father-headed family structure, parental control over the sex education of their children and adherence to traditional values to lower rates of adolescent sexual behavior. Dolores Curran (1983) studied top traits of successful families as ranked by 554 family counselors. The results were as follows:

1. communicate and listen
2. affirm and support family members
3. respect all people
4. develop a sense of trust
5. share time
6. share responsibility
7. have a sense of right and wrong
8. have rituals and traditions
9. share a religious core
10. respect privacy
11. value service to each other and to others
12. help out in problems

George Rekers (1985) reported on the research of Dr. Nick Stinnett who surveyed 3000 strong families and concluded that the key traits were: 1. commitment to family, 2. spending time together, 3. good communication, 4. expressing appreciation, 5. spiritual commitment, 6. solving problems (The Family).

Students who valued the work ethic, attached a high importance to education, and were religious outperformed their peers by 12 to 18 percentile points on standardized tests (The Family, 1986).

B. Parental Attitudes

Grotevant & Cooper (1985) reported that for boys, the father-son interaction was the key in identity development. Boys in late adolescence need to make decisions in consultation with their fathers, but with the boy making the actual decision. Girls needed interaction with both parents, but seemed to be slightly more dependent on their mothers during late teens.

Most mothers of children under the age of 18 did not work full-time outside the home; in fact, only 41% did. Of married mothers with children under six years, only 33% worked full-time for any period during the calendar year, and only 23% worked full-time year round. Close to half of the working women with young children would have preferred to remain at home with their youngsters, but felt they could not afford to do so (The Family, 1986).

Howard Hendricks writes, "During the adolescent years instruction becomes indirective rather than directive. That is why it is so important to be available" (Kessler, 1987).

George Rekers of the University of South Carolina cites studies showing that "the father's active involvement in the family has a unique and highly beneficial influence upon the social, psychological, and moral development of children and adolescents. A positive and continuous relationship with one's father has been found to be associated with a good self-concept, higher self-esteem, higher self-confidence in personal and social interaction, higher moral maturity, reduced rates of unwed teen pregnancy, greater internal control, and higher career aspirations" (Regier, 1987).

A court judge in Denver who has handled over 28,000 delinquency cases says, "The lack of affection between father and mother is the greatest cause of delinquency I know." (Quoted in Kessler, 1987, p. 130.)

Thus, it appears most parents would like to be good leaders for their children. In fact, most think they are doing well in communicating with their children. A Louis Harris poll shows that 52% of adults believe drug abuse is the major problem of teens (NYT, Sept. 25, 1986). 61% of parents believe they communicate with their children better than their parents communicated with them (NYT, Sept. 26, 1986).

But the reality is that many families are in trouble. Worst affected are single-parent families, especially those headed by a mother. But many two-parent families are also experiencing similar problems due to misperceptions and mistaken behavior patterns of fathers and mothers.

II. VALUES REGARDING THE FATHER-TEENAGER RELATIONSHIP

A. Introduction

Ronald Reagan, in his Proclamation of National Family Week, November 15, 1984, said, "Strong families are the foundation of society. Through them we pass on our traditions, rituals, and values. From them we receive the love, encouragement, and education needed to meet human challenges. Family life provides opportunities and time for the spiritual growth that fosters generosity of spirit and responsible citizenship."

In November of 1986 the White House Working Group on the Family reported to the President, "Parental nurturing and education of the young is our most important national investment. It is the fundamental task of humanity". They added, "Strong families make economic progress possible by passing on the values central to a free economy."

Will and Ariel Durant summarized their study of history by observing that "the family is the nucleus of civilization" (The Family, 1986).

The issue of parental or public responsibilities to future generations has been discussed in philosophical literature also. Thomas Swartz (Obligations to Future Generations, 1979) says, " ... we have no obligations to provide widespread benefits to our descendants."

Other philosophers disagreed. Gregory Kavka (1981) said that we do have obligations to future generations and tries to spell out the nature of those obligations. Any actions which we take that affect the lives of future people, either directly or indirectly, raises the issue of how it will affect them. He concluded by designing a Maximizing Principle that states that any action we take which might cause restricted lives for our descendants should be avoided, in order to maximize both their and our lives.

Derek Parfit (1981) responded to Kavka's Maximizing Principle by saying that the principle must be modified by adding that we cannot be required to experience great sacrifice.

Another philosopher (Clinton, 1987) responds to the above argument by developing a Total Value Principle which works to balance the maximum good for both generations.

Of course, a great deal has been written to support traditional values and the traditional patterns of family life in the United States. There is simply not space to review it all here. But the basis of the American traditional family life is found in the teachings of the Bible.

B. Biblical Values

Much has also been written about biblical values for the family. This section will review some specific biblical texts and describe their implications for family life.

Exodus 20:12 sets forth the fifth of the ten great commandments for Israel: "Honor your father and your mother, that your days may be prolonged in the land which the Lord your God gives you". This first commandment with a promise assumes that the father will be known and will be leading the son in right ways. The son is to honor his parents for their life and model.

Deuteronomy sets forth the Law of God for Israel in practical terms. In chapters 6-12 there are nine references to the father as being responsible to pass on to the next generation both the religious and cultural heritage of the nation. Most of these are commands from God to the father. The commands include not only the children, but servants in the house, aliens who reside with the family, and slaves. Since the father was also responsible to maintain order and to provide for the physical well-being of his household, it was clear that he did not have to do all the work (of either education or labor) by himself. He could and did delegate the actual work of education, to his wife or to the local rabbi or to a servant in the house who was qualified. But the father was responsible before God and before the city elders for the outcome.

According to Deuteronomy 24:17-22, individual Israelites were to care for aliens, orphans and widows. The care for orphans included their education as well as their physical welfare.

In Judges 13 Manoah and his wife (the parents of Samson) are commended for their attitude. At the announcement of Samson's coming birth, Manoah prayed, "teach us what to do for the boy who is to be born".

Psalm 72:4 is a prayer that the king will "vindicate the afflicted people, save the children of the needy, and crush the oppressor". The government is to pick up the duty when the father is not able to do so.

In Psalm 146:6-9 God is praised as the one who "supports the fatherless and the widow". They are His concern, along with the establishment of justice in the land.

Ecclesiastes 12:1 is the advice of a wise father to his son about how to conduct himself in life, beginning while he is young. "Remember also your Creator in the days of your youth, before the evil days come and the years draw near when you will say, 'I have no pleasure in them.' " The father reminds his son to act responsibly in the present to prepare for the future.

In Micah 2:1-9 the Lord condemns those who use economic or political power to the disadvantage of strangers, widows and orphans. He promises to remove the power of such people and to leave them with nothing.

Ephesians 6:4 continues the same ideas for Christians. "Fathers, do not provoke your children to anger; but bring them up in the discipline and instruction of the Lord." Fathers have the responsibility of raising the children correctly and kindly.

Hebrews 12:6 says that fathers are to discipline their children in such a way as is good for the children and so that the children will be able to respect their fathers. Fathers are to be role models for children.

There are many other passages which teach the rights of children, the proper forms of communication, what content should be taught, etc. This brief study will have to suffice to show the direction we have indicated: fathers carry the major responsibility for educating the children and preparing them to live life successfully. Note that education included personal (mental, moral, emotional, physical, spiritual), social, vocational, and religious life.

C. Leaders' Comments

Christian leaders have also commented on these responsibilities. Charles Swindoll writes, "Because parents are the first significant others to be near a child and because they fashion the child's environment, they have tremendous opportunity to mold his personality" (Kessler, 1987).

Gordon MacDonald makes it even more to the point. "Throughout childhood and adolescence, there are key times when a child needs certain affirmations from his father. If a father fails to provide them at those times, a void is left that can probably never be filled any other way or by any other person. If a father is not available to a child who is going through adolescence, the child often experiences increased feelings of rejection. When a child seldom or never hears his father say 'Well done' he is likely to struggle all the way from his teens to mid-life" (Kessler).

Larry Richards writes, "There are five areas of critical concern where teens are forced to go through changes and take on a more significant role." These are delineated as (1) developing an independent identity, (2) developing interpersonal relationships, (3) developing boy-girl relationships, (4) decision-making (developing values and integrity), and (5) developing a relationship with God (Kessler, 1987). This is seconded by Bruce Barton. "The way through identity crisis is for teenagers to decide values and make choices about the future. If he does not move ahead with a settled sense of identity, he will not be able to give and receive love in the context of friendships, work or marriage" (Kessler, 1987).

These authors illustrate the need for the father and the mother to be present in the home and family and to be a positive model for the teenager. If this is not possible, then we may expect to find serious problems, not only in deviant teenage behavior, but also in adjustments to coping with life in the adult world.

The statistical evidence of teenage problems without a father in the home is clear. Consistently, there are serious problems in these homes to a greater extent than in homes where the father is present. Presence alone does not ensure success in raising children. The father and the mother have the responsibility of raising their children properly. Lack of realistic expectations and evaluations of the home situation leads to misperceptions and failure for adequate communication and training to take place.

III. PUBLIC POLICY IMPLICATIONS

What has been the role of government in the development of the present state of affairs of the homes of America? What should be the role and responsibilities of government? These are serious questions which should be more real to every government policy-maker than they are to most parents. The government policy-maker carries the responsibility for the intervention of his agency and procedures and will be judged based on his contribution or interference. Parents and other citizens carry the responsibility for concern and action.

The Family: Preserving America's Future (1986) contains the following information.

> Everywhere the equation holds true: Where there are strong families, the freedom of the individual expands and the reach of

the State contracts. Where family life weakens and fails, government advances, intrudes, and ultimately compels. (p.1)

Private choices have public effects. The way our fellow citizens choose to live affects many other lives. (p.3)

Intact families are good. (p.3)

Public policy and culture in general must support and reaffirm these decisions (to support the values and behaviors of traditional families). (p.3)

A pro-family policy must recognize that the rights of the family are anterior, and superior, to those of the state. Government does not create the family, though it has an obligation to protect it. (p.4)

But law and policy should presume the reasonableness of parental action, and the authority of the home should be respected except in cases of substantial risk of harm. (p.4)

Will this program, this change, this law be fair, supportive, and encouraging to the families of America? Does it justify the financial burdens it would impose upon household income? (p.4)

Although government cannot mandate cultural change, public officials can, as opinion leaders, influence its direction. (p.4)

The family is the primary training ground for individual responsibility, for self-sacrifice, for seeking a common goal rather than self interest. (p.10)

These and other decisions by the Supreme Court have crippled the potential of public policy to enforce familial obligations, demand family responsibility, protect family rights, or enhance family identity. (p.12)

Good families, rich, poor or in between, provide encouragement and support to their children, but no excuses. They teach character. They insist upon standards. They demand respect. They require performance. (p. 23)

In a similar vein, William Bennett, in a speech to the Fourth Annual Meeting of Networking Community-Based Services, Washington, D.C., June 10, 1986, said, "First, public leadership must do what public leadership is supposed to do: Lead. That is, public leadership must affirm with no apologies the values and ideals which our tradition has affirmed as good. We must speak up for the family .... We must say too that a husband and wife raising children together is preferable to a mother or father doing the job alone".

This seems to be powerful acceptance by governmental officials that the traditional family is desperately needed today for the future of our country.

But many other leaders are not willing to accept this responsibility. Armand M. Nicholi, Jr. says, "The data [concerning the adverse effects of absentee parents] are unacceptable because they conflict with currently popular trends and because they demand radical changes in our lifestyle and in our priorities" (*Changes in the American Family*, nd). He goes on, "No human interaction has greater impact on our lives than our early family experience. If one factor influences the character development and emotional stability of a person, it is the quality of the relationship he experiences as a child with both of his parents. A parent's inaccessibility either physically, emotionally, or both, can exert a profound influence on the child's emotional health" (Nicholi, p. 2).

The problem here is to find a way to help government to be responsible for the impact of the programs it creates or maintains. Arthur Simon writes, "The will is more crucial and more stubbornly evasive than the necessary technology. And the will must be expressed in millions of individual efforts but translated into national policy decisions as well" (1987).

How can positive influence be brought to bear on government leaders to make responsible decisions and programs?

First, we need to encourage the many government leaders who do manifest such responsibility. We need to help them gain platforms for further influence.

Second, we need to help legislative leaders understand the critical situation which exists and the true implications for the future of our country if the tide is not turned. This can be done by positive, helpful discussions, letters, and expressions of concern, both in the district and in the Congress.

Third, those who are qualified to give statistical advice or legal advice must take the time and effort to help find a solution. They must make themselves available. For example, Section I of this paper shows that single-parent families, in general, do not do nearly so well at raising mentally and emotionally healthy children as do two-parent families. This fact should influence legislation and procedures from divorce and custody issues to legislation concerning welfare and other forms of support to single parent families. We can work to prevent family dissolution and to build in compensating factors where family breakdown is inevitable (although studies show that even a stepfather or big brother does not nearly make up for the absence of the natural father in the life of children).

Fourth, government leaders must listen and must learn to act based on positive family values. To accomplish things in the public sector requires reasonable compromise, but not to the violation of the public good, nor of the leader's integrity. One case in point might be the need for stronger parental consent laws related to teenage sexuality. In Section I we saw that the vast majority of girls who become pregnant during teen years will do so again, unless they adopt different values (not just different methods). Their private lives impact public policy every day in the form of payments and subsidies, as well as the loss of educated contributors to American life.

Fifth, the executive branch needs to monitor all programs and evaluate them based on their contributions to the positive development of the family (a family strengths approach). Also, programs which are negative in effect at any level need to be reformed or cut. Someone has to take the initiative to make some hard decisions based on the reality of social facts and traditional family values. This action needs to be taken by people in the executive and legislative branches of government. They need to act based on the research and on the traditional American family values which have now been proven in practice. Then, their initial action needs to be integrated into the laws and practices of the land.

Sixth, the judiciary, especially the Supreme Court, must weigh every decision within the present social context, but with values that are deeper than the socially changeable mores of the moment. Judiciary decisions so affect the interpretation of law and the implementation of programs that good laws can be frustrated in effect and bad laws protected, unless great care and deliberation is given.

Seventh, if we believe any good can come through government programs, we citizens must also act based on social research and biblical values and then take the responsibility to see that all channels of influence and integration are pursued. Family action councils, lobbyists, and personal involvement are necessary, working together.

Without this coordination and effort, little can be done to turn the direction of present programs around. All of us who are concerned must work and plan together for our nation and for our children's heritage.

BIBLIOGRAPHY — CHAPTER 12

Barnes and Olson."Parent-Adolescent Communication." *ERIC*, *56*: 438-47.
Beal, Dean. *The Impact of Parental Divorce on Young Adults.* San Bernardino, CA: International Leadership Council, 1987.
Bell and Avery. "Family Structure." *Journal of Marriage and the Family*, *47*(1985): 503-08.
Bennett, William. Speech to the Fourth Annual Meeting of Networking Community-Based Services. Washington, D.C., June 10, 1986.
Clinton, Stephen M. *The Problem of Future Generations as it Relates to Environmental Ethics.* San Bernardino, CA: International Leadership Council, 1987.
Curran, Dolores. *Traits of a Healthy Family.* Minn.: Winston, 1983.
Dornbusch, et al. "Single Parent Extended Households and Control of Adolescents." *ERIC*, *56*: 326-41.
Greif. "Single Fathers." *Journal of Marriage and the Family.* *47*(1985): 185.
Grotevant and Cooper. "Patterns of Interaction and Identity Development." *ERIC*, *56*: 415-28.
Kavka, Gregory. "The Paradox of Future Individuals" *Philosophy and Public Affairs*, *11*(1981): 2.
Kessler, Jay. *Parents and Teenagers.* Youth for Christ, 1986.
Nicholi, Armand M., Jr. *Changes in the American Family.* Family Research Council, nd.
Olson, David. *Families.* Beverly Hills: Saga, 1983.
Parfit, Derek. "Future Generations: Further Problems." *Philosophy and Public Affairs*, *11*(1981): 2.
Regier, Gerald. *Welfare Reform and the Family.* Family Research Council, 1987.
Rekers, George. *Family Building.* Logos Research, 1985.
Schwartz, Thomas. "Obligations to Future Generations." *Theory and Decision*, *11* (1979).

Simon, Arthur. *Christian Faith and Public Policy*. Grand Rapids: Eerdmans, 1987.

Strommen and Strommen. *Five Cries of Parents*. Harper, 1985.

The Family: Preserving America's Future. A Report to the President from the White House Working Group on the Family, Gary Bauer, Chairman. United States Department of Education. November, 1986.

Unless otherwise specified, all quotations are from the New American Standard Bible (NASB).

13

TEEN S.T.A.R.: SEXUALITY TEACHING IN THE CONTEXT OF ADULT RESPONSIBILITY

Hanna Klaus, M.D., F.A.C.O.G.
Executive Director, Natural Family Planning Center

M.U. Fagan, ACSW; M.L. Bryant, M.Ed.; S. Dausman; N. Dennehy, RGS, Ph.D.; J. Dornbos, FSC, STM; R. Kern, MHA; R. Kiesewetter, RN; M. Begley, M. Div.; H. Monmonier, OSB, BS; J.L. Martin, MS.

INTRODUCTION

Teenage pregnancy and sexual behavior have not decreased, despite the ever increasing availability of contraceptives and increasingly energetic exhortations to maintain premarital chastity. Since neither the provision of contraception nor the exhortation to preserve chastity serve adolescents' needs to integrate their now-present biological capacity to procreate into their operational self-concepts, we utilized experiential learning about fertility to facilitate the integration of biologic maturity with adolescent emotions, cognition, capacity, life goals and behavior.

Contraception dichotomizes sex and procreation, thus facilitating fragmented, often solely or largely genital, relationships which do not lead to growth. While teens are often exposed to exhortation to moral (chaste) behavior, many have not yet reached the level of personal integration to accept this teaching, even when disposed to do so, because they are immersed in the adolescent personality task of establishing their ego identity. This requires at least a theoretical distancing from the "parental ego" in order to discover which values are their own, and which are passively incorporated from their parent(s). These youngsters cannot "hear" adults when they say that genital union can only have its full meaning within marriage, because they still need to master the preliminary adolescent personality tasks. A high priority for teens is to understand their sexuality as well as their procreative capacity. It seemed to us that until youth can "own" their fertility more than just intellectually they cannot integrate their sexuality and become mature. Only after coming to terms with the fact that one is now biologically capable of becoming a mother or a father, can awareness of this capacity be integrated into choices about present behavior which are consistent with future life goals. Our pilot program was designed to discover whether young women could be taught to recognize their fertility patterns by mucus self-detection, to monitor the effect of understanding their fertility on their sexual behavior in the context of gender-specific value-oriented curricula, and to monitor the effect of parental involvement on client continuation and behavior.

SUMMARY OF PILOT STUDY [1]

Material and Methods

With client (teen) and parental permission, and consent to client-teacher confidentiality, 235 self-selected volunteer women 15 to 17 years of age were recruited into seven U.S. and one Guatemalan study sites. Two hundred subjects were drawn from multiethnic U.S. sites— six from Catholic schools or youth groups, and one from an inner city Sunday school. Thirty-five students came from a rural school in Guatemala. After obtaining informed consent and parental permission, personal information questionnaires and psychometric tests were administered to the study subjects, which consisted of 31 SES-matched control subjects from the general population and 31 control subjects for 2 family planning clinics. Tests were repeated after 12 months. Exit data included (incompletely reported) sexual behavior for the index year.

TABLE 1

Selected Sociodemographic Parameters of Study (S)
General Control (GC) and Family Planning Control (FPC) Subjects

	U.S.			GUATEMALA	
	S	GC	FPC	S	GC
Subjects N	200	31	31	35	12
		Race %			
black	20	29	55		
white	38	64	45		
hispanic	7.5	6.4		100	100
Asian/other	1	1			
No entry *	33.5				

TABLE 1

Selected Sociodemographic Parameters of Study (S)
General Control (GC) and Family Planning Control (FPC) Subjects

	U.S.			GUATEMALA	
	S	GC	FPC	S	GC
		Religion %			
Catholic	60.5	58	10	97	100
Protestant	11	32	57	3	
None	0.5		13		
No entry *	26.5	3	3		
other	0.5	6.4	16		

* Clinic regulations forbade query.

Chronologic and menarcheal ages, income and education of study and control subjects were comparable. [1]

In the context of a comprehensive, value-oriented curriculum which also included information about all methods of family planning, study subjects were taught to recognize and record their cervical mucus patterns via the Billings ovulation method of natural family planning. [2] Females recorded their cycle patterns and consented to a "contract" of group confidentiality and of honest reporting (in private follow up) of any genital contact. Simultaneously, each group used the curriculum to explore the emotional, physical, intellectual, social and spiritual implications of growing into womanhood. Classes met at least every two weeks for the first 3-4 months, then at monthly intervals except during school holidays. Contact with students varied from barely 2 semesters to 2+ years. Post program follow up was conducted at two and three years after the shortened programs, and one year after a fifteen-month program.

Results

Of the 244 U.S. subjects who signed consent forms, 200 (82%) entered the program. Parents gave verbal consent at the rural Guatemalan boarding school. Thirty-five girls completed the two-year study.

Sexual Activity and Pregnancy

Table 2 summarizes initiation, continuation and discontinuation of sexual intercourse (coital dynamics) of the first U.S. cohort. Only 18 (9%) of the U.S. entrants reported prior sexual activity. Five U.S.

TABLE 2

Dynamics of Coital Activity
Comparison of U.S. Acceptors(S), Drop Puts(DO) & General Control Subjects(GC) with U.S. population, 1982(NSFG)
Baseline — Signed Consents N — 244; Acceptors N — 200

	Age	S N(%)	DO[1] N(%)	GC N(%)	NSFG %	S/DO P	S/GC P	S/GP P	GC/GP P
Intake	<17	175 (87.5)	25 (57)	28 (90.4)					
	17+	25 (12.5)	15 (34)	3 (9.6)					
	unk.		4 (9)						
Previously	<17	162 (92.5)	21 (84)	21 (75)	74.5	N.S.	<0.05	<0.05	N.S.
inactive	17+	20 (80.)	12 (80)	1 (33)	43.7	N.S.	<0.001	<0.001	N.S.
Previously	<17	13 (7.4)	4 (10)	7 (25)	25.5	N.S.	<0.01	<0.001	N.S.
active	17+	5 (20.)	3 (20)	2 (66.6)	56.3	N.S.	<0.001	<0.001	N.S.
unkn.			4 (9)						

Cumulative Activity to 12 months/or end of Observation Segment [2]

	Age	S		GC	NSFG				
Remained	<17	158 (90)		17 (60)	74.5		<0.001	<0.05	N.S.
inactive	17+	20 (80)		1 (33.3)	43.7		<0.001	<0.001	N.S.
Became	<17	4 (2.28)		4 (14.3)	25.5		<0.001	<0.001	<0.05
active	17+	1 (4)		0	53.6		—	<0.001	—
Became	<17	6 (3.4)		1 (35)			<0.001	—	—
inactive	17+	3 (12.)		0			*3	—	
Remained	<17	7 (4)		5 (17.8)	25.5		<0.001	<0.001	N.S.
active	17+	1 (4.)		2 (100)	53.6		<0.001	<0.001	N.S.

1 — DO (drop outs) data fragmentary, not entered into life table.
2 — 55 subjects were in programs which only allowed observation 7 months.
3 — * no data for comparison, but "became active" / vs. "became inactive" P — 0.001.

Reprinted with permission of the *Int J Adol Med & Health Care*

subjects initiated sexual activity during the program. Data of sexual activity and pregnancy are incomplete for the U.S. general control subjects, necessitating comparison with the general population. None of the (35) Guatemalan subjects reported activity prior to or during the program. Four pregnancies occurred in the control school population during the study interval.

Life table analysis of cycle data, sexual exposure and conception showed that the single, planned pregnancy which occurred at ordinal cycle 14 yielded a pregnancy rate of .44%, or 4.4/1000 women years.

(Comparable U.S. rate for the same year was 88.0/1000 women years.) The 55 subjects who could only be followed for 8 months were included in the long term follow up of 64 subjects for 1309 menstrual cycle/months over 1-3 years. Nine percent initiated intercourse in the interim. There were 3 pregnancies: 1 planned and 2 after suspended use of the method suggesting possible desire for pregnancy. An admittedly risky attempt to calculate a Pearl rate yielded a figure of 2.7% years.

1986-87 PROGRAMS: TEEN *STAR* FOR YOUNG WOMEN, TEEN *STAR* FOR YOUNG MEN, JUNIOR HIGH AND POSTPARTUM CURRICULA.

Methodology

Recruitment of 434 additional subjects from gender-separated and coeducational junior and senior high schools and postpartum service settings followed the initial pattern of approaching parents, inviting teens and obtaining the subjects and, in the case of unemancipated minors, one parent's consent.

Coeducational groups were taught in gender-separated groups for classes of 2-8 volunteers to permit participants to learn about their own sexuality and fertility. The later classes were taught jointly. Classes in a boys' high school met weekly, girl's and coed classes biweekly. Intake information and follow up of cycles was similar to the pilot procedures. The Nowicki-Strickland locus of control scale [3] was administered at intake and at the end of the course.

Results

Completed questionnaires were tallied and responses were described using frequency analysis and percent change of mean for groups so examined, as shown in Table 3.

TABLE 3
Effects of the TEEN *STAR* curriculum on selected parameters.

Group (n)	Age	M/F	% sexually active before	during Teen STAR	attitude toward premarital sexual activity
A (60)	17	F	data not complete		+
B (45)	17	M	data not complete		+
C (107)	17	M	51	n/a	n/a
D (94)	17-18	M	47	34	+
E (47)	15-16	F	7	3	+
F (13)	15-17	MF	n/a	0	0
G (53)	13-14	MF	0	0	n/a
H (15)	16-18	F-PP	100	27	n/a
434					

* "+" indicates a predominance of attitudes regarding premarital sex congruent with the direction of the Teen *STAR* program; n/a = not available; PP = post-partum. (4 mothers had been put out of the parental home and were living with their boyfriends.)

No pregnancies occurred.

PARENT INTERACTION
Format:

A letter which described Teen STAR was sent to all parents by the person in charge of the school, class or group from which subjects were to be recruited. The letter invited them to attend an information session where the program goals, objectives, procedures and an overview of the curriculum were presented. The Billings method was explained, and the need for confidentiality discussed. Meeting attendance and interaction contributed to the parental involvement (P-I) score:

PARENTAL INVOLVEMENT SCORING GRID

PERMISSION	POSITIVE FEEDBACK ENCOURAGEMENT	PARENT-TEEN INTERACTION REPORTED (by either)
0	0	0
+1 written	+1 pleased	+1 presented
+2 attends meeting	+2 desires program extension	+2 growth, change reported

-1 withdrew daughter without dialogue with teacher
-2 withdrew daughter after dialogue with teacher

Total points = P.I. score, computed at end of interaction with student.

Results

Perhaps due to the novelty of the program, the level of parental attendance and interaction in our pilot study was very high. Not surprisingly, some parents expressed fear that the program would simply facilitate premarital sex. After discussion, they permitted their daughters to participate. By the second meeting the parents had few questions but offered much support. They reported changes in daughters' behavior beginning at the third cycle. Typically reported changes were clearly away from "following the group" to "making one's own individual decision". Frequently, they reported that their daughters avoided activities where sexual encounters were likely. Preparation of the boys' curriculum was in response to a parent's request.

Parent meetings continued to draw high attendance in the subsequent smaller cities' programs. Very few parents attended in large cities despite written invitations with telephone follow up. The only objection came from a father of a large family who thought we were teaching population limitation, which afforded us the opportunity to reiterate the program's goal: free and fully informed choice. At the follow up meeting parents of males reported that while their sons did not talk about their class, the mothers knew when class met because the boys were noticeably more considerate to them and to their sisters.

Effect of Parental Involvement on the Teen's Sexual Behavior

The pilot project correlated acceptors' coital history and subsequent activity with their parent(s)'s involvement (PI score). The disparity of the groups precludes factor analysis, but inspection suggests that when parents showed their concern by an action, such as attending an extra meeting, this appeared to reflect a general level of effective concern. Subjects whose parents had a score of greater than 3 were and remained sexually inactive.

Parental involvement at the big city high school from which 108 male seniors were drawn was almost nil beyond written permission. Nearly half the students reported sexual activity prior to the program. In view of the low level of parental involvement it seems unlikely that the reduction of activity from one half to one third in the available data set can be attributed to parental interaction.

Data for the small city sites are insufficient for interpretation.

Psychometric Tests

The before and after Nowicki-Strickland locus of control test scores among previously sexually active and inactive subjects were no more discriminatory than the Loevinger ego strength and human figure drawing tests which had been administered to the study, general control and family planning clinic control subjects. One third of each group matured, one third regressed, one third did not change. See discussion.

DISCUSSION

Group Composition and Parental Involvement.

The requirement of parental permission may have excluded those subjects at highest risk, but since we were performing research on minors, parental permission was required. It is difficult to assess whether parental involvement was a barrier to recruitment, yet Zabin et al. [7] found that only 18% of teens who attended a family planning clinic rated not telling parents as their highest priority for selecting the clinic.

The pilot study and control groups were well matched for chronologic or menarcheal age. Eighty-five percent of the subjects were drawn from Catholic schools. Reported prior coital activity was 9%

lower than the 25% reported for the Catholic females aged 15-17 years [1], yet it seems likely that in the absence of intervention the level of sexual activity would have reached at least 25%. (One mother asked to enroll her daughter prior to the junior year "because that's when the girls lose their virginity".)

Learning Dynamics

Teen *STAR* approaches the prevention of teen pregnancy by learning about and highly valuing one's capacity to procreate. Instruction in basic reproduction is joined to discussion of the personal, social, intellectual and spiritual implications of sexuality and the exercise of genitality. This affords body-person integration which is radically different from the fragmentation of the genital act into sexual and procreative functions posited by the use of contraception. While the rate of premarital sexual intercourse is over 50% beyond age 16 in our general population, the presumption that teens who have become sexually active will continue to be active is not borne out by our reported experience. Clearly, each act is a free choice. Given additional reasons to consider, many young women and men do not consider a relationship whose fulness is not yet realizable, because they are too immature, or too unschooled to be able to marry and establish a home. It is interesting that nearly all the senior males who were already sexually active wrote that the program came much too late in their education. In light of this recommendation the program is now being directed to younger students.

The requirements of parental consent and client-teacher confidentiality attempt to balance the developmental tasks of adolescence with parental responsibility; the early adolescent begins to separate from parents by belonging to an isosexual peer group and keeping secrets. In middle adolescence the values of the (usually) heterosexual peer group outrank those of the parents. By late adolescence teens begin to make their own decisions, and quite often return to the parental values unless the intervening generational struggles have been so confrontational that they have fixed the teen in an intermediate stage.

Unless parents have begun the sexual education of their children prior to the children's puberty, someone other than the parent needs to shoulder the task initially, because teens are unable to "see" their parents as sexual persons. Once the topic is opened up, parents can express their values and expectations. The Teen STAR curriculum is designed to build just such bridges, and has shown that parental involvement which does not violate privacy facilitates growth. [One can speculate that the inverse, the exclusion of parents seen when contraceptives are (legally) provided to teens without parental knowledge or consent, may prolong middle adolescence. The secrecy and consequently emotionally-charged relationship fosters prolonged dependency on adolescent contraceptive clinic clients which the workers note but apparently do not investigate. [4]]

None of the instruments utilized to date to measure emotional growth have reflected the trend toward maturity our subjects showed: moving away from peer group pressure, making their own decisions and assuming responsibility for them. The literature is replete with correlations of contraceptive compliance with psychosocial information and high self-image, [5] yet the papers cite as "successes" teen women with a high self-image who, having failed to use their oral contraceptives, abort their babies. Perhaps it is time to look beyond the available scales to explain the reasons for the continuing high teen pregnancy rate, tied into the much higher failure rate of contraceptives in teens which is based partly on inconsistent use and nonuse. [6] Granted that many teens conceive because they wish to, however, the high rate of teen abortions is indubitable evidence that, at least in the area of sexual behavior, a conscious desire to avoid pregnancy does not, of itself, counterbalance youthful romance in all its complexity. Perhaps the holistic thrust toward body-person integration is more powerful than the intellectual division between sex and procreation.

Our questionnaires need far more refinement before their value can be judged. However, the clear maintenance of primary chastity, reduction in previously-begun coital patterns, and relatively low pregnancy rates (0.44% during the pilot project, 2.75% in the pilot project post-program 2 year follow up, and 0% — ie., no pregnancies — in the group presently reported) indicate that the program has merit.

END NOTES — CHAPTER 13

1. Klaus, H., Bryan, L.M., Bryant, M.L., Fagan, M.U., Harrigan, M.B., Kearns, F. (in press). Fertility Awareness/Natural Family Planning for Adolescents and their Families: Report of a multisite project. *International Journal of Adolescent Medicine and Health.*
2. Billings J. (1983) *The Ovulation Method*, Seventh Ed. Melbourne: The Advocate Press.
3. Nowicki, S., Strickland, B.R. (1973). A Locus of Control Scale for children. *Journal of Consulting and Clinical Psychology, 40*:148-154.
4. Street, R. (Dec. 1984).Young Mothers Program, John Hopkins University Medical Center, Tenth Anniversary. Oral presentation.
5. Litt, I., Glader L. (1987).Follow-up of Adolescents Previously Studied for Contraceptive Compliance. *Journal of Adolescent Health Care, 8*:349-351.
6. Grady, W.R., Hayward, M.D., Yagi J. (1986). Contraceptive Failure in the U.S.: Estimates from the 1982 National Survey of Family Growth. *Family Planning Perspectives 188*:18(5) 200-209.
7. Zabin, L.S., Clark S.D. (1983). Institutional Factors Affecting Teenagers' Choice and Reason for Delay in Attending A Family Planning Clinic. *Family Planning Perspectives, 15:25-29.*

Acknowledgement:

Major support for the pilot study was provided by the Joseph P. Kennedy Jr. Foundation.

PART V

THE FAMILY AND THE STATE

14

THE ANTI-FAMILY ECONOMY

Joseph Sobran
Senior Editor, National Review

Editor's Note: The following is the edited transcript of an oral presentation.

The title I chose for this talk is a rather forbidding one: "The Anti-Family Economy". Those of you who know my work know I'm not an economist; but by economy I don't mean what we usually mean. I mean something more general, more in the etymological sense of a household.

A few years ago a Treasury Department study found that the actual value of the personal tax exemption amounted to less than one-fifth of its original value when it was established in 1948. This has been the result of what we've come to know as "bracket creep". Bracket creep is what I call "liberalism's invisible hand" — the way inflation moves us up into higher tax brackets. [According to the liberal state], gradual income tax was supposed to hit the rich harder than the rest of us, but, thanks to bracket creep, the richest are unaffected. People in the top brackets couldn't get into higher brackets, by definition; but everyone else could. So eventually blue collar workers were being taxed at rates that were originally aimed at rich people. The result of this was a tax revolt, among other things, but the implications weren't so widely noticed as they ought to have been. Usually we hear this discussed in terms of classes — the middle class was being squeezed.

In *Newsweek Magazine* a few years ago, a French woman was complaining about the policies of the Mitterand government. She said, "The government promised to make the rich pay. Now they tell us that we are the rich." These things tend to strike people who are not the original targets of them. This is an argument the American Civil Liberties Union makes for free speech, but nobody seems to make it for a flat-rate nondiscriminatory income tax.

But there's something deeper going on than just the economic phenomenon of bracket creep. The family itself is being squeezed, and it's not merely accidental. It is not fully intentional or conspiratorial, but there is a definite pattern of neglect, even what liberals would call in other contexts a pattern of discrimination. There's a revolution in progress — a quiet, piecemeal revolution. The squeeze is not on the middle class, as such; it's on the family. What we're seeing, in many ways, is the gradual imposition of a whole new form of social order. This is a revolutionary age, and the United States is not exempt from the general currents of revolution. In fact, revolutionary assumptions permeate our public language now in a way they never did before.

Igor Shafarevich, a great Russian writer and a friend of Alexander Solzhenyisyn, has written a wonderful book called *The Socialist Phenomenon*. According to Shafarevich, the socialist phenomenon is not something new. Socialism isn't just a new idea about how to organize an economy. It's actually a deep-rooted pathology that breaks out time and again in human history. He sees signs of it in the ancient world — in China, Egypt, and Mesopotamia. He sees it in the high Middle Ages, and then again at the time of the Reformation. They didn't call themselves socialists. The word itself is modern, but the phenomenon is perennial. And it's broken out again in our own time, especially since the middle of the nineteenth century.

In America you can't sell anything labelled "socialism"; socialism has to travel under other colors here. Rhetorically, its general form is liberalism — at least, it appropriates liberal rhetoric. Most of those people we call liberals have increasingly gone over toward socialism, with very little resistance. In America, you notice, socialism always comes in this piecemeal way. I like to say that communism is wholesale socialism and liberalism is retail socialism.

Our revolution — and we're having one — is being smuggled in under bland pragmatic rhetoric one step at a time and the family is one of the principle targets. The rhetoric of American socialism is reformist rather than revolutionary. It always purports not to be abolishing or destroying things, but to be improving and redefining them. This is a consistent pattern.

There's an interesting correlation, by the way, in that the people who insist that they're not socialist (they prefer to be known as "domestic progressives", or "liberals"), almost consistently tend to be those most favorably disposed to communism and those most fiercely opposed to anti-communism.

This is not to imply that these people even realize what they are. They don't think of themselves as socialists. They think of themselves as pragmatic reformers. It's just that their reforms always tend toward a socialist model and they furiously resist any attempt to move away from it. They want to increase government's share of the wealth, and they get angry at anyone who suggests tax cuts, for example. Everything is an occasion for a tax increase. Whatever the malady, the cure is always the same, which indicates to me that the cure is ideological, not pragmatic at all. It only masquerades as pragmatic.

I've called this phenomenon the "hive". I liken the whole socialist phenomenon to a gigantic beehive, with the queen bee in Moscow and the workers scattered around the world, organized by the queen, but not necessarily directed by the queen. As Shafarevich points out, the three perennial targets of socialist movements are religion, property, and the family. Religion is persecuted, property is expropriated, and families are broken up.

The socialist impulse takes a different form, even psychologically, in America. In America the hostility of the socialist hive against religion takes the form, among others, of an insistence on the separation of church and state to a remarkable, vindictive degree — i.e., the attack on school prayer. There are always plausible, pragmatic reasons given.

The significance of the individual liberal measure has to be seen in the context of this total movement toward the socialist model. It can't simply be taken on its own immediate pragmatic terms. The rationale always shifts.

The "hive" identifies religious freedom with the separation of church and state. However, it is totally indifferent to the persecution of religion abroad. It is not scandalized by the persecution of religion in the Soviet Union, for example; its concern for religious freedom is selective. This is always one of the marks of an ideology — the apparent double standard. I always say that behind every double standard is an unacknowledged single standard.

The religious people in this country have tended to sense a real anti-religious animus, and they've generally given it the name of secular humanism. Ironically, secular humanism was a euphemism originally used by secular humanists — by unbelievers, people hostile to religion. When it was picked up by Jerry Falwell, suddenly they renounced it.

This is a typical pattern because the people I'm describing are, in a sense, semantic nomads. They don't like to be pinned down as to meaning and they will move on to a new set of terms. They don't like to talk about socialism as such. They have a resistance to blunt language; a preference for the peculiar euphemism.

The area of religion is one of the most fascinating aspects of this phenomenon because we find more and more people who were formerly within organized religion adhering to anti-religious sentiments — to "secular humanism".

Nominally, the old liberalism simply wanted separation of church and state. Within the church, the church's standards would continue to be sovereign, because the church was a private institution. But now, all private institutions themselves are to be remade on the socialist model. And they're all to be assimilated.

The second of the three things that the socialist phenomenon always attacks is the realm of property. We find that the reforms of liberalism take place under such respectable rubrics as "fighting poverty" and "seeking social justice" (which always turns out to be more and more redistribution, no matter what its impact on the production of wealth or on the family). George Gilder has been particularly eloquent on the way redistribution supplants the male role, makes the man useless, and thereby destroys the family. For instance, we've seen the illegitimacy rate among black Americans triple in the last twenty-five years, during the very time when ostensibly the most was being done to help them.

There is a furious resistance at any attempt to stop or reverse the socialization of wealth. On the semantic front, wanting to keep your own wealth is now called "greed". However, there's no such thing as excess when it comes to socialism. The state is never guilty of greed — it can never take too much. It's only the desire for private wealth that's called greed, and even wanting to keep your own earnings is condemned as selfishness.

It is not an overstatement to call this a moral revolution. We always think about sex when we hear about moral revolution. That's only part of it.

We come to the family, now, and its relation to the socialist phenomenon. Shafarevich points out that in all instances of the socialist outburst of which he is aware, the family comes under attack in a special way. There's always a demand for sexual freedom. This is always on the agenda.

Shafarevich's point is that sexual freedom makes people interchangable. It reduces them all to biological units and releases them from the bond of the family and the tribe. One's only remaining identity, then, is not familial but political. One is related to the state, not clearly related to anyone else. Whether this item on the agenda is called "free love" or "sexual freedom", it amounts to the same thing. A lot of other things go with it — for example, abortion on demand, the grimmest of all.

One of the great typical phenomenon of the liberal form of socialism is the shifting rationale. A pragmatic reason is always given, but today's pragmatic reason may contradict yesterday's. At first the argument for legal abortion was, "Abortion is bad. It's an evil. But the way to contain the evil is to legalize it so that it can be controlled and supervised and made hygienic". As soon as abortion was legal, we started hearing that one cannot say whether it's right or wrong — no one knows when life begins. We moved to the agnostic stage. The next thing you knew, abortion was a right, it was a good thing, and should be maximized, not minimized. The state should subsidize abortion.

This was a new argument, made by the very same people who had been admitting that abortion was evil and saying that its evil would best be minimized by legalization. Then legalization turns out not to be enough for them. And they have no sense of inconsistency about it because the reasons are shed as a snake sheds its skin. They move from one reason to another.

It's the leftward direction of motion that is important, and not the reason given at any particular moment. For instance, gay rights is a logical extension of the attitude that sex is not for procreation, sex need not be part of a sacred familial bond, that people are interchangable, and there's nothing wrong with promiscuity. The drive for "safe sex" in the age of AIDS suggests that the goal is not to save the nation's health, but to save the sexual revolution. The feminist agenda is to eliminate men. In fact, some of the more overt feminists have argued that reproduction ought to be achieved by high-tech means, that there should be no act of love between man and woman and there should be no natural childbirth. We've seen the family again redefined by those who hate it. And this, too, is part of the total program, part of the new progressive order.

We also see the advent of what we call population policy. It is now widely assumed that part of the role of the state is to control our numbers as if we were a herd of cattle. It does this gingerly, trying not to make too apparent the ways in which this clashes with our traditional freedoms. This is the reason for the euphemisms that are typically used.

As you are aware, China has mandatory birth control, and

mandatory abortion right up until the end of pregnancy. You find progressive-minded people in this country making excuses for the Chinese policy. The same people who insist that they are pro-choice and not pro-abortion will make excuses for mandatory abortion in China. Their goal is to legitimate abortion. And maybe, ultimately, they'd be willing to make it mandatory here, too. I don't suggest that this is a conscious goal, but they have no objection to it when they see it performed by a regime they regard as progressive. The state increasingly takes the role of provider and usurps in this respect the role of the father and of the family.

The rights of children — not against the state so much as against their own parents — is another item on the anti-family agenda. The American Civil Liberties Union, the greatest example of the style of liberalism that I'm talking about, has supported the right of children to sue their parents and, of course, to get contraceptives and abortions without their parents' knowledge or consent.

In all this we see the drive to reduce the child to an unaffiliated unit — not anyone's child, but simply a member of the polity, a member of the new progressive social order.

One example is in Sweden, where it's now illegal to spank your children. The family there is reduced to the lowest administrative unit of the state. The family has no autonomous dignity — divorce is easy, sex is completely untrammelled and abortion is available on demand. Here's what so-called progressive tendencies in America are tending toward; this is the gravitational pull; this is the way you can predict what liberalism will be up to next. Every move is done under pragmatic reformist rhetoric.

It is the tendency of all programs to go this way. Welfare ceases to be a mere emergency measure and becomes the model of the distribution of wealth. Civil rights ceases to mean what civil rights used to mean to all of us — equal respect from the state — and becomes a set of policies of maximum coercion by the state directed against the family. Education becomes secularized, and kids are subjected to what's known as sex education, of which parents are rightly distrustful, suspecting as they generally do a hidden agenda of the new morality. The "new morality" is the morality that fits into the progressive order. It's not just the commercialized sex of Hugh Hefner, but the reduction of the individual to a mere political unit, with no transcendent identity, no relation, no sacred bonds to parents or family.

In fact, Marxist sociologist Alvin Gouldner rejoiced that the public schools are, without parents even realizing it, weaning children away from the influence of parents and religion and making children "rational", initiating them into what he called the "culture of critical discourse". Children are taught to think critically about their families and about religion, but they are not taught to think critically about socialism. The presuppositions of secular socialism are treated as ultimates.

Education used to mean an initiation of the young into the ways of their parents. Now, it has come to mean the opposite. It has come to mean subverting. The school has increasingly been turned into an anti-family instrument without most people's realizing it. The very title of one recent book, *Teaching as a Subversive Activity*, suggests that it is good to teach the young to dissent and to protest, regardless of the content of the dissent and protest.

One of the key words of the anti-family economy is "compassion" — a nice word. Who can object to compassion? It's intrinsically a good thing. And yet it takes on a special overtone for the progressive community. It stands for a new kind of obligation — an obligation to surrender your wealth, that it may be given to total strangers — a purely political obligation. It's interesting that the aborted child is not an object of this sort of compassion. There is a massive liberal denial that any pain is felt, for example, by a child who is being aborted. Of course, the child is supposed to be called a fetus. We're taught to use a rather antiseptic set of words — i.e., "fetus", "termination of pregnancy" — for that kind of killing.

So at the same time that new duties to total strangers are imposed on us, we're relieved of duties to our next of kin. This is the constant pattern of modern liberalism. And this is why I say it tends toward socialism. You can get divorced, you can abort your children, you can engage in sodomy — you have almost total freedom in those respects, but your obligations to surrender your wealth so that it will be distributed to people that you've never heard of are increasingly absolute.

I like to refer to the IRS as the business end of liberal compassion. It does not take a lackadaisical attitude toward people who don't comply. In fact, The IRS is one of the few state agencies that the ACLU doesn't seem to be interested in taking on. The IRS is essential to the establishment of the progressive order. It is the great instrument of redistribution, and, therefore, it is spared all the criticism that civil libertarians direct against other agencies of the state, especially the local police.

The anti-family program is fostered by a complex but closely interrelated set of attitudes. We're hardly aware of these. The sovereign prejudices of our time are not the prejudices everyone is conscious of, but precisely the ones they're not aware of. Everyone is on the alert for racial prejudice, but the progressive prejudices pass so casually that we're hardly aware of them. They are built into the bland language that we all use every day, such as "civil rights" and "social justice". These terms are not analyzed or contested. People don't ask if they mean what they purport to mean.

We have a lot of language that implicitly condemns our past as medieval and neanderthal. Anyone who wants to defend the past is accused of being "backward". The very language that we use is now deeply biased against our own traditions. It's one of the most amazing prejudices I know of. A whole new social order is emerging that presumes that our past was bad, and that we should all be in favor of change ("change" being undefined but always taking a particular form).

These prejudices go unchecked. We are dimly aware of them. I find myself detecting these anew every day. I keep finding that I've been accepting them myself against my own will, that they've been permeating my own speech very often. In the news media they're ubiquitous, but they really have their home in the academy. The old country club prejudices have been replaced by the new faculty club prejudices. Those are the ones we haven't yet learned to criticize.

It reminds me of a remark of one of my heroes, G.K. Chesterton: "Men can always be blind to a thing as long as it's big enough". And these prejudices really are big enough. They're ushering in a whole new social order that most people are hardly aware of.

Editor's note: Following are edited questions from the audience, addressed by Mr. Sobran.

Question: What do you think is the ultimate goal of those who call themselves progressive and who want to break down the identifying marks of the community — family, church and neighborhood?

Mr. Sobran: I don't know that they have an ultimate goal. I think a lot of them have a certain vision of an ecstatic community with no institutions inhibiting them. Eric Voegelin talks about this in his brilliant book *The New Science of Politics* — the idea that we can all be brothers with no differentiation. That's the positive side. But I actually think that the driving force of it is hate — the kind of hate we're not on the lookout for. The kind of hate that used to be known as envy, for example, plays a large role in it.

Envy used to be regarded and recognized all around as one of the seven deadly sins. You see it in the story of Cain and Abel, or Iago and Othello. Everyone understood envy until this century, for some reason. Generally speaking, envy doesn't get diplomatic recognition as a sin. But it's natural to man to rebel. We have to have a commandment that says, "Honor thy father and thy mother". There's no commandment that says, "Get three square meals every day". We do that automatically. But the law is wise enough to recognize in children this tendency to rebel, to neglect their parents — a tendency to ingratitude. The beginning of history as we know it is rebellion.

In the old days, those who defected — social misfits and malcontents — tended to be loners. The priest who left the priesthood would hide out. If you abandoned your family you went to another town and changed your name — now you go on the Phil Donahue Show! Defectors have reached critical mass. They have formed what I call the communion of apostates — they're in touch with each other, they form a movement, and they have this kind of anti-community that they are intent on imposing on everyone else.

This negative side needs a lot more recognition. Much of the liberal rhethoric is directed against the rich. It's not just in favor of the poor — it doesn't even want to make the poor well off, it simply wants to impoverish the rich. Chesterton speaks of "the modern and morbid habit of always sacrificing the normal to the abnormal". I think that's one of the great drives of our time.

Question: How can we overcome the fact that the liberal socialist has the media on its side, and the other side is not heard?

Mr. Sobran: I don't see it as a problem of two parties that way. It has become a convention, a deep-seated prejudice. You can't say we're going to take the media away from people who have prejudices and give them to people who don't. These things are so deeply operative that it's going to take a change in the entire culture to effect it. I think the media would be fine if they only knew how to report the news straight, if only they were made aware of their own prejudices.

Question: What do you see as the most dangerous trends among conservative leaders?

Mr. Sobran: I suppose we always have to be on the lookout for acquiescence, for giving up too soon. For example, I think a lot of people have failed to recognize that the sexual revolution is very serious. They've tended to think that you can be flippant about sex and it's not really connected to the political struggle. Not to recognize how important the sexual revolution is to the total revolution trivializes the political. If you don't see the sexual revolution as part of a revolution, you won't see the total revolution. You just think that politics is about tax rates, but it is much deeper than that. It is about a total order of things.

So I think that lack of comprehension is one thing that bothers me about some conservatives. They say that as long as a candidate is good on taxes and national defense, his views on abortion don't matter. I'm not saying I would simply vote for a guy who had the right position on abortion but wanted high taxes and little national defense. But I am saying that all those things have to be integrated, and they all matter.

Question: Words creep into our vocabulary which war against our heritage. How stubbornly should we stick to old terminology, especially in our communities, as we work with people?

Mr. Sobran: Well, it's a matter of judgment. It's good to keep the old words alive as much as possible. I was just reading a review in *Time Magazine* of the new edition of the Random House dictionary, which apparently is saturated with feminist ideology.

There's a very deliberate effort in some quarters to insist that people follow a new usage. The new dictionary prints a lot of obscenities, slang terms and words that used to be regarded as solicisms and grammatical mistakes, and it okays them. At the same time it follows the positivist philosophy of simply recording the language and not making prescriptions, it makes political prescriptions that you should use gender-neutral language whenever possible, for example. So the same people who profess to be relativists are always smuggling in their own new dogmas. I've seen that time and time again.

ABOUT THE AUTHORS

William J. Bennett, Ph.D., J.D. is United States Secretary of Education. Secretary Bennett holds a doctorate in political philosophy from the University of Texas and a law degree from Harvard Law School. In 1981, he was selected by President Reagan to be Chairman of the National Endowment for the Humanities, where he served until assuming his current position.

Stephen M. Clinton, Ph.D., has a Master's degree in Counseling, completed his doctorate in Systematic Theology at the California Graduate School of Theology, and has done an additional two years of post-doctoral study in Philosophy at the University of California at Riverside. Dr. Clinton is author of numerous scholarly articles and has published three books.

Abigail Rian Evans, M.Div., Ph.D. is Senior Staff Associate and Director of New Programs at the Kennedy Institute of Ethics at Georgetown University, and Director of Health Ministries at the National Capital Presbytery. Dr. Evans holds graduate degrees in theology from the University of Basel, Switzerland, and Princeton Theological Seminary, and a Ph.D. in Philosophy/Bioethics from Georgetown University. She has been an ordained Presbyterian minister for 25 years.

Hanna Klaus, M.D., F.A.C.O.G. serves as executive director of the Natural Family Planning Center of Washington, D.C., Inc. She is also an obstetrician gynecologist and Associate Clinical Professor of Obstetrics and Gynecology at George Washington University.

John S. Lyons, Ph.D. is an Assistant Professor at Northwestern University Medical School in Chicago, Illinois. Dr. Lyons received his Ph.D. from the University of Illinois, Chicago.

Vernon H. Mark, M.D., F.A.C.S. is an Associate Professor at Harvard Medical School, and Director Emeritus of Neurosurgery at Boston City Hospital. He is a national expert on AIDS. He and his wife have authored *The Pied Pipers of Sex* (Haven Books, 1981). In addition to his medical degree, Dr. Mark holds an M.S. in Neuroanatomy and Neuropathology.

Rita L. Marker is a lecturer in Human Life Studies and Co-director of the Human Life Center at the University of Steubenville in Steubenville, Ohio.

Gerald P. Regier is President of the Family Research Council of America in Washington, D.C. He is a graduate of Michigan State University. He previously served in the Federal Department of Health and Human Services as Associate Commissioner of the Administration for Children, Youth and Families. In this position he directed the Family and Youth Services Bureau and assisted in the formation of family policy in a wide variety of Social Service programs. He has served on numerous review boards, task forces and panels on family policy issues, and speaks frequently before universities and congressional hearings.

Joseph Sobran is Senior Editor of the *National Review*, a syndicated columnist appearing regularly in the *Washington Times*, and a radio commentator on CBS Radio's "Spectrum."

Joseph R. Stanton, A.B., M.D., F.A.C.P. received his medical degree from Yale University. In addition to his career as a physician and Clinical Associate Professor in Medicine at Tufts University School of Medicine, Dr. Stanton is author of numerous papers on euthanasia, abortion, and *in vitro* fertilization.

Robert Strom, Ph.D. is Professor of Education and Human Development at Arizona State University in Tempe, Arizona, and Director of the Office of Parent Development International. He received a Ph.D. in Educational Psychology from the University of Michigan, with post-doctoral study in Developmental Psychology at both Oxford and Cambridge.

Peter Uhlenberg, Ph.D. is Associate Professor of Sociology at the University of North Carolina, Chapel Hill. Dr. Uhlenberg received his Ph.D. in Demography from the University of California at Berkeley, and has authored numerous publications on the subject of aging.

Lynn D. Wardle, J.D. is Professor of Law at J. Reuben Clark Law School, Brigham Young University, and was educated at Duke Law School, Durham, North Carolina. He has written numerous publications including *A Lawyer Looks at Abortion* (with Mary Anne Q. Wood, (BYU Press, 1982).

Everett L. Worthington, Jr., Ph.D. is an Associate Professor of Psychology at Virginia Commonwealth University. He is a licensed Clinical (Counseling) Psychologist and has published numerous research articles on childbirth, transition to parenthood, and counseling.